Faction Displayed: Reconsidering the Impeachment of Dr Henry Sacheverell

Edited by
Mark Knights

Wiley-Blackwell
for
The Parliamentary History Yearbook Trust

© 2012 The Parliamentary History Yearbook Trust

Wiley-Blackwell is now part of John Wiley & Sons

Registered Office
John Wiley & Sons Ltd, The Atrium, Southern Gate, Chichester, West Sussex, PO19 8SQ, United Kingdom

Editorial Offices
350 Main Street, Malden, MA 02148-5020, USA
9600 Garsington Road, Oxford, OX4 2DQ, UK
The Atrium, Southern Gate, Chichester, West Sussex, PO19 8SQ, UK

For details of our global editorial offices, for customer services, and for information about how to apply for permission to reuse the copyright material in this book please see our website at
www.wiley.com/wiley-blackwell

The right of Mark Knights to be identified as the author of the editorial material in this work has been asserted in accordance with the Copyright, Designs and Patents Act 1988.

Wiley also publishes its books in a variety of electronic formats. Some content that appears in print may not be available in electronic books.

Library of Congress Cataloging-in-Publication Data
Faction displayed : reconsidering the impeachment of Dr Henry Sacheverell / edited by Mark Knights.
   p. cm.
   All but two of the articles in this volume were originally papers given at a conference, held at the Palace of Westminster, on the 300th anniversary of the verdict given against Dr Henry Sacheverell on 23 March 1710.
   Includes bibliographical references and index.
   ISBN 978-1-4443-6187-2 (alk. paper)
  1. Sacheverell, Henry, 1674–1724. 2. Great Britain–History–Revolution of 1688–Public opinion.
3. Great Britain–Politics and government–1660–1714. 4. Religion and politics–Great Britain–History–18th century. 5. Great Britain. Parliament–History–18th century. 6. Sacheverell, Henry, 1674–1724–Trials, litigation, etc. I. Knights, Mark. II. Parliamentary History Yearbook Trust.
   DA497.S3F33 2012
   941.06'7–dc23

2011052082

A catalogue record for this title is available from the British Library
Set in 10/12pt Bembo
by Toppan Best-set Premedia Limited

1   2012

CONTENTS

ACKNOWLEDGEMENTS

The editor would like to thank: Paul Seaward, Director of the History of Parliament, for his help in organising the conference 'Contesting Revlution: The Trial of Dr Henry Sacheverell and the Impact of the Revolution of 1688', on 23 March 2010, from which some of this volume derives; the trustees of the History of Parliament Trust, and, in particular, Lord Cormack, for their support of the conference; Warwick University, which contributed financially; and those who attended, for their questions and comments. I would also like to thank the editor of Parliamentary History for his support throughout the process of putting this volume together.

BIBLIOGRAPHICAL NOTE

Many of the authors in this volume cite items from the printed ephemera that the Sacheverell trial generated. Details of these publications are to be found in Francis Falconer Madan, *A Critical Bibliography of Dr Henry Sacheverell*, ed. W.A. Speck (Laurence, KA, 1978). The item numbers from this bibliography are given in the footnotes to the articles in this volume after the title of each publication as in the following example: *The Parliament of Women* [Madan 617], unless the title of the publication is given in the text, in which case only the Madan item number is cited in the footnotes.

LIST OF CONTRIBUTORS

Brian Cowan teaches British and European history at McGill University in Montreal, Canada, where he holds the Canada research chair in early modern British history. He received his PhD in history at Princeton University in 2000, where he studied with Peter Lake. He taught at the University of Sussex and Yale University before moving to Montreal in 2004. He is the author of *The Social Life of Coffee: The Emergence of the British Coffeehouse* (2005) as well as editor of *The State Trial of Doctor Henry Sacheverell*, which will be published in Parliamentary History's Texts & Studies series. He is currently writing a companion volume, entitled *Dr. Sacheverell's False Brethren: Celebrity Politics and the State Trials of Early Modern Britain*. Along with Elizabeth Elbourne, he currently edits the *Journal of British Studies* for the North American Conference on British Studies.

D.W. Hayton, FSA, MRIA, is professor of early modern Irish and British history at Queen's University Belfast. He has written widely on the political history of Ireland and Britain in the early 18th century and was the principal editor of the History of Parliament volumes on *The History of Parliament: The House of Commons 1690–1715* (5 vols, Cambridge, 2002).

Geoff Kemp is senior lecturer in politics at the University of Auckland. A former UK newspaper journalist, in 2001 he gained a PhD at King's College, Cambridge, with a thesis on 17th-century ideas of press freedom. He was general editor of the four-volume *Censorship and the Press, 1580–1720* (2009), in collaboration with Jason McElligott, Cyndia Susan Clegg and Mark Goldie. His other publications include a bibliography of Sir Roger L'Estrange and an essay on New Zealand media and democracy.

Mark Knights is professor of history at the University of Warwick. His most recent book *The Devil in Disguise: Deception, Delusion and Fanaticism in the Early English Enlightenment* (Oxford, 2011) includes a chapter on the Sacheverell trial and seeks to place political and religious developments in a wider context of science, gender relations, fiction, visual representation and witchcraft. His earlier books *Politics and Opinion in Crisis, 1678–1681* (Cambridge, 1994) and *Representation and Misrepresentation in Later Stuart Britain: Partisanship and Political Culture* (Oxford, 2005) explored the public sphere and its manipulations by partisans. He has published numerous articles, including several exploring political discourse, the most recent of which have been part of a wider collaboration of scholars engaged in discussions about a social and cultural as well as a political history of keywords and concepts. He is now working on a number of projects, including petitioning and corruption in the early modern period.

Eirwen E.C. Nicholson is an independent scholar and historian based in Richmond, Virginia. Originally from the Isle of Wight, England, she has an MA from the University of Cambridge and a PhD from the University of Edinburgh and has held teaching and research fellowships at Yale University and the University of St Andrews. Her work has focused on the visual culture of 17th and 18th century Britain and has been published in a wide range of scholarly journals and books. She is currently writing a book entitled 'Pulpit Idol: Dr Sacheverell, Religion and the Commercialisation of Politics, 1710'.

Steve Pincus is Bradford Durfee professor of history at Yale University. He has published widely on early modern British history and is now working on a book on the origins of the British Empire c.1650–c.1785.

W.A. Speck is emeritus professor of history at the University of Leeds and special professor in the School of English at Nottingham University. His publications relevant to the Sacheverell affair include *Tory and Whig: The Struggle in the Constituencies 1701–1715* (1970), *Society and Literature in England 1700–1760* (1983), *Reluctant Revolutionaries: Englishmen and the Revolution of 1688* (Oxford, 1988), *The Birth of Britain: A New Nation 1700–1710* (Oxford, 1994) and *Literature and Society in Eighteenth-Century England: Ideology, Politics and Culture 1680–1820* (1998).

Daniel Szechi is a graduate of the University of Sheffield and St Antony's College, Oxford and was appointed professor of early modern history at the University of Manchester in 2006. He is a fellow of the Royal Society of Edinburgh and the Royal Historical Society. He has published extensively on jacobitism and the early-18th-century British Isles and his most recent books include *The Dangerous Trade: Spies, Spymasters and the Making of Europe* (Dundee, 2010), *1715: The Great Jacobite Rebellion* (2006) and *George Lockhart of Carnwath 1689–1727: A Study in Jacobitism* (East Lothian, 2002).

Introduction: The View from 1710

MARK KNIGHTS

The articles in this volume, planned to mark the tercentenary of the impeachment of Dr Henry Sacheverell on 23 March 1710, reassess the importance of his trial. Sacheverell's attack on the revolution of 1688, and the principles which underpinned it, allows us to question how far, 20 years later, a whig revolution had prevailed. The articles suggest that the revolution continued to be contested; that in 1710 the high church tory vision temporarily triumphed; that the flood of print showed the importance of religious dispute in shaping the public sphere; that the debate over Sacheverell connected Westminster and the public, not just in England but also in Ireland; that there was an important disagreement between high and low church about how to respond to the press's licentiousness, part of a story about the shift away from prepublication censorship towards regulation of print and copyright; that the print controversy over the trial was vituperative, 'impolite' and traded lies and misrepresentations; that Sacheverell's critics sought to associate him with harlots in a bid to suggest that his strong influence over women was unhealthy; that Sacheverell, on the other hand, deliberately depicted himself as a martyr; and that, for all its religious heat, 1710 was also important for an early enlightenment debate about political economy, since the tory vision on Church and state also embraced a reoriented foreign policy and that this contest over imperial visions had important consequences for the development of the colonies after 1714.

Keywords: Sacheverell; Glorious Revolution; public sphere; press; censorship; gender; moderation; political economy; empire; Ireland; ideology; early enlightenment

1

All but two of the articles in this volume were originally papers given at a conference, held at the Palace of Westminster, on the 300th anniversary of the verdict given against Dr Henry Sacheverell on 23 March 1710. Sacheverell's parliamentary trial was the sensation of its day. It provoked rioting in London and a huge flood of printed works, recounting the impeachment and debating the Doctor's controversial views. 'Perhaps there never was an Instance, since our happy Constitution was in being, of such a Ferment as we have seen in our Days, raised upon such Grounds, and in so Critical a Time', remarked one pamphleteer.[1] Sacheverell's attack on 'Revolution principles' opened a wide-ranging review of the ideas and practices that had underpinned the years 1688–9: religious toleration and the legitimacy of resistance were the two most important themes but the debate widened to include the freedom of the press, the financing and aims of war, the grounds of authority and the nature of monarchy. Indeed, the impeachment was also something of a turning point. In the short term, it led to the

---

[1] *The Voice of the Addressers* (1710) [Madan 717], 5.

demise of the administration, headed by Godolphin and Marlborough in collaboration with the whigs, and to a landslide tory victory at the subsequent general election in October.[2] That victory brought an end to the long war against France, which had become increasingly to be seen as a whig war, and tories capitalised on Sacheverell's attack on the self-interested monied men who financed it. Victory also led to a revival of high church tory ideology. In 1711, legislation against 'occasional conformity' – the practice of occasionally attending a Church of England service in order to qualify for political office – which had proved so controversial in the first years of Anne's reign, was finally passed.[3] It seemed as though the whigs and low churchmen were not only on the defensive, but had been routed. In the medium and longer term, however, 1710 looked very different: a temporary, pyrrhic victory for a high church tory ideology that was subordinated by the Hanoverian succession in 1714 and its long whig legacy.

Looking back on 1710 is, thus, instructive in all sorts of ways. It allows us to re-examine what, 20 years on from 1688–9, the significance of that revolution had been for contemporaries and why it remained so contentious; and it allows us, from our vantage point 300 years later, to assess how far the events and debates of 1710 marked continuity or change. What follows in this introduction is an attempt to sketch out both these dimensions, drawing on the articles in the collection in the process.

A secondary purpose of the volume is to embrace a broad definition of parliamentary history. The trial of Henry Sacheverell was very much a parliamentary event: it was initiated in parliament, run by parliament, conducted in Westminster Hall, and resulted in parliamentary elections and a change of government.[4] But it was also much more than that. The significance of the impeachment cannot be fully understood without seeing the parliamentary debates in conjunction with a much wider public debate, a lot of which commented on events at Westminster. That debate is, in part, recoverable from the huge amount of print and correspondence that the affair provoked, as well as from the visual and material culture it spawned.[5] And the public debate was wide-ranging, examining issues of ideological conflict in a wide context that included the informal and formal rules governing what it was tolerable or polite to say and write, the nature of 'moderation' as a cultural or political mode of behaviour, and the expected roles of women in relation to Church and state. The articles that follow focus to a large degree on this extra-parliamentary dimension. This concern to link parliament to its public through a cultural form of parliamentary history is desirable because the significance of the trial lay outside Westminster as much as inside it. Moreover, such an approach can help relate parliamentary history to a wider historiography. Over the last 20 or 30 years we have been offered a history of political culture, of the way in which parliament acted as 'point

---

[2] M.E. Ransome, 'The General Election of 1710', *Bulletin of the Institute of Historical Research*, xvii (1939), 95–7; *The History of Parliament: The House of Commons, 1690–1715*, ed. Eveline Cruickshanks, Stuart Handley and D.W. Hayton (5 vols, Cambridge, 2002).

[3] John Flaningham, 'The Occasional Conformity Controversy: Ideology and Party Politics, 1697–1711', *Journal of British Studies*, xvii (1977), 38–62; Mark Knights, 'Occasional Conformity and the Representation of Dissent: Hypocrisy, Sincerity, Moderation and Zeal', *Parliamentary History*, xxiv (2005), 41–57.

[4] The best introduction to the trial remains Geoffrey Holmes, *The Trial of Doctor Sacheverell* (1973).

[5] F.F. Madan, *A Critical Bibliography of Dr Henry Sacheverell*, ed. W.A. Speck (Lawrence, KA, 1978); Mark Knights, 'Possessing the Visual: The Materiality of Visual Print Culture in Later Stuart Britain', in *Material Readings of Early Modern Culture*, ed. James Daybell and Peter Hinds (2010).

of contact' with a wider public, as much as a history of an institution.[6] This has both stimulated and reflected an increased interest in the formation of popular political attitudes, the means by which contemporaries learnt of, and engaged with, the world of Westminster, the type of political discussions and discourse that ensued, and the part played by events at Westminster in a wider framework of an emerging empire.

2

What then, from the vantage point of 1710, had been the significance of the revolution of 1688–9? It is certainly clear what Sacheverell thought.[7] In his controversial sermon *The Perils of False Brethren* he argued that the period since the revolution had seen the Church thrust into danger by toleration, dissenters and lukewarm churchmen; and he believed that two central tenets of the Church, passive obedience and non-resistance, had been subverted by resistance theories and the notion of popular sovereignty, both of which undermined that prop of the Church, the monarchy. Sacheverell thus discerned – and protested against – a shift in religious and political culture and in the ideology that underpinned it.

This shift had a long gestation but had accelerated in the period since the revolution of 1688. The change in religious culture, he feared, was profound. He saw many who equated the Church with 'Priestcraft and Popery in Masquerade'.[8] Such men, he thought, ridiculed and abused the Church. More than that, however, he identified a growing number of the lukewarm, those who were really of no religion, 'a secret sort of reserv'd Atheists'.[9] Thus he talked of the threat from 'hypocrites, Deists, Socinians and Atheists'.[10] Toleration, too, had weakened the Church. The national Church, he argued, was in grave danger from those who wanted to make it a 'heteregeneous mixture of all persons of what different faith soever', a soup of protestants, '*Jews, Quakers, Mohometans* and anything', all allowed entry by a policy of 'moderation and occasional conformity'.[11] Such an enfeebled and incoherent institution, he warned, would fall prey to 'universal scepticism and infidelity', thereby ensuring the triumph of popery which had been working so long to defeat protestantism.[12] Sacheverell's sermon thus brought together the fears underlying the potent rallying cry of 'the Church in danger'.

[6] See, e.g., Miles Taylor, 'British Politics in the Age of Revolution and Reform, 1789–1867', *Historical Journal*, xlv (2002), 661–77; *Negotiating Power in Early Modern Society: Order, Hierarchy and Subordination in Britain and Ireland*, ed. Michael J. Braddick and John Walter (Cambridge, 2001); Michael J. Braddick, *State Formation in Early Modern England, ca. 1550–1700* (Cambridge, 2000); Joanna Innes, *Inferior Politics: Social Problems and Social Policies in Eighteenth-Century Britain* (Oxford, 2009). The notion of parliament as a point of contact was used by Geoffrey Elton in 'Tudor Government, the Points of Contact, 1: Parliament', *Transactions of the Royal Historical Society*, 5th ser., xxiv (1974), 183–200.
[7] For the high church context see G.V. Bennett, *The Tory Crisis in Church and State, 1688–1730* (Oxford, 1975).
[8] Henry Sacheverell, *The Perils of False Brethren* (1709) [Madan 57], 13.
[9] Sacheverell, *Perils of False Brethren*, 14.
[10] Sacheverell, *Perils of False Brethren*, 8.
[11] Sacheverell, *Perils of False Brethren*, 24.
[12] Sacheverell, *Perils of False Brethren*, 26.

But he also attacked the ideology, 'the New-fangl'd Terms of Modern Philosophy', behind this threat.[13] One danger that he identified was the doctrine of resistance, since this undermined the state. 'The Grand Security of our Government, and the very Pillar on which it stands', he thundered, 'is founded upon the steady belief of the Subject's Obligation to an Absolute and Unconditional Obedience to the Supreme Power, in all things lawful, and the utter Illegality of Resistance upon any pretence whatsoever.'[14] This doctrine of obedience, he lamented, had been displaced by ideas about the 'Right Liberty and Property of the PEOPLE' who, liberated from authority, could cancel their allegiance at will and call their sovereign to account. Sacheverell likened those who defended that principle of resistance to those who approved of 'the horrid Actions and Principles of Forty One', in other words to the 'Republican faction' which had brought about the civil war.[15] The 'New-fangl'd Notion of Self-Defence', Sacheverell claimed, would justify 'all the rebellions that ever were or can be'; and would reduce the monarch to 'the breath of his Subject's nostrils, to be blown in or out at their caprice and pleasure'.[16] The government, he urged, should suppress such dangerous ideas with the sword and condemn them through Church and parliament. Otherwise republican notions amongst the dissenters would result in rebellion, just as they had done in 1642: 'the Old Leaven of their Fore-Fathers is still working in their present Generation' and their 'Poison still remains in this brood of Vipers, to Sting us to Death'.[17]

Sacheverell's indictment of the religious and political shifts since the revolution, nevertheless, went much further. For as well as castigating dissenters for undermining both Church and state, the Doctor suggested that as great a danger came from the 'pretended friends and false brethren' of the Church, the low churchmen who had espoused whiggish political and cultural principles. The culture of 'moderation', a key plank of the whig programme of toleration and one which related closely to the ideal of 'politeness', was thus, he suggested, a veil for those interested in 'nothing but Getting Money and Preferment'.[18] Subordinating their principles to self-advancement and mate-

---

[13] Sacheverell, *Perils of False Brethren*, 12. For the political thought of the period see Justin A.I. Champion, 'Political Thinking between Restoration and Hanoverian Succession', in *A Companion to Stuart Britain*, ed. Barry Coward (Oxford, 2003), 474–91; Justin A.I. Champion, *Republican Learning: John Toland and the Crisis of Christian Culture, 1696–1722* (Manchester, 2003); John Greville Agard Pocock, *Virtue, Commerce, and History: Essays on Political Thought and History, Chiefly in the Eighteenth Century* (Cambridge, 1985); John Marshall, *John Locke, Toleration and Early Enlightenment Culture* (Cambridge, 2006); Mark Goldie and Robert Wokler, *The Cambridge History of Eighteenth-Century Political Thought* (Cambridge, 2006).

[14] Sacheverell, *Perils of False Brethren*, 17.

[15] Sacheverell, *Perils of False Brethren*, 17–18.

[16] Sacheverell, *Perils of False Brethren*, 19–20.

[17] Sacheverell, *Perils of False Brethren*, 18.

[18] Sacheverell, *Perils of False Brethren*, 14. For the culture of politeness see A. Bryson, *From Courtesy to Civility: Changing Codes of Conduct in Early Modern England* (Oxford, 1998); N. Phillipson, 'Politics and Politeness in the Reigns of Anne and the Early Hanoverians', in *The Varieties of British Political Thought 1500–1800*, ed. J.G.A. Pocock (Cambridge, 1993); L. Klein, 'The Political Significance of "Politeness" in Early Eighteenth Century Britain', in *Politics, Politeness and Patriotism*, ed. G. Schochet (Washington, DC, 1993); L. Klein, 'Coffee-House Civility, 1660–1714: An Aspect of Post-Courtly Culture in England', *Huntington Library Quarterly*, lix (1997), 30–51; L. Klein, 'Liberty, Manners and Politeness in Early Eighteenth Century England', *Historical Journal*, xxxii (1989), 583–604; L. Klein, *Shaftesbury and the Culture of Politeness* (Cambridge, 1994); L. Klein, 'The Third Earl of Shaftesbury and the Progress of Politeness', *Eighteenth Century Studies*, xviii (1984–5), 186–214; L. Klein, 'Politeness and the Interpretation of the British Eighteenth Century', *Historical Journal*, xlv (2002), 869–98; Marku Peltonnen, 'Politeness and Whiggism, 1688–1732', *Historical Journal*, xlviii (2005),

rial gain, such men were ready to 'Fall down and Worship the very Devil himself, for the Riches and Honours of this World'.[19] They turned all religion into 'State-Craft and Imposture' and destroyed 'All Common Honesty, Faith and Credit in the World', setting up in their place 'an Universal Trade of Cousenage, Sharping, Dissimulation and downright Knavery'.[20] Covering their treachery with 'Plausible Pretences of Friendship' they were thereby 'capable of doing much more Mischief than a bare-fac'd and professed Enemy'.[21] The Church was thus in danger from ranks of hypocrites who professed to uphold the Church only as a cover to pursue their own self-interest.[22] Sacheverell saw a conspiracy afoot, involving catholics, dissenters, low churchmen and whigs, who had joined forces to undermine Church and state. Sacheverell's attack thus questioned the whole culture ushered in by the revolution, a shift, as he saw it, towards atheism, irreligion, republicanism, hypocrisy and self-advancement veiled by a dangerous veneer of worldly 'moderation' that his own zeal and passion was intended to challenge.

Sacheverell thus attacked revolution principles head on, provoking a parliamentary trial in order to defend them. The preamble to the articles of impeachment made it abundantly clear that he was being tried for slandering the revolution of 1688: 'Whereas his late Majesty King William the Third, then Prince of Orange, did, with an arm'd force, undertake a Glorious Enterprize, for delivering this Kingdom from Popery and arbitrary power', it began, 'and divers Subjects of this Realm, well affected to their Country, join'd with and assisted his late Majesty in the said Enterprize . . . the happy and blessed Consequences of the said Revolution are the Enjoyment of the Right of God's True Religion establish'd among us, and of the Laws and Liberties of the Kingdom, the uniting her Majesty's Protestant Subjects in Interest and Affection by a legal Indulgence or Toleration, granted to Dissenters'.[23] The articles went on to list Sacheverell's seditious views: 'that the necessary means used to bring about the said happy Revolution were odious and unjustifiable' and that there had been no resistance in 1688; that toleration was 'unreasonable' and 'unwarrantable'; 'that the Church of England is in a condition of great peril'; and that the low church and whiggish administration of Church and state 'tends to the destruction of the constitution'. Sacheverell was thus charged with harbouring a 'wicked, malicious and seditious intention' to undermine the government, create division and incite rebellion. In explaining the charges, the prosecution stressed that the Doctor was on trial because he aimed 'to Traduce and Condemn the late Happy Revolution' and its key doctrines of resistance against tyranny and religious toleration.[24]

In pressing home these charges, the whig prosecution inevitably put forward a vigorous defence of its own values. This led to a type of double trial: an explicit one of the Doctor

---

[18] *(continued)* 391–414. For a literary dimension on the creation of whig culture see Abigail Williams, *Poetry and the Creation of a Whig Literary Culture 1681–1714* (Oxford 2005); *Augustan Critical Writing*, ed. D. Womersley (1997).

[19] Sacheverell, *Perils of False Brethren*, 32.

[20] Sacheverell, *Perils of False Brethren*, 33.

[21] Sacheverell, *Perils of False Brethren*, 33.

[22] This theme is explored in more depth in Mark Knights, *The Devil in Disguise: Deception, Delusion, and Fanaticism in the Early English Enlightenment* (Oxford, 2011), which has a chapter on the Sacheverell affair.

[23] *A Compleat History of the Whole Proceedings . . . against Dr Henry Sacheverell* (1710) [Madan 511], 11–12. It passed no one's notice that the Doctor had chosen 5 November, the anniversary of William's landing, 'to preach against the Revolution' (p. 37).

[24] *Compleat History*, 32.

and an implicit one of revolution principles and revolutionary culture. The impeachment presented two very starkly different accounts of the revolution and its achievements. This was nowhere more apparent than in disputes over the central question of resistance. Countering Sacheverell's attack on resistance theory, Robert Walpole argued that 'to plead for Resistance' was 'to assert and maintain the very Being of our present Government and Constitution; and to assert Non-resistance, in that boundless and unlimited sense in which Doctor Sacheverell presumes to assert it, is to Sap and Undermine the very Foundations of the Government'.[25] Establishing a right of resistance was so important because a good deal more flowed from it, including the protestant succession and the war against France. Denying a right of resistance, the managers of the prosecution argued, questioned the queen's own right to sit on the throne and implied that she owed it to a usurpation of the crown.[26] It also questioned the direction of foreign policy. The military hero, General Stanhope, in attacking the high church tory principles of 'Passive Obedience, Jus Divinum, an Hereditary Indefeasible Right of Succession', argued that, far from undermining the state and Church, as Sacheverell had alleged, the ministry had funded a necessary, 'long and expensive war' against catholic France which aspired to be 'the Universal Monarchy of Europe'.[27] Managers also queued up to uphold another key revolution principle, the toleration of 1689, in the plainest terms. Lord William Powlet asserted that 'the good Effects of the Wisdom of the Legislature in making that Act had been seen' and Spencer Cowper insisted that 'Indulgence was requir'd from them as Christians and as men professing Humanity and Good Will towards one another'.[28] Whereas Sacheverell and his high church brethren defined a false churchman as one who *upheld* the toleration, it was the Doctor, the prosecution maintained, who was unchristian in his intolerance, desiring 'nothing more at heart than to destroy the present Church'.[29] The Doctor, they suggested, wanted a 'Church that would destroy all those who brought about, and had since supported, the happy Revolution. A Church, which upon Anti-Christian principles, profess'd Burning for Conscience-sake . . . A Church that would turn all the Blessings they enjoy'd under the present Administration into all those Miseries they had got rid of by the late glorious Revolution'.[30] The high churchmen, the prosecution alleged, were the real false brethren.

Sacheverell was also said to have breached the culture of politeness and moderation that the whigs sought to promote. He had, the prosecution alleged, delivered a 'harangue' full of 'Malice, Bitterness, Reviling, Insolence, endeavouring to raise in his Auditors the Passions [he] himself put on'.[31] He had 'instilled groundless Fears and Jealousies',

---

[25] *Compleat History,* 69. The grounds on which resistance could be justified did vary. General Stanhope argued 'that there was not, at that Time, any Nation or Government in the World, whose first Original had not receiv'd its Foundation either from Resistance or Compact' and that the latter implied a right to the former (p. 84) but not everyone subscribed to that view.

[26] *Compleat History,* 83–4, for Stanhope on this point.

[27] *Compleat History,* 88, 91. A high church tory printed image celebrated Stanhope's victory in the summer of 1710 but contrasted that with his role as a manager for the prosecution, suggesting that he had 'Regain'd that Honour which thy Tongue had lost': ['To the Immortal Memory of that Renowned Manager', British Museum, Satires 1530].

[28] *Compleat History,* 110–11.

[29] *Compleat History,* 127.

[30] *Compleat History,* 127.

[31] *Compleat History,* 131.

stigmatised his enemies with 'opprobrious titles', and used 'Passion, Heat and Violence' to spread 'Hideous Representations of an Evil Government'.[32] He 'fir'd the Zeal of the People, alarm'd their Passions', spoke 'a bold Falshood' and indulged in 'Bitterness, Reviling, Wrath, Clamour and Evil-Speaking'.[33] He was a trumpet of sedition. Sacheverell thus violated the cultural norms of polite, moderate, sober, rational discourse that the whigs had sought to instil in their campaign to quell religious persecution and to promote a more civil and commercial society.

The trial thus presented two very polarised positions – essentially two rival conspiracy theories in which the Church and state were either the victims of an unholy alliance of dissenters, atheists, republicans and self-advancing hypocrites or, alternatively, of bigoted high church zealots who wanted to revive persecution, tyranny and possibly a Stuart restoration. The year 1710 with its white heat of ideological conflict, was thus the apex of the 'rage of party'. That rage was so bitter because low church, 'revolution' principles were pitted against remarkably resurgent high church ones. Daniel Szechi's transcription and discussion of Lord North and Grey's notes for a speech during the trial show how ardently one high church tory subscribed to the traditional notions of non-resistance and passive obedience as the guarantor of Church and state. He was far from being alone. The vehemence of the high church tory reaction, which eventually led to the collapse of the government and victory at the subsequent election, was testament to the strength of the enduring popular adherence to the Church of England that John Morrill found for the 1650s, and John Spurr for the restoration period, and what was morphing into, for the other end of the 18th century, what Mark Philp has called 'vulgar conservatism'.[34] But as the latter suggests, this was not so much godly politics as a politically-charged mindset shaped by religious ideas and civil war myths. This was abundantly clear in the flood of addresses presented to the queen in the immediate aftermath of the trial, where it is evident that loyalty to the established Church fused with love of the monarchy and hatred of republicanism. Many of these addresses read as lessons in political and religious loyalism. Thus the address from St Albans abhorred 'schismatical, anti-monarchical and republican principles' and promised to 'curb and suppress all irreligious, immoral, seditious and rebellious tenets'.[35] The address from Cirencester, where some townsmen had burnt an effigy of King William, defended passive obedience as a fundamental and essential part of the constitution.[36] Minehead's address condemned 'how the Republican principle of resistance is of late openly taught', a notion that was 'inconsistent with reason and scripture' and Denbighshire's attacked the 'traiterous and damnable positions which assert the legality of deposing or resisting princes'.[37] Helston, which claimed not to have a single dissenter in its midst, attacked the 'popish, schismatical and fanatical

[32] *Compleat History*, 137.

[33] *Compleat History*, 142–4.

[34] John Morrill, 'The Church in England, 1642–49', in John Morrill, *The Nature of the English Revolution* (Harlow, 1993), 148–75; John Spurr, *The Restoration Church of England, 1646–1689* (New Haven, CT, 1991); Mark Philp, 'Vulgar Conservatism 1792–3', *English Historical Review*, cx (1995), 42–69; see also J. Gregory, 'Transforming the Age of Reason into an Age of Faiths: Or, Putting Religions and Beliefs (Back) into the Eighteenth Century', *Journal for Eighteenth-Century Studies*, xxxii (2009), 287–305; see also Lee Horsley, 'Vox Populi in the Political Literature of 1710', *Huntington Library Quarterly*, xxxviii (1975), 335–53.

[35] John Oldmixon, *History of Addresses, part 2* (1711) [Madan 712], 156–9.

[36] Oldmixon, *History of Addresses, part 2*, 170–1.

[37] Oldmixon, *History of Addresses, part 2*, 176, 202.

doctrines of resisting lawful princes'.[38] Hindon's referred to 'antimonarchical principles in every corner of this kingdom'; Fowey's attacked those who derived the queen's title 'from the sole gift of the people'; and Newcastle-upon-Tyne's condemned the 'original power and right of resistance in subjects'.[39] The address from Essex attacked the trilogy of anti-monarchical, atheistical and republican principles, and condemned men who tried 'to render the Imperial crown of these realms precarious by insinuating that when your Majesty or your successors shall do what they shall construe to be a breach of an Imaginary contract, the subjects are discharged from their allegiance'.[40] The addresses are proof both of how far whig revolution principles had penetrated and also how far, in some quarters, they were consequently resented, resisted and refuted.[41]

John Odmixon and Daniel Defoe tried to explain these addresses away as an example of what the latter called the people 'playing Bo-Peep with their Sovereign', making meaningless professions of opinion.[42] There may well be something in the idea that the addresses were inconstant panegyrics; but the articulation of high church tory public sentiment could not be so easily brushed aside. That Defoe felt compelled to write a 91-page tract attacking the addresses and Oldmixon a two-volume history of addresses was testament to the perceived need to counter their impact. The Sacheverell trial thus revealed both an enduring and passionate loyalty to the Church and the doctrines of obedience to authority and non-resistance, often articulated through a visceral hatred of 'republicans' and 'atheists', and an equally ardent desire by their opponents to defend, justify and even to impose revolution principles. What 1710 suggests, then, and this is a prominent theme in Bill Speck's article, is not a revolution complete but a revolution that was still contested 20 years after its central event of the flight of one king and the crowning of another.[43] In the short term, 1710–14 seemed like a tory reaction which was on a par with that of 1681–5, a reassertion of high church tory values in Church and state.[44] With hindsight, of course, the high church tide was unable to sweep all before it for long; but between 1710 and 1714, to many whigs it seemed as though it might.

3

Sacheverell's impeachment was a moment when contemporaries assessed and contested the impact of the revolution of 1688–9. What, then, do we as historians make of the furore of 1710 and its significance?

---

[38] Oldmixon, *History of Addresses*, part 2, 212.

[39] Oldmixon, *History of Addresses*, part 2, 235, 243, 292.

[40] Oldmixon, *History of Addresses*, part 2, 254.

[41] See, e.g., Huntington Library, San Marino, CA, Stowe MS 57: James Brydges to Drummond, 15 July 1710; 'the republican notions that were so openly asserted and maintained upon the late tryall have allarmed to ye highest degree ye whole kingdom, and you may see their sense from the addresses that have been sent up from all parts of it, which are ye strongest in their expressions and ye most numerous I remember to have read'.

[42] Daniel Defoe, *A New Test of the Sence of the Nation* (1710), 2–7, 89.

[43] Steve Pincus, *1688: The First Modern Revolution* (New Haven, CT, 2009), ch. 14, suggests that from the perspective of 1696 a whig revolution looked complete.

[44] The period is explored by Daniel Szechi, *Jacobitism and Tory Politics 1710–14* (Edinburgh, 1984).

The impeachment has important things to tell us about print and the public sphere, two themes which have generated much discussion over recent years.[45] Several contributions to this volume focus on the national debate surrounding the impeachment, expressed through a vibrant print and material culture. Bill Speck's article analyses the bibliographical work of the Madans (to which he has himself added considerably) in cataloguing the outpouring of print, from which we have a very clear idea of the extraordinary magnitude, diversity and range of the printed controversy. With over a thousand items, and with some huge print runs – Sacheverell's sermon was itself a publishing sensation, selling hundreds of thousands of copies – it outnumbered earlier print debates.[46] Arguably, the first major flexing of the press's muscles after the expiry of the Licensing Act in 1695, 1710 was, nevertheless, important for debates over censorship and regulation of the press. Sacheverell was himself prosecuted for what he had said, and then silenced after the judgment against him, but he also sought to attack what he saw as the press's attacks on the Church and even to reanimate the 1683 Oxford University decree which had burnt a number of offending works. Seeing censorship debates through the lens of the Sacheverell controversy, Geoff Kemp's article suggests, highlights differences within the clerical response to the lapse of licensing. While some, such as Sacheverell himself, clearly thought that the press had become a danger to the Church – and his defence catalogued the pamphlets that sought to undermine it – others within the Church sought regulation rather than censorship. Thus one of Sacheverell's 'perfidious prelates', Archbishop Tenison, sought to tackle heresy, not through the restoration of prepublication licensing but through regulation of imprints, a deliberate ploy to frustrate the intolerance of the high churchmen, and this policy was closer to the landmark press legislation of 1710, the passage of the copyright law. Kemp thus suggests that debates between the different wings of the Church over the press mirrored the low church–high church divide that characterised the Sacheverell controversy.

The debates also shed interesting light on the nature of the public sphere, which could be manipulated for partisan advantage. Brian Cowan shows how Sacheverell was skilful in presenting himself as a persecuted, censored martyr, drawing on older memories of

---

[45] Both themes have generated voluminous literatures. For discussion of print culture see Mark Knights, *Representation and Misrepresentation in Later Stuart Britain: Partisanship and Political Culture* (Oxford, 2005); Joad Raymond, *Pamphlets and Pamphleteering in Early Modern Britain* (Cambridge, 2003); Jason Peacey, *Politicians and Pamphleteers: Propaganda during the English Civil Wars and Interregnum* (2004); Paula McDowell, *The Women of Grub Street: Press, Politics and Gender in the London Literary Marketplace, 1678–1730* (Oxford, 1998). For discussions of the public sphere in this period see Mark Knights, 'How Rational was the Later Stuart Public Sphere?', in *The Politics of the Public Sphere in Early Modern England*, ed. Peter Lake and Steven C.A. Pincus (Manchester, 2007); Mark Knights, 'Public Politics in England c. 1675–c. 1715', in *The English Revolution c.1590–1720: Politics, Religion and Communities*, ed. N. Tyacke (Manchester, 2007); Peter Lake and Steve Pincus, 'Rethinking the Public Sphere in Early Modern England', *Journal of British Studies*, xlv (2006), 270–92; Brian Cowan, 'Mr Spectator and the Coffee House Public Sphere', *Eighteenth Century Studies*, xxxvii (2004), 345–66; Brian Cowan, 'What was Masculine about the Public Sphere?: Gender and the Coffeehouse Milieu in Post-Restoration England', *History Workshop Journal*, li (2001), 127–57; Brian Cowan, 'Geoffrey Holmes and the Public Sphere: Augustan Historiography from Post-Namierite to the Post-Habermasian', in *British Politics in the Age of Holmes: Geoffrey Holmes's British Politics in the Age of Anne 40 Years On*, ed. Clyve Jones (Oxford, 2009).
[46] There were 192 tracts published in 1689–92 over the 'allegiance controversy', though the total volume of print relating to the revolution was much larger than that; there were 215 anti-papal tracts published in the reign of James II: Mark Goldie, 'The Revolution of 1689 and the Structure of Political Argument', *Bulletin of Research in the Humanities*, lxxxiii (1980), 473–564.

another martyr for the Church, Charles I.[47] Cowan stresses how much of the later Stuart period could be seen in terms of rival martyrologies – even if Sacheverell's pretensions as a martyr were ridiculed by his critics who condemned his hypocritical and theatrical posturing. Cowan also explores how the Doctor's affecting impeachment defence, his apologetic oratory, his conduct when travelling to the trial and his publications, worked carefully to generate public sympathy. He was deliberately playing to the gallery, cultivating and milking the widespread sympathy for the Church and depicting himself as entirely orthodox in order to defuse the central charge that he was a seditious incendiary. For Cowan, the impeachment became a spectacle, a piece of public theatre using Westminster as the stage, and one in which those in the audience were as much participants and judges as were the lord chancellor and the other peers who had formal votes.[48] The public sphere was, thus, a theatrical one, one in which players could even be given lines by others (many thought Sacheverell's defence speech was not his own work), and one that could be manipulated by clever rhetorics and representations that could be used both to deepen and to undercut partisan attacks, so long as they tugged on deeply-felt heartstrings of the audience.

Cowan notes how the Doctor was able to move his female auditors to tears, and his ambiguous 'appeal' to women is explored more fully in Eirwen Nicholson's article.[49] She highlights how the public discussion of Sacheverell had deeply sexualised overtones: to his detractors, the Doctor's 'appeal' to female 'admirers' was more than ideological and he became a dangerously-charged, adored idol. His portraits were bought and reverenced; consumer items, such as fans, were produced, that were aimed at women buyers; women attended his trial; and they followed his progress. As an object of female fascination and worship – and in a culture in which partisanship was increasingly sexualised for the scandal that could be thrown at opponents – Sacheverell became associated in prints – visual as well as verbal – with prostitution. This endured, so that William Hogarth's harlot has a portrait of the Doctor on her wall. The participation of women in the consumer culture generated by Sacheverell's celebrity suggests a public sphere in which women could participate but at the risk of their reputation.

The public sphere was also capable of extending across borders and boundaries, as David Hayton's article shows. Coming only two years after union with Scotland, the Sacheverell controversy united England and Ireland through a common set of responses. Hayton shows that although in Ireland references to Sacheverell himself were relatively rare, the Dublin press reprinted a good deal of English Sacheverellania and, in part as a result of this, two partisan proxies caused similar waves. The high church cleric, Francis

[47] There were at least four different versions of a print depicting Sacheverell holding a portrait of Charles I: Knights, 'Possessing the Visual', 110.

[48] One visual satire of the period, *Faults on Boath Sides*, depicts Hoadly astride an ass on stage. Sacheverell's sermon had assured any 'turn-coat' who had 'got upon the stage' that, after acting his part he would be 'hiss'd off': Sacheverell, *Perils of False Brethren*, 41.

[49] Politics were infused by gender issues, as Rachel Weil has shown in *Political Passions: Gender, the Family and Political Argument in England 1680–1714* (Manchester, 1999). For the association between prostitution and politics see also Melissa Mowry, *The Bawdy Politic in Stuart England 1660–1714: Political Pornography and Prostitution* (2004); Susan Wiseman, *Conspiracy and Virtue: Women, Writing, and Politics in Seventeenth Century England* (Oxford, 2006); Laura Rosenthal, *Infamous Commerce: Prostitution in Eighteenth-Century British Literature and Culture* (Ithaca, NY, 2006); Sophie Carter, *Purchasing Power: Representing Prostitution in Eighteenth-Century English Popular Print Culture* (Aldershot, 2004).

Higgins, and Sir Constantine Phipps, one of the Doctor's defence counsel and, from 1710, a whig-hating lord chancellor of Ireland, became the focus of controversy, not just in England but also in Dublin. Both, like Sacheverell himself, depicted themselves as champions (and martyrs) for the Church, tapping into the same values in Ireland as the Doctor had done in England.

The graphic prints used by Hayton, Nicholson and Cowan also suggest that the public sphere was innovating in terms of its appropriation of visual emblems and material culture.[50] Sympathetic portraits were an intrinsic part of the publishing strategy adopted for Sacheverell's sermon and subsequently for his defence. These provoked hostile portraits and satirical images of the Doctor in what was becoming an increasingly dialogic visual debate. Half a century before Wilkes's more famous use of topical prints and consumables, visual and material propaganda were being used to construct and undermine public, controversial images.

The articles by Hayton, Nicholson and Cowan also problematise the secular nature of the Habermasian public sphere. They show that in England and Ireland, the emerging public sphere could be strengthened and shaped by religiously-inflected debate, even if it was also highly politicised. The highly-charged and contested nature of belief and forms of worship necessarily swelled, and at times triggered, extensive public discussion. Similarly, Habermas's stress on the *rational* nature of the public sphere is questionable, given the zeal and passion generated by the controversy.[51] Sacheverell disliked dissenting zeal; but he sought to replace it with zeal for the established Church, a type of emotional piety that was to recur in the 18th century as a reaction to the attempts to make religion sober and reasonable. Bill Speck also reminds us about the riots that occurred during the trial – the most serious disorder on London's streets since the revolution. So we have a public sphere that was full of passionate, furious, railing and sometimes violent debate (prompting ever louder calls for a more polite form of interaction); one which was about religion, or at least about the political and cultural implications stemming from a religious controversy; one which was highly aware of the gendered or even sexualised nature of public 'conversation'; and one which sought to make use of images and material culture as well as words. This is not quite the public sphere that Habermas conceptualised but it is recognizable throughout the 18th century and, arguably, a good deal earlier than that.

Steve Pincus's article, nevertheless, suggests that the public sphere also embraced a vigorous and contested debate about political economy (state policy towards wealth creation) and empire.[52] His piece is a salutary reminder about the importance of a more

---

[50] I have also explored this in 'Possessing the Visual' and *The Devil in Disguise*, ch. 5. Brian Cowan's *The State Trial of Doctor Henry Sacheverell* (Parliamentary History Texts & Studies) also contains a discussion of a volume into which a contemporary inserted visual material.

[51] Knights, 'How Rational was the Later Stuart Public Sphere?'.

[52] For discussions of political economy see Pincus, *1688*; Julian Hoppit, 'The Contexts and Contours of British Economic Literature 1660–1760', *Historical Journal*, xlix (2006), 79–110; Julian Hoppit, 'Checking the Leviathan, 1688–1832', in *The Political Economy of British Historical Experience, 1688–1914*, ed. Donald Winch, Donald Norman and Patrick O'Brien (Oxford, 2002); Julian Hoppit, 'The Myths of the South Sea Bubble', in *Transactions of the Royal Historical Society*, 6th ser., xii (2002), 141–65; Julian Hoppit, 'Political Arithmetic in Eighteenth-Century England', *Economic History Review*, 2nd ser., xlix (1996), 516–40; Istvan Hont, *Jealousy of Trade: International Competition and the Nation-State in Historical Perspective* (2005); Ted McCormick, *William Petty and the Ambitions of Political Arithmetic* (2010); Perry Gauci, 'The Clash of Interests: Commerce and the Politics

secular set of debates that, nevertheless, intersected with the more religiously- and politically-inspired ones. The controversies of 1710 and the years that immediately followed were as much (Pincus might argue 'more') about the nature of wealth and how best to promote it as they were about religion. Pincus argues that there were competing tory and whig conceptions of wealth, the economy and empire, leading to radically-different visions of Britain's national interest and strategic aims. For the tories, for whom he suggests wealth was finite, extending an empire that could embrace the gold mines of Spanish America was highly attractive. For the whigs, by contrast, such a vision was a chimera; wealth was not finite because it was founded in labour, and commerce, not conquest, was the key to national prosperity. Pincus suggests that these contrasting viewpoints were in sharp conflict in Anne's reign and that 1710 marked an important point in the competition between these visions of empire. The tory backlash after the Sacheverell trial led to the abandonment of a whig war that had sought to militarily defeat, and economically restrict, France in favour of schemes of South American conquest and peace with France, even if that meant sacrificing commercial advantages won during the war. Pincus thus reminds us that foreign and economic policy was contested; that these contests can be mapped on to the bitter partisanship of the period; and that the results of the contests, particularly after a return to whig policies in 1714, helped to shape the development of a North America and West Indian empire. He adds a useful corrective to the idea that the rage of party and the Sacheverell controversy should simply be viewed in terms of religious and constitutional conflict; rather, the ideological debates reflected in the Sacheverell controversy also found expression in competing economic visions.

The public debates about political economy, about the role of the Church and monarchy, about the nature of resistance and the origins of political authority also suggest that we might consider 1710 as part of an early enlightenment.[53] At first sight this does not seem a promising line of enquiry. A furore about a cleric who promoted religious intolerance and a defence of an 'ancien regime' yoking of Church and state does not sound likely terrain in which to find enlightenment ideals. Nevertheless, the use of the press to popularise and disseminate ideas; a keen debate about the nature of wealth, foreign policy and the national interest; the invocation and participation of the public in debates which contested religion, politics, and the place of women; the attack on the 'priestcraft' of the high churchmen and the defence of toleration; the justification of popular sovereignty and a right to resist tyranny; a debate over censorship; and the idealisation of rational, moderate, discourse amid the clamour and railing of zealous, prejudiced fanatics, are all recognizable features of an early enlightenment. The Sacheverell affair reminds us that the early enlightenment was a process of contestation – the revolution principles valued by the low churchmen and whigs were vigorously contested

---

[52] *(continued)* of Trade in the Age of Anne', *Parliamentary History*, xxviii (2009), 115–25; Thomas Leng, 'Commercial Conflict and Regulation in the Discourse of Trade in Seventeenth-Century England', *Historical Journal*, xlviii (2005), 933–54.

[53] I explore this theme at greater length in *The Devil in Disguise*, especially ch. 5. See also Champion, *Republican Learning*; Champion, 'Political Thinking between Restoration and Hanoverian Succession'; Justin A.I. Champion and Lee McNulty, 'Making Orthodoxy in Late Restoration England: The Trials of Edmund Hickeringill, 1662–1710', in *Negotiating Power in Early Modern Society: Order, Hierarchy and Subordination in Britain and Ireland*, ed. Michael J. Braddick and John Walter (Cambridge, 2001), 227–48, 302–5; Marshall, *John Locke, Toleration and Early Enlightenment Culture*.

as part of an ongoing struggle, a process in which statements of principle provoked challenge and counter-attack, which, in turn, stimulated restatement or refinement of ideas in a process that was difficult to close down. The lively intellectual and cultural contests triggered by Sacheverell were part of a dialectical enlightenment in which two sides participated, shaping the arguments of the other as they engaged with them.

One key enlightenment debate concerned the nature and demonstrability of truth; and the Sacheverell affair – symptomatic of partisanship more generally – raised this concern very forcibly. The verse under one of the most popular images of the Doctor, which depicts him holding a portrait of Charles I, reads:

> To preach up Truth, some say tis not a time
> False Brethren allwaies think ye Truth a Crime
> But since ye Truth offends, I'll vex you more
> And shew ye Face of Truth you've wrong'd before.[54]

The image and its text thus suggested that Charles I had been martyred for adhering to the 'Truth' and that Sacheverell, too, was its martyr.[55] But both Charles I and Sacheverell could be seen as perverters of the truth and the hail of criticism directed at Sacheverell fundamentally questioned the truth of his assertions. The Doctor could be seen in two diametrically-opposed ways: as a valiant defender of the Church and state or, quite the reverse, as a fanatic and trumpet of sedition. Determining truth in a polarised polemical battle was no easy task. Moreover, not only was the true ideology or even the true character of any politician or cleric difficult to discern; the debate over Sacheverell also destabilised the capacity of language to convey truth. To return for a moment to the addresses presented to the queen, Defoe thought that they were a mere 'rhapsody of words' that had no meaning, rendering all language useless as a signifier of things. He argued that the addresses threatened the meaning of words to the point of 'non-signification'[56]

> This new system of having No Meaning at all, brings em off as clever as a gun, and washes them as white from the scandal of talking nonsense to the Queen as can be. For having only muster'd up a Rhapsody of Words, which they meant for nothing; and which they hoped no doubt that her Majesty wou'd take for nothing; the want of truth in them was a thing of no signification, for what can it signify whether words that have no meaning have any truth in them or no?[57]

Truth and meaning had so disappeared from the 'common conversation of men' that they had become like 'froth upon your drink'. As another pamphlet put it, the addresses

---

[54] See above, n. 47.

[55] This paragraph highlights themes explored at more length in Knights, *Representation and Misrepresentation* and *The Devil in Disguise*.

[56] Defoe, *A New Test of the Sence of the Nation*, 3, 7, 13, 17. The BL copy at 101.c.44 has a manuscript date of 3 Aug. 1710.

[57] Defoe, *A New Test of the Sence of the Nation*, 55. Cf. Benjamin Hoadly, 'Queries of the Utmost Importance', in *A Collection of Several Papers Printed in the Year 1710* (1718), 88.

contained 'false stories invented, persons and actions misrepresented, charges of disloyalty, heresy, disaffection to the church, or whatever implied reproach, whether true or false'.[58]

Identifying truth and sincerity was also apparent in the debate about the culture of self-interest that Sacheverell had identified as pervading attitudes to religion and politics. The whigs and low churchmen, he claimed, proceeded 'upon no Principle, but meer Interest and Ambition'.[59] His supporters agreed. 'It is as plain as the Sun', wrote one high church pamphleteer, 'that they are for no others Interest but their own'.[60] Another pro-Sacheverell pamphlet depicted a dream (or nightmare) in which a devilish (whig) beast was accompanied by 'a powerful man . . . with a huge Purse hanging by his side . . . a true servant unto the Idol Mammon', clearly attacking Lord Treasurer God-olphin (as Sacheverell had) as the leader of a system of corruption.[61] On the other side, Sacheverell's prosecution and critics alleged that it was Sacheverell and the high church-men who were self-interested. The Doctor, they said, was a man interested in power who used religion as a tool to oust the whig government and undermine the national interest, engaging in a form of 'priestcraft'.[62] The 'ferment' whipped up by the sermon 'could tend to nothing but the ruin of the Protestant Interest', fumed one pamphleteer.[63] Sarah Cowper, mother of the lord chancellor who presided over the Doctor's trial, believed that Sacheverell and his fellow high churchmen wore a 'mask' or 'vizard' which obscured 'a Mercenary Sort of people without Conscience'. Indeed, she was so disillusioned by high church self-interest that her allegiances began to shift. She had 'never felt so Bitter Zeal against any, as These [Sa]Cheverell Miscrants: who make me that was a Staunch Church: Woman become one of the Staggering Party'.[64]

Unmasking or drawing back the curtain to reveal the true selfish and sinister intent of partisan rivals thus became a vital task in order to undeceive the people about hypocrites who threatened them. This, again, was what Sacheverell thought he was doing.[65] The 'false brethren' that he attacked were a dangerous self-contradiction, 'maintaining an irreconcilable war betwixt the outward and inward man', a mixture of 'inconsistency and nonsense' whose 'habitual hypocrisy' would undermine religion, society and the state. The false brethren, he urged, should 'throw off the mask' or be unmasked by others.[66] The hypocrite was often thought of as masked or cloaked or hidden behind a curtain (a visual code that can be found in many of the images of the period). Unmasking, uncloaking, pulling back the curtain were all ways in which 'truth' or the true self could be uncovered. And that act was often a dramatic, even theatrical one – on which many a play, plot, or image turned. Dror Wahrman has located the birth of the 'modern self'

[58] *The High Church Mask Pull'd off or Modern Addresses Anatomized: Designed Chiefly for the Information of the Common People* (1710) [Madan 722], 3.

[59] Sacheverell, *Perils of False Brethren*, 33.

[60] Patrick Drewe, *The Church of England's Late Conflict with, and Triumph over the Spirit of Fanaticism* (1710) [Madan 657], 53.

[61] *Aminadab: Or, the Quaker's Vision* (1710) [Madan 419], 5–6.

[62] William Bisset, *The Modern Fanatick* (1710) [Madan 987] – a work which had three parts; *A Character of Don Sacheverellio* (1710–14) [Madan 987, 1005, 1108].

[63] [Arthur Maynwaring], *Four Letters to a Friend in North Britain, Upon the Publishing the Tryal of Dr Sacheverell* (1710) [Madan 555], 17.

[64] Hertfordshire Archives and Local Studies, Panshanger MS, DE/P F33, p. 190: 20 July 1710.

[65] See also Knights, 'Occasional Conformity and the Representation of Dissent'.

[66] Sacheverell, *Perils of False Brethren*, 42–4.

in the later 18th century and related it to a sudden revolution in the theatricality of outer selves; but we can find this masked self alive and embedded in politico-religious culture very much earlier.[67]

As a high point in the rage of party, the parliamentary impeachment of Henry Sacheverell thus throws light on the nature of partisanship, popular loyalties to Church and state, a revised notion of the public sphere, a gendered culture of moderation and politeness, competing visions of political economy, and some of the preoccupations about truth and selfhood of the early enlightenment. If the Sacheverell trial is not an event to 'celebrate' it is, nevertheless, an important one to mark and remember.

[67] Dror Wahrman, *The Making of the Modern Self: Identity and Culture in Eighteenth-century England* (New Haven, 2006).

The Current State of Sacheverell Scholarship

W. A. SPECK

This article reviews the literature on the Sacheverell affair as it stood when it was delivered as a paper to the symposium held in March 2010 to commemorate the 300th anniversary of his impeachment. The basic narrative and prevalent interpretation of its significance were established by the late Geoffrey Holmes in his monograph *The Trial of Doctor Sacheverell* published in 1973. Holmes placed it in the context of a crisis in Church and state brought about by the Glorious Revolution and its aftermath. This led to the formation of the party conflict between high church tories and low church whigs. When the whigs, led by the junto, came to power between 1708 and 1710, their ascendancy provoked a reaction from tories claiming that the established Church was in danger. It was in this context that Sacheverell preached his provocative sermon on 5 November 1709, which brought on his impeachment for high crimes and misdemeanours. Holmes's detailed account of the trial, together with his separate analysis of the 'Sacheverell riots', have been generally accepted as definitive. Consequently, scholarly attention has tended to shift to the cultural aspects of the affair such as poems on affairs of state and political prints. These investigations have led, in turn, to attempts to establish an appropriate methodology for analysing their significance.

Keywords: revolution (of 1688); nonjurors; dissenters; deists; high church; low church; whigs; tories; occasional conformity

When Geoffrey Holmes's *The Trial of Doctor Sacheverell* appeared in 1973, it proved to be as definitive a study of the impeachment as his *British Politics in the Age of Anne* had become of the political system in the early 18th century. Both replaced previous accounts and have yet to be superseded. Certainly when I narrated the trial in *The Birth of Britain: A New Nation 1700–1710* (1994), which I dedicated to Geoffrey's memory, my narrative was based on his book. Again the life of Sacheverell which I contributed to *The Oxford Dictionary of National Biography* (2004) owed much to the account of the Doctor's career provided by Holmes, who would surely have written the entry himself had he lived.

There were many discussions of the impeachment in biographical and political studies of the period, the more outstanding, before they were replaced by Holmes, being those in Sir Keith Feiling's *A History of the Tory Party 1640–1714* (1924) and G.M. Trevelyan's *England under Queen Anne* (3 vols, 1930–4). Yet, curiously, only two specific studies of the trial had been published before 1973. The first had appeared in the very limited edition of *A Bibliography of Dr. Henry Sacheverell* by Falconer Madan, of which a mere 100 copies had been printed in 1884. The other, *The Sacheverell Affair* by Abbie Scudi, published in 1939, was a major contribution to the series in which it appeared, Columbia University Studies in History, Economics and Public Law. It was, however, totally eclipsed by that of Holmes.

He placed the trial in the context summed up by the slogan 'The Church in Danger'. Thus the impeachment was not just a political affair but was also 'a symptom of the malaise which had stricken the Church of England by Sacheverell's day'.[1] It set in during the reign of James II. Under Charles II the anglican church had flourished in a way which was to make 'good King Charley's Golden time' long remembered as an age in which 'zealous high churchmen' like the vicar of Bray 'got preferment'. The time-serving vicar boasted that he had then preached the traditional anglican doctrines of divine right kingship, passive obedience and non-resistance. James II's attack on anglicans, however, brought the golden age to an abrupt end. Their loyalties came to be divided between the Church and the crown. When the revolution occurred in 1688 many put their loyalty to the Church before their oaths of allegiance to the king. The doctrines of divine right and passive obedience were clearly compromised in the process. A minority of churchmen continued to uphold them and remained loyal to James II. They seceded or were expelled from the established Church, bringing about the nonjuring schism. The non-jurors pricked the consciences of the majority who continued to conform and took the oaths to William and Mary. As Holmes observed: 'to say that nine-tenths of the Anglican clergy "conformed" after the Revolution tells us nothing about the contortions of conscience and the mental reservations which conformity . . . involved'.[2]

Assailed by nonjurors for their apostasy from the traditional teachings of the Church, anglicans also found themselves under attack from dissenters in the 1690s. The Toleration Act seemed to open the floodgates to the licensed establishment of dissenting conventicles. The presence of dissenting ministers in their parishes lawfully competing with them for the cure of souls did much to feed the paranoia which led anglican clergymen to believe that the Church itself was in danger.

As if to be besieged by nonjurors and dissenters was not enough, they also found themselves challenged in their basic beliefs by deists, freethinkers and socinians. Holmes even claimed that rational religion was 'intellectually the most powerful force of the day'. 'Yet even Deism seemed almost respectable', he continued, 'when compared with the flow of sceptical, blasphemous or downright atheistical literature . . . encouraged by the effective end of press censorship in 1695.'[3] The established clergy bore the brunt of these attacks, 'priestcraft' becoming a cant word for their alleged insidious influence.

Instead of presenting a united front to their adversaries, however, churchmen became deeply divided into high church and low church parties. Holmes traced the division to the Convocation controversy of 1697–1701. High churchmen yearned to return to the golden age of good King Charley's days, when anglicans had been united and dissent had been proscribed. They regarded the Toleration Act as a strictly limited measure, no more than an 'indulgence' or 'exemption'. It certainly should not be taken to legalise the foundation of dissenting academies and schools, which one high church tory denounced as 'nurseries for rebellion'.[4] Nor should 'occasional conformity' be allowed to undermine the anglican monopoly of offices held under the crown or in borough corporations. The high church party demanded the revival of Convocation to re-establish the Church's

---

[1] Geoffrey Holmes, *The Trial of Doctor Sacheverell* (1973), 1.

[2] Holmes, *Trial of Doctor Sacheverell*, 23.

[3] Holmes, *Trial of Doctor Sacheverell*, 25–6.

[4] Sir John Pakington, quoted in Holmes, *Trial of Doctor Sacheverell*, 38.

authority and put it back on an equal footing with the state. And it looked to parliament
to pass legislation making occasional conformity a criminal offence. Low churchmen, by
contrast, accepted that there was no going back. The Church of England had been
'partially disestablished' by the Erastian ecclesiastical settlement in the revolution. Toleration should be welcomed and dissenters treated as fellow christians, not as heretics.
Their schools and academies were lawful, while even occasional conformity was not the
heinous crime which high churchmen denounced as 'abominable hypocrisy' and 'inex-
cusable immorality'.[5] Low churchmen co-operated with dissenters in societies for the
reformation of manners which high churchmen like Sacheverell denounced as 'mongrel
institutions'.[6] 'The least edifying of all the spectacles presented by a Church divided into
High and Low factions', Holmes observed, 'was the prostitution of the pulpit, particularly
in Queen Anne's reign, to blatantly party ends. Henry Sacheverell's crime of 1709 was
but the offence of hundreds of his fellow-divines writ large.'[7]

The parties were not confined to the clergy but had their political allies in the whig
and tory parties. Thus whigs espoused the low church and tories the high church.
Without the bitter partisanship between them the impeachment and trial would never
have gone ahead. Between 1702 and 1704, when the tories had a majority in the house
of commons, the whigs used their superiority in the Lords to block three bills aimed at
outlawing occasional conformity. The cry 'the Church in danger' was raised by tory
candidates in the subsequent general election held in 1705, which resulted in a narrow
whig victory. Shortly after the elections, an anonymous high church tract appeared with
the provocative title *The Memorial of the Church of England*. It accused the ministry led by
Lord Treasurer Godolphin of endangering the Church by dispensing with high church
tory ministers and turning to whigs in a misguided policy of 'moderation'. 'They have
forfeited the esteem and affection of the whole body of the Church Men', asserted the
author, probably James Drake, 'to make themselves Heads of a Prick-ear'd Faction.'[8] In
December 1705, tories in both houses of parliament proposed motions that the Church
was in danger from the government. Though the motions were defeated, the slogan was
not silenced. On the contrary, it became more strident when the Godolphin ministry,
which in 1705 contained not a single member of the whig junto, yielded to pressure
from their supporters to admit them into office. The pressure became irresistible when
the whigs won a clear majority at the general election of 1708. By 1709 four of the five
members of the junto – Orford, Somers, Sunderland and Wharton – were in the cabinet.

It was, therefore, no coincidence that the whigs were in power when Dr Sacheverell's
notorious sermon was preached in St Paul's on 5 November 1709 before the lord mayor,
aldermen and citizens of London. The mayor, Sir Samuel Garrard, had been a tacker, that
is one of those high church tory MPs who had also earned notoriety for themselves by
supporting an abortive bid to tack the occasional conformity bill to the land tax bill in
1704. It was one of the mayor's duties to invite a preacher to deliver a sermon before
the city fathers on 5 November. The day was chosen for its double significance as the
anniversary of the Gunpowder Plot and of the landing of William of Orange in Torbay

[5] William Bromley, quoted in Geoffrey Holmes, *British Politics in the Age of Anne* (1967), 99.
[6] Henry Sacheverell, *The Character of a Low-Church Man* (1702) [Madan 7], 11.
[7] Holmes, *Trial of Doctor Sacheverell*, 32.
[8] [James Drake], *The Memorial of the Church of England* (1705), 21.

in 1688. Garrard deliberately chose a high-flying firebrand to provoke his overwhelmingly whig colleagues on the aldermanic bench and in the common council. By 1709 Sacheverell was well known for his high church rants against whigs, dissenters and 'fanatics' of all kinds. He had come by this reputation in Oxford soon after his appointment to a fellowship of Magdalen College in 1701. On 31 May 1702, he delivered a sermon in St Mary's on the theme of 'the political union' between Church and state. It began as a standard exposition of the theme 'that religion is the grand support of Government'. Towards the end, however, it degenerated into a tirade against dissenters, who formed 'a party which is an open and avowed enemy to our communion'. They were sectarians 'against whom every man that wishes [the Church's] welfare ought to hang out the bloody flag and banner of defiance'.[9] The publication of this sermon attracted notice throughout England that summer, and particularly in London. It provoked John Dennis to publish *The danger of priestcraft to religion and government*. It was also to inspire Daniel Defoe's *Shortest Way with the Dissenters*, the title page of which proclaimed that it was 'taken from Dr. Sach—ll's sermon'. Sacheverell entered the lists in the general election held in the summer of 1702. He defended the high church tory knight of the shire for Worcestershire, Sir John Pakington, against the alleged attacks of Bishop Lloyd of Worcester. Lloyd was denounced in a pamphlet *The Character of a Low-Church-man . . . humbly offered to all the electors of the ensuing Parliament and Convocation*. Those clergymen involved in the elections to Convocation were advised to beware of 'false brethren' in their midst. Thus Sacheverell's use of the text 'in perils amongst false brethren' in 1709 was anticipated several years before in an election pamphlet, and was even employed for a sermon he preached in Oxford in December 1705.

By then Sacheverell was well known as a high church zealot, not afraid to speak his mind against those he saw as threats to his brand of anglicanism. As long as his overblown rhetoric and scathing denunciations were confined to Oxford, or on occasional excursions to the provinces, as when he delivered the assize sermon at Leicester in 1706, they could be tolerated as the ravings of a deluded don. But when he got a living in St Saviour's Southwark in the spring of 1709, it was another matter, for now he had a pulpit within the metropolitan area of the capital. That summer he preached another assize sermon, this time at Derby. When this was published in October it caused a stir, not least because of words Sacheverell used in the dedication. He claimed that 'now . . . the principles and interests of our Church and communion are so shamefully betrayed and run down', and deplored 'the secret malice and open violence they are persecuted with'.[10] These words were hot from the press when Sir Samuel Garrard invited him to preach at St Paul's on 5 November.

Holmes sets the scene splendidly. 'During the prayers and hymns which preceded the sermon Doctor Sacheverell sat with his fellow-clergy. He offered the thanksgiving prayer himself, significantly with 'not a word of the two great mercies of the day' (i.e., the discovery of the Gunpowder Plot and William's arrival in Torbay). But otherwise he remained half-oblivious of the service, locked away in a private world, working himself up into the mood of frenzied anger and near-hysteria which an Oxford audience would at once have recognized as presaging a storm. His immediate neighbour, never having

---

[9] Henry Sacheverell, *The Political Union* (1702) [Madan 1], 5, 59.
[10] Henry Sacheverell, *The Communication of Sin* (1709) [Madan 48], dedication.

seen him before and 'little suspecting him to be the Bloody Flag Officer', was utterly astonished 'at the fiery red that over-spread his face . . . and the goggling wildness of his eyes'.[11] The bulk of Sacheverell's sermon hit out at the familiar targets of his previous effusions. Indeed much of it could well have been a rerun of the one he had preached on the same text, 'in perils among false brethren', in December 1705. Many of the false brethren in Church and state were the usual suspects, low churchmen and whigs. Even Godolphin, clearly alluded to by the preacher's reference to 'wily Volpones', could have featured in the earlier version, since he had been referred to as 'Volpone' in William Shippen's poem *Faction Displayed* in 1704.[12] But the sermon had somehow to be adjusted to the anniversaries of Guy Fawkes's plot and William of Orange's landing. 'At the start it took Sacheverell under three minutes to dispose of the Gunpowder Plot and the Papists', observes Holmes, 'and even here, by bracketing 5 November with 30 January [the anniversary of the execution of Charles I] as days of equal significance in the English calendar, he was able to brand the dissenters as being no less abhorrent than the Guy Fawkes's Day conspirators.'[13] He contrived to hook the commemoration of 1688 to a defence of the traditional anglican doctrine of 'the utter illegality of resistance upon any pretence whatsoever'! 'Our adversaries think they effectually stop our mouths, and have us sure and unanswerable on this point, when they urge the Revolution of this day in their defence. But certainly they are the greatest enemies of that, and of his late Majesty, and the most ungrateful for the deliverance, who endeavour to cast such black and odious colours upon both.'[14]

It was his denial that there had been resistance in the revolution which led to Sacheverell's impeachment. Such a blatant attack on the whig view of 1688 could not be ignored by a party which had a majority in both houses of parliament. Although alternatives were scouted, the ministers decided to impeach the preacher. Holmes effectively defends that decision from the charge often made against it that it was rash and ill-advised. He also shows how the unexpected delay in starting the trial played into the hands of the tories. It was originally to take place at the bar of the house of lords on 9 February. But then on 4 February it was voted to be held in West-minster Hall. Resulting arrangements to accommodate 400 MPs as well as all peers, who were allowed up to seven guests each, led to the start being postponed until the 27th.

Holmes vividly recreates the theatrical atmosphere in which the trials took place over three-and-a-half weeks before about 2,000 spectators. There were four articles of impeachment, for which 20 managers were appointed by the Commons to uphold the charges against Sacheverell before the Lords. The first, and by far the most important, accused Sacheverell of having suggested and maintained 'that the necessary means used to bring about the . . . happy Revolution were odious and unjustifiable; that his late Majesty, in his Declaration disclaimed the least imputation of Resistance; and that to impute Resistance to the said Revolution is to cast black and odious colours upon his

---

[11] Holmes, *Trial of Doctor Sacheverell*, 63.

[12] *Poems on Affairs of State: Augustan Satirical Verse 1660–1714*, general ed. George deForest Lord (7 vols, New Haven, CT, 1962–75) [hereafter cited as POAS], vi [ed. Frank H. Ellis (1970)], 669.

[13] Holmes, *Trial of Doctor Sacheverell*, 64.

[14] Henry Sacheverell, *The Perils of False Brethren* (8vo, 1709) [Madan 58], 12.

Majesty and the said Revolution'.[15] The defence of the right to resist by the managers became a classic statement of whig principles. Burke was to draw on the trial proceedings to remind his contemporaries of these in *An Appeal from the New to the Old Whigs* (1791).

Burke quoted extensively from speeches made by managers who spoke to the first article, but overlooked those which addressed the remaining three. Holmes provides highlights from them all. Like Burke, he quotes from General Stanhope, whom he considered the ablest of the managers on the first article, and Robert Walpole. It was the young Walpole who famously said: 'surely my Lords it cannot be necessary to prove Resistance in the Revolution, I should as well expect your Lordships would desire me, for form's sake, to prove the Sun shines at noon day'.[16] Although three managers dealt with the second, that Sacheverell had impugned the Toleration Act, in Holmes's view: 'it was [Sir Peter] King . . . who totally dominated'. 'The Doctor, he concluded, had not only incited the Church's own hierarchy to undermine the legal Toleration, guaranteed by parliament and the Crown, but had by implication repudiated the royal supremacy over the Church.'[17] The third and fourth articles accused Sacheverell of asserting that the Church and constitution were in danger under Her Majesty's administration. The only speech which Holmes analyses at length is that of Sir Thomas Parker on the fourth. He held this to be 'a display which for intellectual quality and power of analysis can rarely have been matched in any British political trial.' 'The pity is', he added in a footnote, 'that in a narrow compass one can do it no sort of justice. To savour it to the full one must read the original from start to finish.'[18] That is undoubtedly true. Parker's forensic skills drew out the ideology underlying Sacheverell's sermon, which could only be made compatible with a repudiation of the revolution and support of the pretender's claim to the throne. Nowhere in it, Parker pointed out, had the Doctor denounced jacobites as 'false brethren'.

In defending Sacheverell, therefore, Sir Simon Harcourt had his work cut out to demonstrate that the Doctor's high church toryism was distinguishable from jacobitism. One ploy was to argue that resistance to the sovereign was never justifiable, but that sovereignty lay not with the monarch alone but with the crown in parliament. 'Eminent historians of late Stuart England', Holmes observes, citing Feiling and Trevelyan, 'have written that Harcourt's speech "put the classic case for the new Tory school".'[19] Against this, he insists that this was far from being the main plank in Harcourt's defence. That was to maintain that Sacheverell accepted that there could be exceptions to the doctrine of passive obedience and non-resistance and that the revolution was one such, though 'no Anglican divine could have been expected to mention such an exception while enunciating a basic precept'.[20] Given that the sermon was unequivocal that there had been no resistance in 1688, this was something of a *non sequitur*. At one stage Harcourt took refuge in the obscurantism of Sacheverell's style, confessing that: 'I can't easily compre-

---

[15] *The Tryal of Dr Henry Sacheverell* (8vo, 1710) [Madan 467], 8–9.

[16] *Tryal*, 94.

[17] Holmes, *Trial of Doctor Sacheverell*, 146.

[18] Holmes, *Trial of Doctor Sacheverell*, 150.

[19] Holmes, *Trial of Doctor Sacheverell*, 183.

[20] Holmes, *Trial of Doctor Sacheverell*, 188.

hend him myself'.[21] Harcourt had to cease being counsel for the defence when the writ announcing his return to parliament as MP for Cardigan was served, having been deliberately delayed for 12 days so that he could defend the Doctor against the first charge. Rebutting the managers on the other three charges was left to lesser lights. In Holmes's view they made rather heavy weather of it, and the day was only saved by Sacheverell himself, who was allowed to make a speech in his own defence. This was much more restrained than was his sermon, having been heavily influenced by more prudent high churchmen, such as Francis Atterbury. It was, however, delivered with such emotional intensity that it left many in the hall, men as well as women, in tears. Nevertheless when the managers replied on behalf of the Commons they 'took apart the case for the Defence brick by brick, until at the end there was very little, even of Harcourt's work, left standing'.[22] They had never effectively addressed Sacheverell's bold claim that there had been no resistance in 1688, which was the main charge against him.

In the end the trial was more a political than a judicial process. Brute votes in a very partisan house of lords were to decide the outcome. Where the ministers had wanted a harsh punishment, with a bar on preferment, a fine and even imprisonment, Sacheverell was only banned from preaching for three years, while his sermon was burned by the common hangman. That mild sentence was delivered in Westminster Hall on 23 March 1710, 300 years ago to the day. Holmes, the authority on politics in the age of Anne, provides a definitive analysis of the manœuvrings which led to a majority on the verdict that the Doctor was guilty as charged, but which fell apart on the sentence. The key lay with the queen. Holmes had established the crucial role played by Anne in the politics of her reign in his magisterial monograph on them. In his account of the trial he showed how her view that the Doctor had delivered a foolish sermon and deserved to be punished for it, but that the punishment should be lenient, influenced a number of peers whose votes were instrumental in the verdict and sentence.

His expertise on the political context also informs what is, in some respects, the most novel aspect of the book, the chapter on 'the night of fire'. This narrates the riots which occurred in London overnight on the 1st and 2nd of March. It led to an analysis of the events in a paper which was first aired at a conference on social control held in Newcastle upon Tyne in January 1973, the year in which the book appeared. An 'expanded and modified version' was published in *Past & Present* in 1976, reprinted in 1984 in *Rebellion, Popular Protest and the Social Order in Early Modern Britain*, edited by Paul Slack, and again in 1986, in *Politics, Religion and Society in England, 1679–1742*, a collection of Geoffrey Holmes's articles. The narrative and analysis were pioneering investigations into the activities of the London crowd in the early 18th century. By comparing the social status of some of those brought to trial afterwards with that of rioters later in the century he was able to demonstrate that those involved in the Sacheverell riots were of significantly higher social status than were the Wilkite or Gordon rioters. Holmes concluded that they constituted a Church mob, mainly from the targets they attacked, which were dissenting chapels. The methodical way in which they demolished one, that of Daniel Burgess, convinced him that the demonstrations, far from being spontaneous, were highly-organised and even financed by men of substance.

[21] Holmes, *Trial of Doctor Sacheverell*, 186.
[22] Holmes, *Trial of Doctor Sacheverell*, 202.

The attack on Burgess's conventicle inspired an anonymous verse:

Invidious Whigs, since you have made your Boast,
That you a Church of England Priest would roast,
Blame not the Mob, for having a Desire
With Presbyterian Tubs to light the Fire.

This was published, along with several other verses about the Sacheverell affair, in *Poems on Affairs of State: Augustan Satirical Verse 1660–1714: Vol. 7: 1704–1714*, edited by Frank Ellis, which appeared in 1975.[23] Yale University Press performed a splendid service to students of late Stuart history in general, and of the Sacheverell trial in particular, when it brought out this sumptuous edition under the general editorship of George deForest Lord. It was lavishly produced, permitting editors to annotate the poems chosen for publication with elaborate footnotes. Frank Ellis took full advantage of this latitude, volumes 6 and 7 which he edited resembled Jack Fisher's celebrated description of the archetypal learned monograph as 'a thin rivulet of text meandering through wide and lush meadows of footnotes'.[24] The four lines just quoted were accompanied by a full-page introduction and 13 lines of footnotes. Frank was aware of his own extravagance in this regard. One poem he chose for volume 4, *High Church Miracles*, which was dated 9 June 1710 by Narcissus Luttrell, and might have been written by Defoe, contained 26 lines of verse and an 'Explanation' of 60 lines of prose. Ellis observed of this: 'that such a high proportion of footnotes to text was found necessary in 1710 may justify to some degree the high ratio in the present volume'.[25] As one who was hired as a footnoteman for volume 7, I plead guilty to swelling their number. Notwithstanding the availability of the volume for 35 years, it has rarely been cited by historians. I suspect this is only partly due to lack of knowledge of the existence of the Yale series. It also reflects a methodological problem – how to make use of this kind of material? In any hierarchy of sources used by historians to document political realities it comes so far down as to be almost instantly discounted. Much of it is anonymous, ill-informed, biased, libellous and utterly unreliable. Ellis, a literary scholar interested in the poems as literature rather than as historical documents, was not concerned to evaluate their reliability as sources. Instead, as he explained in the introduction to volume 6, covering the years 1697 to 1704: 'in annotating these poems no attempt was made to be objective. The aim instead was to provide Tory commentary for a Tory poem and Whig commentary for a Whig poem.'[26] This editorial policy was continued in the annotation of volume 7, which completed the series down to 1714. Thus an anonymous high church attack on the seven bishops who voted against Sacheverell was footnoted from tory and jacobite sources. For example, its reference to 'Time-serving Trimnell', the bishop of Norwich, was glossed by reference to the rabid tory, Thomas Hearne's, remark that he was one

---

[23] POAS, vii, 393.

[24] F.J. Fisher, 'The Sixteenth and Seventeenth Centuries: The Dark Ages of English Economic History', *Economica*, new ser. xxiv (1957), 2–3.

[25] POAS, vii, 442.

[26] POAS, vi, p. xxxv.

of 'these degenerous Clergymen . . . that . . . renounce the divine right of the Episco-pat'.[27] Six bishops voted for the Doctor, inevitably giving rise to the notion that they 'have left the Church at sixes and sevens'. This observation was made in a tory poem on the six who were referred to as 'save-alls'. Ellis admitted that this was 'pure pan-egyric' but upheld the anonymous panegyrist's claims in footnotes. Thus Hearne was again pressed into service to 'document' his eulogy of George Hooper, the bishop of Bath and Wells.[28] When a whig poem 'on the sentence passed by the House of Lords on Dr Sacheverell' referred to him as a 'deluded Tool' a footnote cited James Stan-hope's jibe during the trial that he was 'an inconsiderable tool of a party'.[29] This allegation reflected whig suspicions that Sacheverell had been groomed by tory poli-ticians before delivering his sermon, but there is no evidence to substantiate the allegation. In the introduction to volume 7, Frank justified this editorial policy, explaining that: 'as in the preceding volume of this series, no attempt was made to provide "objective" commentary . . . The purpose of the commentary is not to balance the books, or set the record straight, but to make a political satire intelligible in its own terms.'[30] What he was aiming at was a methodology for contextualising extremely biased and partisan poems. Although this approach was novel to me, a historian trained to evaluate sources as evidence of objective realities, it was invaluable for developing a method for dealing with literary products as historical documents rather than as creative literature.

So was my editing of F.F. Madan's *A Critical Bibliography of Dr. Henry Sacheverell*. I had been commissioned to edit it by the executors of the late Frank Madan, who made provision in his will for its completion. Although I began work on it in 1967, it was not until 1978 that it appeared in print. The delay was due to difficulties in getting such a specialist work published. Indeed without the help of Henry Snyder, who persuaded the University of Kansas Press to publish it, the bibliography might never have seen the light of day. In retrospect, I do not think I thanked Henry enough for his assistance at the time and I am pleased to set the record straight now.

Frank Madan performed a remarkable service to scholars interested not just in the trial but in almost any aspect of early-18th-century British history. First he recorded twice as many titles than had been listed by his father, Falconer Madan, in his *Bibliography of Dr Henry Sacheverell*, published in 1884. This was thanks to the son's widespread investigation of the holdings of libraries on both sides of the Atlantic. These days when one can sit in one's study and access ECCO (Eighteenth Century Collections on Line) and other websites, it is easy to acquire a comprehensive listing of works relevant to an episode like Sacheverell's impeachment. Younger scholars might not appreciate the difficulties of locating and tracking them down in the era BC (before computers). It will be interesting to see how far Brian Cowan's electronic edition of the bibliography extends its coverage. Something of the range of Frank Madan's researches can be gleaned from the entries for 23 March 1710, the date of the sentence being passed on Sacheverell. There are five titles listed under it, all concerned with speeches made in the house of lords during the trial.

[27] POAS, vii, 419.
[28] POAS, vii, 425.
[29] POAS, vii, 441.
[30] POAS, vii, pp. xxxix–xl.

Two are located in the British Library, one in Cambridge University Library, one in Indiana University Library, while one was in the possession of Lord Rothschild. His dating of the appearance of titles was also impressive. As I noted in the introduction: 'it is remarkable that he was able to assign dates to so many. Apart from the godsend of the date added by Narcissus Luttrell . . . and diligent scrutiny of newspapers and entries in Stationers' Hall, internal evidence is usually the only clue to the time of publication.'[31] The range of materials was also remarkable. The bibliography incorporates not only pamphlets and poems but also addresses, division lists and prints.

The addresses included those which were presented to Queen Anne in the period between the trial and the general election of 1710. There were 141 of them, about 120 from tories. In June there appeared *A Collection of the Addresses* which claimed that by them 'it most evidently appears, that the sense of the kingdom . . . is express for the doctrine of passive-obedience and non-resistance, and for Her Majesty's hereditary title to the throne of her ancestors'.[32] Many urged an immediate dissolution of parliament so that they could capitalise on the high church backlash against the whigs provoked by the impeachment. Some division lists were also published in an attempt to influence the elections. Thus late in September, shortly after the dissolution of parliament, there appeared *The High Church True Blue Protestant list of those worthy members of Parliament who voted for the church and the Queen, and Dr. Sacheverel, these ought to be chosen*. It was accompanied by *The low church black list of the names of those who voted against the Doctor, and are turn'd out. These ought not to be chosen*.[33] Among the attempts to influence public opinion during the election campaigns of 1710 was the triumphal tour of the midlands which Sacheverell undertook on his way from London to Shropshire ostensibly to take up a living at Selattyn offered to him by an admirer. Frank Madan himself intended to publish an account of this as an appendix to the bibliography. Knowing that Geoffrey Holmes was to include a narrative of it in his account of the trial, I edited it out of the published version, and incorporated titles associated with the tour into the main text. In retrospect, it would perhaps have been more appropriate to keep it as a separate section, as the items dealing with the tour became too subsumed in the process. They include favourable commentaries, such as *Dr Sacheverel's progress from London, to his rectory of Salatin in Shropshire*, and hostile observations, including *A new map of the laborious and painful travels of our blessed high church apostle*.

Scholarly work on prints is a relatively recent development. Few historians have made use of those associated with the Sacheverell affair listed by Madan. Among those who have is Eirwen Nicholson. Her PhD thesis at Edinburgh in 1994 was a wide-ranging investigation of 'English Political Prints and pictorial political argument c.1640–c.1832: a study in historiography and method'. She has subsequently gone on to explore further 18th-century visual and material culture in its original politicised context, with an emphasis on its confessional aspects. Drawing extensively on the Madan bibliography she is now preparing a book on Sacheverell from these perspectives, 'Pulpit Idol'. Some of her conclusions about the consumers and spectators of political prints in the 18th century appeared in a seminal article published in *History*

[31] F.F. Madan, *A Critical Bibliography of Dr. Henry Sacheverell*, ed. W.A. Speck (Lawrence, KA, 1978), p. vi.
[32] Madan 213.
[33] Madan 238.

in 1996.[34] It challenged the previously widely-held notion that prints were mass-produced and reached a wide audience. On the contrary, as she demonstrated from the technology available to engravers and printmakers at the time, only small runs of 100 to 600 could be made at any one time. Much fewer were produced than was the case with newspapers and pamphlets. Moreover they were relatively expensive too, and could not be purchased by customers below the level of the elite. The claim that they could be perused by spectators in print-shop windows, coffee houses and other public spheres is also open to challenge. While non-political prints might have reached a wider audience through these channels, political prints were not so accessible.

Among the sources used to substantiate these challenging claims was the bibliography. Thus Dr Nicholson cited it to show that newspapers could be used to document the print trade. 'In the case of the Sacheverell trial, which produced many comparatively cheap prints, the prices suggest an attempt on the part of publishers to exploit an extant market, namely that for the pamphlets and other printed literature on the sermon and the trial.'[35] Her views have provoked criticism, but her thesis is based on very substantial evidence. She has shown the way to a methodology which can 'read' prints as sources which require to be taken at other than face value.

My own absorption in poems on affairs of state and the paper war of 1709–10 led me to conclude that they did not document the 'reality' of politics, but the political ideologies of their authors and how they tried to persuade their target audiences to accept their views.[36] A much more thorough and sophisticated analysis of the latter was undertaken by Mark Knights in his *Representation and Misrepresentation in Later Stuart Britain: Partisanship and Political Culture* (2005). He shows how political propaganda – a term he dislikes though he accepts that it has its uses – misrepresented the virtues of the party it supported and the vices of the party it opposed. Partisans on both sides manipulated language to influence their target audiences. The distinction between truth and fiction was deliberately blurred to the point where 'one's own identity was now rendered uncertain by the partisanship of others'. Knights quotes a pamphlet from the Sacheverell affair, *The Declaration of an honest Churchman upon occasion of the present times*, to illustrate this. 'The trial of the doctor last winter has brought every man upon his trial; and I must no longer take my self for granted, while the world is discussing me . . . With the violent Whigs, I am a Tory; and with the violent Tories, a Whig.'[37]

While the political passions roused by the trial have long subsided, the politics of the protagonists still reverberate 300 years later. The historians who have examined the Sacheverell affair have, no doubt, made every effort to be impartial and objective in their accounts. Yet, just like the very whores who at the time asked potential clients: 'are you for or against the Doctor', the same question can be asked of them. For many, if not

---

[34] Eirwen E.C. Nicholson, 'Consumers and Spectators: The Public of the Political Print in Eighteenth-Century England', *History*, lxxxi (1996), 5–21.

[35] Nicholson, 'Consumers and Spectators', 13.

[36] I first suggested this in a paper I read to the Royal Historical Society in 1971, 'Political Propaganda in Augustan England'. This was published in the *Transactions of the Royal Historical Society*, 5th ser., xxii (1972), 17–32. I developed the approach in several later studies, particularly in two books, *Society and Literature in England 1700–1760* (1983) and *Literature and Society in Eighteenth-Century England* (1998).

[37] Mark Knights, *Representation and Misrepresentation in Later Stuart Britain: Partisanship and Political Culture* (Oxford, 2005), 328.

most, modern scholars adopt the neo-whig attitude observable in Holmes's account, which approves of the junto's decision to impeach the Doctor and applauds the legal stance they took, while suspecting Sacheverell himself of at least crypto-jacobitism. Since *The Trial of Doctor Sacheverell* appeared there has been a reassessment of the jacobites by historians more inclined to take them seriously and even to show sympathy with their cause. The leading exponent of this neo-jacobite school, J.C.D. Clark, is not impressed by whig arguments employed against the Doctor. 'With the trial of Dr Sacheverell in 1711 [*sic.*]', he insists, 'the Whig political theory as laid down in the 1670s was seen to be profoundly compromised.'[38] He also maintains that their notion of popular sovereignty was rooted in ideas of divine right as much as was the tory theory of indefeasible hereditary kingship. So the issues raised in the impeachment of Henry Sacheverell continue to inform the historiographical debate on its significance.

---

[38] J.C.D. Clark, *English Society 1660–1832* (Cambridge, 2000), 134.

The Spin Doctor: Sacheverell's Trial Speech and Political Performance in the Divided Society*

BRIAN COWAN

Henry Sacheverell's speech in his own defence on the eighth day of his parliamentary trial (9 March 1710) was, by all accounts, a show-stopping performance. The speech was an effective political performance at a show trial originally designed to condemn the principles he had enunciated in his controversial 1709 sermons at Derby and St Paul's Cathedral. Sacheverell avoided any forthright or elaborate defence of his beliefs with regard to the legitimacy of resistance during the Glorious Revolution in order to appear humble, orthodox, and loyal to the queen and to the protestant succession. As such, he presented himself as a sort of living martyr for the high church cause. While this strategy was itself deeply controversial, it was also rather successful in spinning the debate from one about 'revolution principles' to one about the persecution of a loyal clergyman. In order to understand the form, the effectiveness and the purpose of Sacheverell's trial speech, one must take its pathetic form and its widespread distribution, both in print and manuscript reports, into account. The sympathy garnered for Sacheverell due to his speech was a public relations success for the tory cause in the short run, but it also entailed a solid commitment to the Hanoverian succession that remained deeply controversial within high church circles.

Keywords: Henry Sacheverell; oratory; performance; house of lords; print culture; 18th-century politics; tories; whigs; resistance; passive obedience; state trials; martyrdom

1

Perhaps the only thing that whigs and tories could agree upon with regard to the parliamentary trial of Doctor Henry Sacheverell is that his speech on the eighth day of the trial (9 March 1710) was the most memorable moment of the whole proceedings. Sacheverell's speech in his own defence was, by all accounts, a show-stopping performance. Both whigs and tories agreed that it showcased the Doctor's highly-honed oratorical skills, and that the content of the speech presented his case in the best possible light. Nearly everyone who was present at the trial marvelled at the pathetic effect it had upon the audience of perhaps 2,000 spectators.[1]

Even the whig bishop of Salisbury, Gilbert Burnet, who vigorously denounced Sacheverell and his doctrines at the trial, begrudgingly admitted that 'the style' of the

* I would like to thank Mark Knights, John Marshall, Noah McCormack and Scott Sowerby for their assistance with the writing of this article. It has benefited from discussions at the conference on 23 Mar. 2010 and feedback from the Department of History seminar at the Johns Hopkins University on 28 Feb. 2011.

[1] For the audience at the trial, see Geoffrey Holmes, *The Trial of Doctor Sacheverell* (1973), 125–6.

Doctor's speech 'was correct' even though he thought it was 'far different from his own' usual style, and that it had a greater effect on the weaker sort amongst Sacheverell's audience than it did on those whose stronger reason could see through Sacheverell's charades.[2] Sir Thomas Parker, one of the managers for the prosecution, similarly owned that the 'speech was extremely well composed' and Sir Peter King, another whig manager, also admitted that 'it was a speech of the finest oratory, that he ever read or heard in any language and deliverd as well, with all due life and courage joyned with due and decent modesty, soe that the Doctor was not wanting in any one thing either in pronuntiation or action that became his gown or the circumstances he was under'.[3] The ferociously partisan whig, Sarah, Lady Cowper, whose elder son, William, presided over the trial as lord chancellor and whose younger son, Spencer, was a manager for the prosecution, noted with some regret that even the printed version of Sacheverell's speech was 'so artfull an[d] elegent . . . that no doubt but it will gain some' converts for the high church cause.[4]

Tory observers were, of course, even more effusive in their praise of the Doctor's performance in his own self-defence at his trial. The tory author of a manuscript account of the trial gushed that Sacheverell:

spoke with a fine Accent & the most agreable Voice, that ever I heard; and behav'd himself with a Modesty becoming a Man before so great a Judicature, and under the Misfortune of a Prosecution from so great a Body, as the House of Commons; with Eloquence and Learning suitable to the Character of a Man in holy Orders; and with a Constancy, and Resolution proper to a Christian, and an Innocent Man; and received from the Breasts of all unprejudic'd Persons, that reward, w[hi]ch the Truth & Sincerity of his Cause seem'd so justly to demand.

He also noted in the margins that 'this Speech was look'd upon by all, even the Whigs themselves, as fine a thing as ever was spoke, and they had no way of shifting off the force of such Evidence & conviction, but the poor pitifull shift of saying, they did not believe it'.[5]

These comments cut to the heart of contemporary reactions to Sacheverell's trial speech. Most of those who listened to it agreed that it had been well delivered. A majority of the even larger number of people who read the text of the speech must have found the political sentiments expressed within it to be acceptably orthodox, especially since Sacheverell's speech unambiguously proclaimed that he had not intended to 'condemn the late happy Revolution' and it contained an explicit avowal of his support

[2] Gilbert Burnet, *The Bishop of Salisbury his Speech in the House of Lords, on the First Article of the Impeachment of Dr. Henry Sacheverell* (1710) [Madan 319]; Gilbert Burnet, *Bishop Burnet's History of his Own Time* (6 vols, Oxford, 1823), v, 444.

[3] *A Complete Collection of State Trials*, comp. T.B. Howell (34 vols, 1809–28), xv, 458; Bodl., MS Ballard 31, f. 82: William Bishop to Arthur Charlett, 8 Mar. 1710.

[4] Hertfordshire Archive and Local Studies, Panshanger MSS, D/EP F29–35 (Sarah Cowper diary in 7 vols), v, 128: 16 Mar. 1710. I am grateful to Anne Kugler for providing me with a copy of her transcript of these diaries, and to Mark Knights for guidance relating to the Panshanger MSS. See also Anne Kugler, *Errant Plagiary: The Life and Writings of Lady Sarah Cowper 1644–1720* (Stanford, CA, 2002), 168; Mark Knights, *The Devil in Disguise: Deception, Delusion, and Fanaticism in the Early English Enlightenment* (Oxford, 2011), ch. 5.

[5] Yale University, Beinecke Library, Osborne MS 13043, f. 16r; also published in *The State Trial of Doctor Henry Sacheverell* (Parliamentary History Texts & Studies), ed. Brian Cowan, with Noah McCormack, ch. 2.

for the legitimacy of Anne's reign and the Hanoverian succession.[6] Such a clear avowal
of his loyalty made it much more difficult for his whig opponents to accuse Sacheverell
of hidden jacobite sympathies. Had one not read his incendiary sermons preached at
Derby and St Paul's Cathedral, and there cannot have been many of the politically-
informed public who had not read at least the latter, one might have justifiably wondered
why this poor clergyman was being prosecuted and what the whole fuss about him was
all about.[7]

The fuss over Sacheverell and his trial speech revolved around the problem of
reconciling appearance with reality in an age of deeply-partisan politics and the shams,
duplicities, deceptions and plots that were associated with political discourse caught in
the midst of the rage of party. As such, the debate exemplified deeply-rooted and
long-standing anxieties regarding the truth and verifiability of partisan claims within later
Stuart political culture.[8] Sacheverell's trial speech was a political performance above all,
and in this he excelled over all of the other competing performances by any of the whig
managers for the prosecution; but even an orator as skilled as he, and even a speech with
content as moderate and generally unobjectionable as this one, could only succeed in
exacerbating the doubts and divisions that plagued early-18th-century English political
discourse.

Both contemporaries and some later historians have tried to distinguish between the
performative aspects of Sacheverell's trial speech and the content of his intended political
and religious message, most often with an eye towards denigrating the importance of the
speech as a performance in order to reveal and explain its 'real' meaning as a means of
exploring Sacheverell's 'actual' political beliefs and strategies. Perhaps for this reason,
Mark Goldie found it to be a 'paradox' that 'one of the most startling features of the
speeches of the prosecution and of the defence is the similarity of the views expressed'
by both sides at the trial. Similarly, J.P. Kenyon thought that Sacheverell's speech 'was at
once evasive and conciliatory' and he expressed some doubt as to whether the Doctor
'really accepted' the arguments presented in his defence at the trial.[9]

To distinguish strictly between form and content only obscures the purpose, the
effectiveness, and, indeed, the meaning of the trial speech for Sacheverell and his
supporters. One need not accept wholeheartedly Marshall McLuhan's contrary claim
that the 'medium is the message' in order to recognize the need to explore the
relationship between the content of the trial speech and the performative media through

[6] State Trials, xv, 374 (quote) and 375; original in The Speech of Henry Sacheverell, D.D. Upon His Impeachment
at the Bar of the House of Lords, in Westminster-Hall, March 7. 1709/10 (1710) [Madan 248]; the BL copy at
shelfmark 1474.d.26(17) has MS emphasis marks in the margins of the text where Sacheverell's professions of
loyalty to the protestant Hanoverian succession are printed, 12–15.

[7] Henry Sacheverell, The Communication of Sin (1709) [Madan 48]; Henry Sacheverell, The Perils of False
Brethren (1709) [Madan 57]. On the dissemination of the latter sermon, see Holmes, Trial of Doctor Sacheverell,
74–5 and the bibliographical note to the Rota edition of Henry Sacheverell, Perils of False Brethren (Exeter,
1974).

[8] See Kate Loveman, Reading Fictions, 1660–1740: Deception in English Literary and Political Culture (Aldershot, 2008); Rebecca Bullard, The Politics of Disclosure, 1674–1725 (2009); Mark Knights, Representation and
Misrepresentation in Later Stuart Britain: Partisanship and Political Culture (Oxford, 2005); Mark Knights, 'Judging
Partisan News and the Language of Interest', in Fear, Exclusion and Revolution: Roger Morrice and Britain in the
1680s, ed. Jason McElligott (Aldershot, 2006), 204–20.

[9] Mark Goldie, 'Tory Political Thought 1689–1714', University of Cambridge PhD, 1977, p. 274; J.P.
Kenyon, Revolution Principles: The Politics of Party 1689–1720 (Cambridge, 1977), 138.

which its message was disseminated to a variety of different audiences, both actual at the moment of the trial and virtual readers of its proceedings in the months to follow.[10] For effective performance, both as oratory and in print, was central to the success and persuasiveness of Sacheverell's speech.

Sacheverell's was a political show trial in the full sense of the term, and as such it is necessary to understand how both the prosecution and the defence played their parts in the drama as it unfolded. Political show trials have recently emerged in the political history of early modern England as an important site for the representation of power to a larger public, and for debates about the nature of that power to be conducted both within the courtroom and more importantly, beyond the court as part of a continuously malleable court of public opinion. This was certainly the case for the show trials of the Roman catholics, Edmund Campion and Margaret Clitherow, under Elizabeth's reign.[11] It was a key element of the celebrated trials in the 1640s of the earl of Strafford, Archbishop William Laud, and above all, of King Charles I.[12] The Restoration era trials of *soi disant* whig martyrs such as Algernon Sidney or Lord William Russell also played a similar role, but Sacheverell's trial was surely the most dramatic since the king's trial in 1649, and it took place in exactly the same venue, Westminster Hall, a fact that Sacheverell's propagandists were keen to ensure that people remembered.[13] Foreign observers in 1710 noted that Westminster Hall had been turned into a 'makeshift theatre' for the purposes of Sacheverell's show trial.[14]

A key element of the political performance of these political show trials is that they were aimed at, and interpreted by, several different audiences at once. This was true, above all, of Sacheverell's trial, where the speeches for both the prosecution and the defence were aimed at the queen, the lords who would ultimately decide on the Doctor's guilt or innocence, the gallery of spectators at the trial, and the politically-engaged reading public that everyone knew would ultimately pore over the printed version of the trial and eventually discuss and debate over its justness and significance

---

[10] Marshall McLuhan, *Understanding Media: The Extensions of Man* (Cambridge, MA, 1994), 7–21.

[11] Peter Lake and Michael Questier, 'Puritans, Papists, and the "Public Sphere" in Early Modern England: The Edmund Campion Affair in Context', *Journal of Modern History*, lxxii (2000), 587–627; Peter Lake and Michael Questier, 'Margaret Clitherow, Catholic Nonconformity, Martyrology and the Politics of Religious Change in Elizabethan England', *Past & Present*, No. 185 (2004), 43–90; Peter Lake and Michael Questier, *Trials of Margaret Clitherow: Persecution, Martyrdom and the Politics of Sanctity in Elizabethan England* (2011).

[12] T. Kilburn and A. Milton, 'The Public Context of Trial and Execution of Strafford', in *The Political World of Thomas Wentworth Earl of Strafford, 1621–1641*, ed. J. Merritt (Cambridge, 1996), 230–51; Sean Kelsey, 'Staging the Trial of Charles I', in *The Regicides and the Execution of Charles I*, ed. Jason Peacey (Basingstoke, 2001), 71–93; Kevin Sharpe, *Image Wars: Promoting Kings and Commonwealths in England, 1603–1660* (New Haven, CT, 2010), 379–84.

[13] The public relations characteristics of later Stuart political trials have been less well-investigated, but see Jonathan Scott, *Algernon Sidney and the Restoration Crisis, 1677–1683* (Cambridge, 1991), 313, 317–47; Lois Schwoerer, 'The Trial of Lord William Russell (1683): Judicial Murder?', *Journal of Legal History*, ix (1988), 142–68; Lois Schwoerer, 'William Lord Russell: The Making of a Martyr, 1683–1983', *Journal of British Studies*, xxiv (1985), 41–71; Melinda Zook, ' "The Bloody Assizes": Whig Martyrdom and Memory after the Glorious Revolution', *Albion*, xxvii (1995), 373–96; Melinda Zook, *Radical Whigs and Conspiratorial Politics in Late Stuart England* (University Park, PA, 1999). On Sacheverell and Charles I, see Kenyon, *Revolution Principles*, 133, and figure 1, p. 32.

[14] *La Clef du Cabinet des Princes de l'Europe*, ed. C. Jordan de Colombier (45 vols, Luxembourg, 1704–26), xii, 334, my translation.

To preach up Truth, some say tis not a time|But since y̆ Truth offends, Ill vex you more
False Brethren allwaies think y̆ Truth a Crime|And shew y̆ face of Truth you're wrongd befó

Figure 1: *Henry Sacheverell and Charles I* (c.1710). Print engraving; BM, Satires 1510. © Trustees of the British Museum.

amongst themselves.[15] While the immediate goal for the prosecution and the defence was to make a convincing case before the queen and the lords at the impeachment, the larger purpose of the trial itself was to provide a public forum for a debate on the nature of the Glorious Revolution and the constitutionality of the Toleration Act of 1689. For this reason, the first two articles of impeachment levied against Sacheverell concerned his traducement of the revolution and his impugning the toleration in his controversial Derby and St Paul's sermons of 1709.

[15] Michael Mendle has demonstrated the general accuracy and reliability of the prints of later Stuart political trial proceedings in 'The "Prints" of the Trials: The Nexus of Politics, Religion, Law and Information in Late Seventeenth-Century England', in *Fear, Exclusion and Revolution*, ed. McElligott, 123–37. On the printing and publication history of Sacheverell's trial proceedings, see *State Trial of Doctor Henry Sacheverell*, ed. Cowan, ch. 1.

This made the prosecution's task much more difficult than it might have first appeared. The whigs in the house of lords had the votes to convict before the trial had even begun, but the outcome in the court of public opinion was not so clear at all. This is why the whig leaders would have preferred to have had Sacheverell tried swiftly at the bar of the house of lords rather than in the much more public forum of Westminster Hall.[16] Whereas the whig managers wished to use the trial as an occasion to defend and legitimate an understanding of the revolution as a case in which the 'necessary means' used to bring it about included resistance to James II's tyranny, and to defend the reasonableness of toleration for protestant dissenters, Sacheverell's tory defence counsel had an easier task. They simply had to make the Doctor appear to be the victim of cruel and unjust partisan attacks; as a clergyman and a doctor of divinity, Sacheverell would appear to be a living martyr for a Church of England in danger of such injustice without even having to say so. For these reasons, Sacheverell did not need to make a forthright defence of his 'real' beliefs regarding the revolution or the toleration, nor did he have to respond directly to the panoply of charges levelled against him by the prosecution. In order to successfully defend himself before the general public in the gallery and well beyond Westminster Hall, he simply had to appear humble, orthodox, and loyal to the queen and to the protestant succession. Sacheverell's speech accomplished all of this, and it did so through a bravura performance that left no one in doubt that he had stolen the stage at his own show trial.

2

When he spoke at his trial, Sacheverell adopted a more conciliatory tone, and a more moderate position, than he had in his firebrand sermons and even his earlier published answer to the articles of impeachment that had been exhibited against him by the house of commons. Sacheverell's sermons were deliberately provocative, and his formal answer to the articles of impeachment had been defiant and entirely non-repentant with regard to his positions on controversial matters such as whether there had been any resistance to the crown during the revolution or whether the Toleration Act should be understood merely as an act of 'exemption' that only temporarily withheld penalties from being applied to dissenters.[17] His trial speech, by contrast, was cast in the form of a humble petition, and it was obviously designed to ply the sympathetic emotions of the crowd.

Reports on its length vary, but it seems that Sacheverell held court with his 'eligant and pathetical speech' for at least an hour, and it may have lasted for as long as two hours. By all accounts, it must have been very moving for many in the audience, as it was said to have drawn tears 'from the eyes of men and women', and it certainly held the queen's attention throughout. Crooke Dodd thought it was 'the most moving, eloquent, and unanswerable speech, that 'ere was heard . . . it made both sex's weep; especially the ladies, in generall were full of sorrow, and their tears flow'd very plentifully'. Tory lords such as the duke of Leeds, the earl of Rochester and the earl of Nottingham were all

---

[16] Holmes, *Trial of Doctor Sacheverell*, 110–13, explains how the initial plans for the trial got out of hand during debates in the Commons on 3–4 Feb. 1710, and thus allowed for a concerted tory campaign to rally public support for the Doctor.

[17] Henry Sacheverell, *The Answer of Henry Sacheverell. D.D. to the Articles of Impeachment* (1710) [Madan 165], 8–17; see also Holmes, *Trial of Doctor Sacheverell*, 105–8.

reported to have 'shewed their tenderness' towards the Doctor through their public tears for him.[18]

Perhaps the most remarkable aspect of Sacheverell's trial speech is what he did not say. He refrained from making any further intemperate remarks about the revolution, or about dissent. He claimed, possibly disingenuously, that his denunciations of the legitimacy of resistance to the supreme power had not been meant to apply to the revolution; although his qualifying aside that this was because during the revolution, 'the supreme power [was not] . . . resisted' at the revolution, must surely have raised some whiggish hackles.[19] With regard to dissent, he denied that he meant to challenge the legality of the toleration, but, nevertheless, he claimed that the act had not 'altered the nature of schism, or extinguished the obligations to Church-communion, which is an evangelical duty, incumbent on all Christians'. Dissent, in other words, was a sin and as such liable to legitimate condemnation by a clergyman, even if it remained legal by the laws of the land: 'the consequence of which guilt may still rest upon their souls, however it may cease to affect their bodies or estates'.[20] These were strongly tory views, to be sure, but they were carefully crafted to ensure that the Doctor appeared to be on the right side of the law, politically correct with regard to the question of the protestant succession of the house of Hanover, and religiously correct with regard to orthodox Church doctrine.

While he did not admit any guilt, Sacheverell insisted that the meanings of his sermons had been misrepresented by the managers for the prosecution. This presented him with an opportunity to offer a new, and more moderate, gloss on his beliefs and some of the more controversial moments in his sermons. He also adopted a strongly apologetic and self-effacing presentation that went a long way towards countering the common whig caricature of the Doctor as a self-serving, self-promoting provocateur. Together, these two moves aimed to spin the terms of the debate away from a focus on Sacheverell's transgressions as an incendiary arch-tory and a demagogue and towards a concern with orthodox doctrine within the Church of England and the duty of its clergy to defend that orthodoxy.

This had been the strategy adopted by Sacheverell's defence counsel throughout the trial. Much of the sixth day had been devoted to a lengthy reading of passages from orthodox sources (including the writings of some divines who were present at the trial, such as the bishops, William Wake of Lincoln, William Fleetwood of St Asaph and, particularly, Gilbert Burnet of Salisbury) that supported the tory doctrines of passive obedience and non-resistance.[21] The seventh day continued in this vein, but now with

[18] BL, Add. MS 70421 (unfoliated): 7 Mar. 1710 (quote), reports the speech as lasting one hour and 20 minutes. See also Bodl., MS Ballard 31, f. 82: William Bishop to Arthur Charlett, 8 Mar. 1710, which reports the speech as lasting over an hour and 15 minutes; *Lettres Historiques* (90 vols, Amsterdam, 1692–1736), xxxvii, 440, clocked the speech at one hour and a half; and Bodl., MS Ballard 34, f. 79: Crooke Dodd to Rev. Thwaite, 11 Mar. 1710, claims that the speech lasted 'up near two hours'. Cf. HMC, *Portland MSS*, iv, 535: [Abigail Harley] to [Edward] Harley, 7 Mar. 1710.

[19] *State Trials*, xv, 366; see also Goldie, 'Tory Political Thought 1689–1714', 290–1.

[20] *State Trials*, xv, 368.

[21] *State Trials*, xv, 270–1, 273–5, 276. Burnet's tergiversations in particular on the issue of justified resistance had occasioned much controversy in the pamphlet wars that surrounded the Sacheverell affair: see *The Royal Martyr and the Dutifull Subject* (1710) [Madan 90], 212, 237–42, 283, 323–5, 571. Compare Steve Pincus's argument that 'there was in fact no tension in Burnet's mind' on the question of lawful resistance, in *1688: The First Modern Revolution* (New Haven, CT, 2009), 419–20.

readings of numerous passages of highly unorthodox or putatively blasphemous passages from books that Sacheverell's defence council claimed were the real target of his invective in his sermons.[22] The whole case for the defence reached its climax with Sacheverell's moving speech on the eighth day.

Sacheverell began by meeting the case for the prosecution on its own grounds. Many whigs had insisted that the trial was not designed to punish Sacheverell the clergyman so much as it was intended to put an end to high church disparagements of the revolution and its heritage.[23] Sacheverell accepted that challenge, and he used his speech to present himself as a defender of the Church and its orthodox doctrine:

> It has been owned by some of the managers for the honourable House of Commons, that though I am the person impeached, yet my condemnation is not the thing principally aimed at. I am, it seems, an insignificant tool of a party, not worth regarding; the avowed design of my impeachment is, by the means of it to procure an eternal and indelible brand of infamy to be fixed, in a parliamentary way, on all those who maintain the doctrine of non-resistance, and to have the clergy directed what doctrines they are to preach, and what not. And therefore, as insignificant as I am in myself, yet the consequences of my trial (if rightly represented to your lordships by some of those gentlemen) are of the highest moment and importance.[24]

The remainder of the speech was divided into three parts. He questioned the methods used by the prosecution to interpret the meanings of his sermons, and protested that he was the victim of impartial and uncharitable readings of his works. He answered each of the articles of impeachment levied against him in turn, insisting in each case that his views were entirely orthodox and free from any particular malice against the revolution, the Act of Toleration, or the current administration. And he concluded with a long and pathetic personal apologia in which he played up both his loyalty to the queen and the protestant succession while also insisting on his prerogative as an ordained man of the cloth to preach orthodox religion and to rebuke sin wherever he found it.[25]

In his concluding apologia, Sacheverell managed to present himself both as a selfless defender of orthodoxy, and yet also akin to the martyrs of the early Church and the early Reformation:

> when I consider that I now stand, and am judged for some of the doctrines of that gospel which God delivered unto our fathers . . . to be maintained inviolably in its primitive simplicity; when I consider, what is the cause for which I am this day called in question; that it is one of those eternal truths, which you are so solemnly commissioned to teach, and earnestly contend for; when I consider, that it is what our blessed Lord and his Apostles sealed with their precious blood, and so many primitive

[22] *State Trials*, xv, 292–344.
[23] E.g., Defoe in the *Review*, vi, no. 118, p. 469: 7 Jan. 1710.
[24] *State Trials*, xv, 364.
[25] Holmes, *Trial of Doctor Sacheverell*, 197–201, provides a faithful summary.

martyrs maintained even in the midst of flames, so many learned bishops, and confessors recommended to posterity in their immortal writings, as the distinguishing badge, and glory of our Reformation.[26]

Sacheverell surely knew that his life was hardly in danger even if parliament decided on the most severe punishment for his high crimes and misdemeanours, but it served him well to remind his audience, and later the readers of his printed speech, of the tradition of christian martyrdom that he stood ready to join.

Much of the politics of the later Stuart era can be understood in terms of a sort of competitive martyrdom, with tories often harking back to the regicide and King Charles the martyr, while whigs constructed their own new secular martyrologies of victims of absolutist tyranny in the years after the death of Charles II and especially after the 1688 revolution.[27] As the debates over Sacheverell's trial and ultimate conviction proceeded, many of his supporters drew explicit connections between his case and that of previous royalist or high church martyrs, such as Charles I and Archbishop Laud.[28] Sacheverell's prayers and meditations were published in imitation of those who had been associated with Charles I during his trial and execution and published in the best-selling royalist hagiography *Eikon Basilike* (1649).[29] Several printed images which were circulated around the time of the trial portrayed Sacheverell in the company of the martyred Charles I. One urged readers to 'view him whose life rebellion took away', while another presented Sacheverell showing 'ye face you've wronged before' to his persecutors.[30]

Sacheverell's trial offered the tories a perfect opportunity to construct their own living martyr, and his speech capitalised on this perspective as much as possible. He concluded his speech with an explicit invocation of his willingness to die for his loyalty to Church and queen: 'For my own part, it matters not what becomes of me, nor is my deliverance, or ruin, of any moment to the world; or, if it be, I am not only ready to be bound, but to die, could I by that do service to my queen, my Church, or my country; neither count I my life dear, so that I might finish my course with joy, and the ministry which I have received of the Lord Jesus.'[31]

---

[26] *State Trials*, xv, 378.

[27] See *Martyrs and Martyrdom in England, c.1400–1700*, ed. Thomas Freeman and Thomas Mayer (Woodbridge, 2007); Andrew Lacey, *The Cult of King Charles the Martyr* (Woodbridge, 2003); Zook, *Radical Whigs*; Melinda Zook, 'Violence, Martyrdom, and Radical Politics: Rethinking the Glorious Revolution', in *Politics and Political Imagination in Later Stuart Britain*, ed. Howard Nenner (Rochester, 1997), 75–95.

[28] See *An Historical Emblematical Fan in Honour of the Church of England, and of Such her Pious Genuine Sons, that with Primitive Bravery have suffer'd for, and Defended her Holy Doctrine in the most perillous Times* (1710), British Museum, Department of Prints and Drawings [hereafter cited as BM], Satires 1525; and *On the Late Martyrs of the Church* [Madan 897], in *A Collection of Poems, &c. for and Against Dr Sacheverell, The Fourth Part* (1711) [Madan 87], 28.

[29] *The pious and devout meditations of Henry Sacheverell, D.D. in the time of his troubles; with his morning and evening prayers before he went to, and came from his tryal at Westminster. Likewise his hearty thanksgiving for his great deliverance. As also, a mournful elegy on the burning his sermons. To which is added, a wonderful prophecy written to King Charles I. a little before he was beheaded, relating to these present times* (1710) [Madan 309].

[30] Madan 957–8 record two related, but different impressions of the print *Portrait of Henry Sacheverell, D.D., holding an Engraved Portrait of Charles I* (1710). Madan 957 is based on a copy from F.F. Madan's personal collection (see BL, Add. MS 88475F), while Madan 958 is also catalogued as BM, Satires 1510. There is another copy in Huntington Library, San Marino, CA, RB283000, xxiii, no. 61. See also *Made and Written by a Youth of 15 Years of Age on the Sight of 3 Pictures Which Hung in his Closet* (nd) [Madan 959 and BM, Satires 1514].

[31] *State Trials*, xv, 379.

By claiming that he was ready to die for the cause of the Church and the queen, Sacheverell managed to have his martyrological cake and live to eat it too. It was no small feat for someone who had earned his reputation as a steadfast proponent of condemning protestant dissenters as schismatic sinners, and who had insisted that the Act of Toleration merely suspended, but did not abrogate, the penal laws against recusansy for the dissenters, to present *himself* as the victim of persecution. His speech was a magnificent demonstration of the flexibility of self-fashioning in a deeply-divided political culture, and a striking example of the ability of each side to spin that self-presentation to partisan advantage.

Sacheverell's pretended claim to martyrdom (without actually dying) did not go unanswered. 'What a profane blasphemous wretch is this Pseudo-Martyr?' Arthur Maynwaring rhetorically asked.[32] A whig broadside print issued not long after the conclusion to the trial, entitled *The Living Man's Elegie or Doctor Sacheverell's Much Lamented Silence, March ye 23 1710* (1710) (figure 2) took direct aim at the Doctor's hypocrisy in claiming all of the glory and reverence accorded to a holy martyr without actually being executed. The text of the print taunted Sacheverell's high church supporters to:

Weep for the Man that did so boldly parte:
That Brethren false were in our Church & State:
For now he's silenc'd and disgrac'd most just;
His sermon's burnt and turned into dust.

At the bottom of the print is a jocular 'epitaph' for Sacheverell, the now censured and false living martyr:

Here lies Sacheverell, who would have thought it,
Jacks and High flyers did not, tho: they wrought it.
From Fiercely Preaching in a railing way
He's now debar'd, then laugh and go your way.

Prints such as this mocked the pretensions of Sacheverell and his supporters to be martyrs-in-waiting for the defence of the established Church. They also invited responses, and the tories obliged with a broadside entitled *An Answer to the Liveing Mans Elegy* (1710) which denounced the author of *The Living Man's Elegie* as a 'foul monster' who dared to 'write an Elegy for him whose name / Were he now dead thy verse could not defame'.[33] They also continued to promote Sacheverell's case as a form of martyrdom by producing elegies for his sermons, which were burned by order of the house of lords as part of his punishment. One tract made a direct anology between the 'Glorious Martyrs [who] fell in former days, / Ending their pious lives with scorching blaze' and

[32] [Arthur Maynwaring], *Four Letters to a Friend in North Britain, Upon the Publishing the Tryal of Dr. Sacheverell* (1710) [Madan 555], 11.

[33] *An Answer to the Liveing Mans Elegy* (1710) [BM, Satires 1545, registration no. 1868,0808.3444; Madan 963].

© *The Parliamentary History Yearbook Trust 2012*

Figure 2: *The Living Man's Elegie or Doctor Sacheverell's Much Lamented Silence, March ye 23 1710* (1710) [Madan 962]; BM, Satires 1527. © Trustees of the British Museum.

the fate of the doctrine of passive obedience which has been 'Martyr'd by the Senates Order'.[34]

The elegy was an established and active poetic genre in the early 18th century, and like so many other genres of the age, it was often infiltrated by partisanship.[35] Political elegies in broadside format, both solemn and serious, were a popular sales item amongst the stock in bookseller's shops. Competing partisan broadside elegies for controversial figures such as Titus Oates, Sir Roger L'Estrange, or John Tutchin, were

[34] *Fire and Faggot, or; an Ellegy on Dr. S–ch–ls Two Sermons* (1710) [Madan 347], 3, 7 (quote). See also the tory tract *An Epitaph on Passive Obedience, Executed for High Treason Against our Sovereign Lord the People* (1710) [Madan 283]; and the whig broadside *An Elegy on the Death of High-Church Passive Obedience and Non-Resistance* (1710) [Madan 284].

[35] David B. Morris, 'A Poetry of Absence', in *The Cambridge Companion to Eighteenth Century Poetry*, ed. John Sitter (Cambridge, 2001), 232–7.

commonly printed upon the occasion of their death.[36] Sacheverell's invocation of his willingness to die for the cause of Church orthodoxy during his trial speech invited propagandists on both sides to exploit martyrdom as a metaphor for the high stakes at issue in the case, particularly when the memories of truly dead heroes for both the whig and tory causes were still very much alive in the political discourse of the day.

Defoe's *Review* played into the hands of Sacheverell's pretence at martyrdom-in-waiting during his trial speech by condemning the Doctor's speech as pure hypocrisy. He drew an analogy between Sacheverell's trial and the prosecution of a blasphemer who denied his crimes during his trial, claiming that his words 'admitted of a quite different construction; that he never meant any thing against the honour or being of God . . . But only against the wrong conceptions ignorant people had entertain'd of these things'. The blasphemer spoke with great eloquence and moved many in the audience to weep, but the more sober judges 'saw through all the hypocrite out-side of his flourishing behaviour'. When they passed their sentence of guilt and condemned him to death, the convicted 'threw [sic.?] off the mask, and burst out in the most horrid blasphemies and most impious gestures at the Majesty of God . . . And in that manner he dy'd'. While the story was designed to expose Sacheverell's speech as an excercise in 'cant and counterfeit', it also reinforced the image of the Doctor as a man willing to die for his beliefs.[37] Later in the year, Jonathan Swift would also revisit the Sacheverell as martyr metaphor in an ironical essay for the tory *Examiner* that claimed that the 'late ministry' had actually prosecuted Sacheverell because 'they had somewhere heard the maxim, that *Sanguis Martyrum est Semen Eclesia* [the blood of martyrs is the seed of the Church]; therefore, in order to sow this seed, they began with impeaching a clergyman'. While Swift hardly flattered Sacheverell when he implied that the Doctor was a 'violent, hot, positive fellow' in the essay, he also clearly signalled the relative success that the martyr imagery had achieved for the tory cause.[38]

Sacheverell's pretended martydrom was, at heart, a carefully-constructed pose designed to present the Doctor in the most sympathetic light. It was, perhaps, the most successful move made by his defence counsel at the trial. By eschewing the more controversial implications of his claims about resistance during the revolution and about toleration for protestant dissenters, Sacheverell and his defence team made the trial appear to look less like a condemnation of his outrageously tory sermons, and much more like a brazen attack by the whig managers for the prosecution on a humble, orthodox clergyman.

[36] E.g., *An Elegy on the Much Lamented Death of Sir Roger L'Estrange* (1704) [ESTC T32553]; *An Elegy, on the Death of the Late Famous Doctor Titus Oates* (1705) [ESTC N626]; *An Elegy upon the Much Unlamented Death of Dr. Titus Oates* (1705) [ESTC N46102]; *An Elegy on the Death of the Late Famous Observator, Mr. John Tutchin* (1707) [ESTC N580].

[37] *Review*, vi, no. 146, p. 582: 14 Mar. 1710. Defoe had already occasioned much controversy by his comparison of the 'dry martyrdom' of James II with the 'wet martyrdom' of Charles I in *Review*, ii, no. 123: 18 Dec. 1705, a phrase that was brought up more than once by the defence during Sacheverell's trial: *State Trials*, xv, 213, 324, 341. Compare BL, Add. MS 70421 (unfoliated): 4 Mar. 1710 and HMC, *Portland MSS*, iv, 534: [Abigail Harley] to [Edward] Harley, 7 Mar. 1710.

[38] *Examiner*, i, no. 23: 28 Dec. 1710–4 Jan. 1711.

3

Most whig complaints against Sacheverell's speech tended not to focus on its content. While it is true that Burnet objected that it did not go far enough in justifying the necessity of resistance in cases of extreme necessity, such as had obtained at the time of the Glorious Revolution, a much more common whig strategy was to denounce the speech as a ruse or, perhaps, even as an outright duplicitous denial of Sacheverell's true beliefs that had been merely stated in order to secure his acquittal, or at least to mitigate his sentence. At the trial itself, one of the managers for the prosecution, Sir Thomas Parker, claimed that the speech obscured Sacheverell's real motives and his real beliefs as stated in his controversial sermons. He claimed that the speech was 'fitted not so much to inform . . . as to move, (wherein his hopes were more justly placed;) not so much to state the question, and clear it, as to divert it'. The whole speech, in Parker's view, was calculated as 'an appeal to the people, and to obtain their acquittal upon [Sacheverell's] own word'. The earl of Wharton also noted that 'there is a different strain between the Doctor's sermon and his speech' and then declared that 'the speech is a full confutation and condemnation of the sermon'.[39] The *Scots Post-Man*, perhaps written by Defoe, judged it to be 'a long studyed, and indeed very superficial speech: in which he made solemn protestations of the innocence of his intentions, used most gross flatterys to the queen and moving expressions to affect the passions of the ladys who appeared mightily to befriend him'.[40]

Whig criticisms of Sacheverell's apparent *volte-face* in his speech were curiously echoed by those from the jacobite wing of the high church cause. Thomas Hearne noted gossip in jacobite circles later in the summer after the trial, that expressed discontent that Sacheverell's defence strategy during the trial was 'directly opposite to the Dr.'s sermon' and for this reason the jacobite true believers concluded that 'neither the Doctor nor any of those that vindicated him have acted like men of conscience or honesty, they having made Passive obedience to be only the Doctrine of the Church of England at some times, and having granted Resistance to be lawfull in some Cases, that is times of Rebellion, such as that at the late Revolution'. For this reason, Sacheverell and his defence counsel were condemned by jacobites for their 'fickleness' and denounced as 'men of no principles'.[41] Other tories saw this as less of a problem, or a contradiction. One tract justified Sacheverell's whole defence case at the trial on the grounds of expediency. It was not designed 'to plead the cause, but to bring off the suppos'd criminal'.[42] While Sacheverell's apparent backsliding on the meaning of his earlier declaration that there was an 'utter illegality of resistance upon any pretence whatsoever'

---

[39] Burnet, *History of his Own Time*, v, 443; *State Trials*, xv, 458; Wharton is in Abel Boyer, *The History of the Life and Reign of Queen Anne* (1722), 429, also in John Oldmixon, *The History of England During the Reigns of King William and Queen Anne* (1735), 437.

[40] *Scots Post-Man*, no. 39: 17 Mar. 1710. On Defoe's involvement with the *Scots Post-Man*, see P.N. Furbank and W.R. Owens, *A Critical Bibliography of Daniel Defoe* (1998), 242.

[41] Thomas Hearne, *Remarks and Collections of Thomas Hearne* (8 vols, Oxford, 1885–1907), iii, 35–6. The argument developed from Charles Leslie's more forthright defence of indefeasible passive obedience in *The Good Old Cause, or, Lying in Truth* (1710) [Madan 447], which refrained from attacking Sacheverell personally.

[42] *A Letter to the Bishop of Salisbury* (1711 [1710]) [Madan 329], 7. See also Goldie, 'Tory Political Thought, 1689–1714', 291, which explores the divisions within tory thought on Sacheverell's defence in detail.

may have lost him some support amongst jacobites, non-jurors and some of the highest flying tories, it effectively checked the strongest whig criticisms of the Doctor and his cause.

As a result of the moderate tone of the trial speech, Sacheverell's critics were not able to easily criticize its content. George Ridpath's rabidly whig *Observator* was obviously flummoxed by the speech's moderation. 'If the Doctor's speech be true', he fulminated, 'every man in England has lost the property of his native tongue, and not one of 'em understands a word of it but the Doctor himself; so that hence-forward we must call black white, and blessing cursing.' In later papers, he further complained that Sacheverell's speech lamely protested that he had 'spoke one thing and meant another' in his sermons. He concluded that 'the Doctor's speech [must be] as full of falshood, as an egg is full of meat, or at least, that the Doctor is a changeling'.[43] While Ridpath was obviously disappointed by the lack of controversial material in the speech, more moderate observers were similarly puzzled. How should one reconcile the Doctor's sermons with his trial speech? One pamphleteer mused that 'the one seems inveterate hot, and in many places, terrible and shocking; the other calm, sedate and moving, and like those soft and gentle showers that succeed violent claps of thunder'. In this case, Sacheverell's turn towards moderation went over well, and the author declared: 'I dare say a week ago a great many people, did not believe [Sacheverell] so well, and so heartily affected to the present government or the Protestant succession, who now are almost of another opinion; what a wonderful turn is here of a sudden.'[44]

Since the trial speech gave them so little content to challenge, Sacheverell's opponents were forced, instead, to focus on its insincerity and its over-theatricality, and above all, to suggest that it was not his speech at all. Some grumbled that the weakness of the Doctor's cause was made evident by 'his resort to art' in his speech.[45] Whig pamphleteers reported that Sacheverell had later 'made a jest' in conversation of his solemn oath before God, the queen and the Lords that he remained steadfast in his loyalty to the revolution and the Hanoverian protestant succession.[46] One extra-illustrated, and whiggish, binding of the Jacob Tonson edition of Sacheverell's *Tryal* along with several other tracts relating to the controversies provoked by his impeachment included a print of the Italian *commedia dell'arte* character Scaramouche pasted in just before the account of the second day of the trial's proceedings. The binder's implication was clearly to draw a parallel between Sacheverell and the roguish clown of the Italian comedies.[47] Arthur Maynwar-

---

[43] *Observator*, ix, no. 18: 15–18 Mar. 1710; no. 19: 18–22 Mar. 1710; no. 21: 25–9 Mar. 1710.

[44] *A True Answer; or, Remarks, Upon Dr. Sacheverells Speech* (1710) [Madan 268], 2, 5.

[45] HMC, *11th Report, Appendix, Part vii*, 117: Thomas L'Estrange to Nicholas L'Estrange, 16 Mar. 1710. The original letter, which contains more material of interest than that which has been calendared, is at the Norfolk RO, LEST/P 20, no. 236. I am grateful to Noah McCormack for discussions regarding this and so many other documents relating to the Sacheverell controversies.

[46] *A Supplement to the Faults on Both Sides* (1710) [ESTC T66273], 45; William Bisset, *The Modern Fanatick* (1710) [Madan 987], 23.

[47] Nicolas Bonnart, *Scaramouche* (c.1678–93) etched and engraved print in BL, Sach. 445, (4) bound together with *The Tryal of Dr. Henry Sacheverell* (1710) [Madan 465], as *Dr. Sacheverell's Trial, Etc. Illustrated*. I am grateful to Mark Knights for drawing my attention to this unique item, and to Dr Moira Goff of the British Library for allowing me to consult it. The volume came from the collections of Horace Walpole the younger (1717–97) of Strawberry Hill, but was apparently in the possession of several other people as well.

ing criticized the overt theatricality of Sacheverell's speech directly. 'Will it acquit him to say that he did not compose his speech, and only perform'd his part like an actor?', he asked. 'Indeed it may be said to resemble a play in one respect, because it was a farce well wrought up, and had a wonderful effect on the weak part of his audience.'[48]

One of the most common accusations was that Sacheverell did not write the speech himself. At the trial itself, Parker referred to the 'composer' of the speech as if to indicate that he did not believe that Sacheverell was the author. He also expressed his desire that this composer had 'given [the speech] a little more resemblance of the Doctor and his Sermon; that he had not calculated so many parts of it for an appeal to the people, and to obtain their acquittal upon his own word'.[49] He thought, in other words, that the speech did not reflect Sacheverell's true beliefs, and that it had been crafted in order to make him appear sympathetic in the eyes of popular opinion.

The charge that Sacheverell's speech had been penned by others quickly became a common refrain amongst whig critics. The day after Sacheverell delivered his speech, William Bishop reported coffee-house gossip amongst city whigs that 'own it was well delivered, but made by the University of Oxford'.[50] In the *Review*, Defoe immediately wrote that the speech was 'borrowed', and later in the year, Arthur Maynwaring's whig tract *Four Letters to a Friend in North Britain, Upon the Publishing the Tryal of Dr. Sacheverell* (1710) developed, at greater length, the charge that the speech was not Sacheverell's own. Maynwaring noted the contradictions between the counter-revolutionary implications of Sacheverell's St Paul's sermon and his declarations of loyalty and modesty at his trial speech before accusing 'these penmen of the speech' of encouraging the Doctor to pronounce 'such solemn appeals made to heaven for the truth of fact, which the whole assembly knew to be directly contrary'.[51] Henceforth, whig authors would commonly refer to the 'author' of Sacheverell's speech as a means of rhetorically distancing it from the more inflammatory sermons.[52]

It would not be long before a guessing game as to who the 'real' author of the speech might have been, began to exercise the minds of many commentators. Francis Atterbury, dean of Carlisle and a well-known high church propagandist, was a likely candidate. Atterbury had advised Sacheverell carefully in preparation for the trial and he sat prominently behind the Doctor during its proceedings, all of which gave the distinct impression that the performance had been coached. The earl of Dartmouth thought the speech was Atterbury's because it was so 'finely written' and hence probably beyond Sacheverell's own limited rhetorical capabilities; the jacobite, Thomas Hearne, agreed.[53] Others believed that the speech had been written by a committee of high churchmen, with Atterbury amongst them to be sure, but also including other prominent tories such as George Smalridge, Doctor Robert Moss, and Doctor John Freind, with the finished product being 'supervis'd and corrected' by Sacheverell's defence counsellors, Sir Simon

[48] [Maynwaring], *Four Letters to a Friend in North Britain*, 9.

[49] *State Trials*, xv, 458.

[50] Bodl., MS Ballard 31, f. 82r: William Bishop to Arthur Charlett, 8 Mar. 1710.

[51] *Review*, vi, no. 146, p. 581: 14 Mar. 1710; [Maynwaring], *Four Letters to a Friend in North Britain*, 9.

[52] [Benjamin Hoadly], *The Jacobite's Hopes Reviv'd by our Late Tumults and Addresses* ([1710]) [Madan 449], 3; [William Fleetwood?], *A Letter to the Reverend Dr. Sacheverel* (1711) [Madan 1000], 19–20.

[53] Burnet, *History of his Own Time*, v, 444 note 'c'; Hearne, *Remarks and Collections*, viii, 224.

Harcourt and Sir Constantine Phipps.[54] Later in the century, John Wesley would claim that his father, Samuel Wesley, then rector of Epworth in Lincolnshire, had composed the speech, and the claim would be repeated in subsequent histories of the Wesley family. No evidence for the assertion has ever been produced, but a substantial oral history regarding the relationship between Sacheverell and the Wesley family developed around this rumour.[55]

Some defenders of Sacheverell attempted to answer the charge that Sacheverell had been given a ghost-written speech in order to bolster his reputation by claiming that it was, indeed, the Doctor's own composition. The tory Speaker of the house of commons in the post-Sacheverell crisis parliament, Sir William Bromley, made a point of announcing that he had seen a copy of the speech written in Sacheverell's own distinctively florid handwriting. More sceptical parties, such as the earl of Dartmouth, were keen to note, however, that this 'by no means proves, that Sacheverel [*sic*.] was its real author'.[56] Upon reading the printed version of the speech, the Reverend Thomas Carte was one of only a very few of Sacheverell's contemporaries to be satisfied that it was 'his own' and even he was quick to add that 'I am satisfied Dr. Atterbury and Smalridge perused it before he spake it.'[57]

Amongst modern historians, only Abbie Turner Scudi has been convinced that the speech's style resembles closely that of Sacheverell's earlier sermons.[58] G.V. Bennett, on the other hand, argued from 'the phraseology, paradoxical manner and quiet emotion' of the speech that Atterbury had 'the chief hand in its composition'.[59] Mark Goldie has given Sir Simon Harcourt substantial credit for co-ordinating Sacheverell's whole defence strategy, one which included, and indeed culminated in, the Doctor's own rousing oratory on the eighth day of the trial. Goldie notes that Harcourt's careful management of the arguments presented in Westminster Hall could only succeed if he 'ignored the fact that Sacheverell himself certainly did not think the Revolution was an exceptional case [of resistance], though the wording of his sermon had been carefully ambiguous'.[60] Given the divisions amongst the tories on the question of the legitimacy of resistance in the revolution documented by Goldie, and the surprise that was generated by Sacheverell's much more equivocal stance towards the issue in his trial

[54] Boyer, *History of the Life and Reign of Queen Anne*, 427; John Oldmixon, *The History of England, During the Reigns of King William and Queen Mary, Queen Anne, King George I* (1735), 435, adds Moss's name to Boyer's list; see also, Nicolas Tindal, *The Continuation of Mr. Rapin's History of England* (7 vols, 1761–3), v, 230; William Rider, *A New History of England* (50 vols, 1761–4), xxxii, 129. On Smalridge's equivocal relationship to the high church cause, see William Gibson, 'Altitudinarian Equivocation: George Smalridge's Churchmanship', in *Religious Identities in Britain, 1660–1832*, ed. William Gibson and Robert Ingram (Aldershot, 2005), 43–59.

[55] John Wesley, *A Concise History of England, From the Earliest Times, To the Death of George II* (4 vols, [1776]), iv, 75; Luke Tyerman, *The Life and Times of the Rev. Samuel Wesley, M.A.: Rector of Epworth and Father of the Revs. John and Charles Wesley, the Founders of the Methodists* (1866); Joseph Beaumont Wakeley, *Anecdotes of the Wesleys: Illustrative of Their Character and Personal History* (New York, 1870), 81.

[56] Burnet, *History of his Own Time*, v, 444 note 'c'; for an example of Sacheverell's handwriting, see BL, Add. MS 4276, f. 111.

[57] Bodl., MS Carte 230, f. 225: Thomas Carte to John Carte, 7 Apr. 1710, quoted in Holmes, *Trial of Doctor Sacheverell*, 196.

[58] Abbie Turner Scudi, *The Sacheverell Affair* (New York, 1939), 90.

[59] G.V. Bennett, *The Tory Crisis in Church and State, 1688–1730* (Oxford, 1975), 116; see also George M. Trevelyan, *England Under Queen Anne* (3 vols, 1934), ii, 53.

[60] Goldie, 'Tory Political Thought 1689–1714', 290.

speech, it seems likely to conclude that he had, indeed, been coached by more astute minds such as Atterbury and Harcourt to adopt a more moderate pose for his own good. Whether Sacheverell himself truly agreed with this counsel, one cannot say for certain, as we have only deeply partisan gossip and hearsay as evidence.

To concentrate too deeply on the authorship of Sacheverell's speech, or, indeed, upon Sacheverell's own true convictions, may be to miss the main point of the whole performance however. The goal of the performance was to arouse sympathy for the Doctor during his supposed time of persecution. The more loyal, the more orthodox, and the more pathetic he could appear to the audience at his trial and to the general public abroad, the greater the support that Sacheverell could garner for himself and for the tory cause in general. The widespread comments that his speech had been so provocative that it moved both the men and women in the audience to tears of sympathy for the Doctor's plight should not be easily dismissed, as many whig commentators, in fact, tried to do so not long after the speech had been delivered and throughout the rest of the 18th century.[61] Burnet's complaint that the speech only had a 'great effect on the weaker sort, while it possessed those who knew the man and his ordinary discourses with horror, when they heard him affirm so many falsehoods with such solemn appeals to God' could not deny that many people, indeed, had been moved to see the Doctor in a more sympathetic light in the wake of his performance.[62]

4

When George Smalridge wrote to Arthur Charlett to report on Sir Simon Harcourt's speech in defence of Sacheverell at the trial, he noted that Harcourt's 'speech you will see in publick [i.e., in print], but you will not be able to conceive half the pleasure from reading, as we did from hearing it'.[63] This comment would have been all the more true in the case of Sacheverell's own speech. The speeches at the trial were all composed and presented with an eye towards their eventual publication in print, but they were also performed with great panache and overt theatricality in the hopes of moving the audience present in Westminster Hall, and that such reactions would be reported by the many observers in private and public observations.[64]

The published versions of the speeches, both in print and in manuscript, were themselves another form of performance for the wider reading public beyond Westminster Hall. Sacheverell himself was keen to exploit this opportunity. Scribal and printed versions of his answer to the house of commons' articles of impeachment had circulated

[61] E.g., *The Correspondence of Sir James Clavering*, ed. H.T. Dickinson (Gateshead, 1967), 70: Anne Clavering to James Clavering, 18 Mar. 1710; Alexander Cunningham, *The History of Great Britain: From the Revolution in 1688, to the Accession of George the First* (2 vols, 1787), ii, 292–3.

[62] Burnet, *History of His Own Time*, v, 444; see also *A Compleat History of the Whole Proceedings . . . against Dr. Henry Sacheverell* (1710) [Madan 511], 84 [part two].

[63] Bodl., MS Ballard 7, f. 36r: Smallridge to Arthur Charlett, [4 Mar. 1710].

[64] Thus General James Stanhope was reported to have spoken 'on this ecclesiastical mattter [of Sacheverell's impeachment] with such vivacity that it is as if he had taken some of his abilities from the military arts', in *Le Clef du Cabinets des Princes*, ed. Jordan de Colombier, xii, 336–7, my translation.

well before the trial had begun.[65] Just days after his speech, Sacheverell's publisher, Henry Clements, printed a tract entitled *Collections of Passages Referr'd to by Dr. Henry Sacheverell in his Answer to the Articles of his Impeachment*, which included much of the substance of the proceedings of his defence counsel on the sixth day of the trial.[66] Within a week of having delivered his speech, Clements had brought to market a published version. The printed version was rather disingenuously dedicated to the house of lords, and Sacheverell complained that 'it hath been my hard fortune to be misunderstood, at a time when I endeavour'd to express my self with the utmost plainness; even the defence I made at your Lordships bar . . . hath been grievously misrepresented'.[67] Ridpath more accurately, if derisively, described its purpose as 'an appeal to the mob'.[68] Sacheverell's speech had been the most effective part of his defence and now it was allowed to circulate amongst readers throughout the country, indeed throughout much of Europe, without the context of the charges laid against him, the arguments for the prosecution, or the deliberations and ultimate decision of the Lords.[69]

The printed version of the speech was, indeed, widely circulated. At least 20 different editions of the speech were published in 1710 alone, including one Latin translation (presumably for a foreign readership), several editions published with his portrait included (as a means of further personalising his plight) and several piracies along with provincial impressions printed in Norwich, Edinburgh and Dublin.[70] The publication of his speech was, technically, a violation of parliamentary privilege to control the printing of its proceedings, but clearly Clements and Sacheverell thought that the public relations benefits from publishing it was worth incurring the wrath of the Lords. At the conclusion of the trial, Clements was, indeed, called into custody to answer for his offence, but it appears that he managed to evade any serious punishment for the offence.[71]

The printing of Sacheverell's speech surely spurred the quick publication of other speeches that had been delivered at the trial. Little more than a week after Clements had begun to sell his copies of Sacheverell's speech, other booksellers quickly rushed into print copies of the speeches of the duke of Buckingham, Lord Guernsey, the duke of Ormond, and the earl of Pembroke.[72] A week later, on 5 April, the whigs had responded by rushing into print Gilbert Burnet's trial speech in defence of resistance theory.[73]

[65] *The Answer of Henry Sacheverell. D.D. to the Articles of Impeachment* (1710) [Madan 165]; [George Ridpath], *Dr. Sacheverell's Speech upon his Impeachment at the Bar of the House of Lords* (1710) [Madan 270], 3. For a surviving example of a handsomely produced manuscript separate copy of Sacheverell's 'Answer', see BL, Egerton MS 3347. One difference between this manuscript version and the printed versions is that the manuscript contains references to the texts that Sacheverell refers to in his 'Answer' in the margins. These references were later included in the printed *Collections of Passages Referr'd to by Dr. Henry Sacheverell in his Answer to the Articles of his Impeachment* (1710) [Madan 237–40].

[66] *Collections of Passages.*

[67] *Speech of Henry Sacheverell, D.D. Upon His Impeachment at the Bar of the House of Lords* [Madan 248], preface.

[68] [Ridpath], *Dr. Sacheverel's Speech*, 5.

[69] The printing of the complete trial proceedings would have to wait several months, until 15 June 1710. On which see, *State Trial of Doctor Henry Sacheverell*, ed. Cowan, and *Tryal*.

[70] Madan 248–67.

[71] Parliamentary Archives, HL/PO/JO/1/81, 430-1: 23 Mar. 1710; *LJ*, xix, 122b.

[72] Madan 277–80.

[73] Burnet, *The Bishop of Salisbury his Speech*.

Print gave Sacheverell's trial performance an extended afterlife that carried on from the day it was delivered right into the contested histories of the trial that would be written, contradicted and rewritten throughout the 18th century. While the trial itself raised issues of tremendous importance for understanding the political and religious settlements that had emerged in the wake of the revolution, Sacheverell's speech at the trial did little to clarify those issues. That, indeed, was its purpose: surely Harcourt and Atterbury, and perhaps even Sacheverell himself, understood that there was little to be gained through orchestrating a direct clash of competing political ideologies at a show trial in which the ultimate outcome was more or less foreordained. This was especially true given the divisions within the tory party itself on many of the issues that Sacheverell had raised, particularly those concerning the legitimacy of resistance at the revolution. Sacheverell's speech, and the representations of it in manuscript and print, developed, instead, the image of the Doctor as a tory martyr. It was a controversial perspective to be sure, but it managed to garner more sympathy for Sacheverell than the firebrand preacher might otherwise have managed to obtain.

This sort of spin worked extremely well in the short run, and it surely contributed to the tory revanche in the latter half of 1710, but it had also entailed Sacheverell's unambiguous and very public commitment to the Hanoverian succession. The consequences of that assurance would only become clear four years later.

The 'End of Censorship' and the Politics of Toleration, from Locke to Sacheverell

GEOFF KEMP

The end of pre-publication censorship in England in 1695 is a milestone in the historical self-image of modern liberal democracy, although historians since at least Macaulay have seen the fall of the Licensing Act as preceding, rather than proceeding from, a principled commitment to press freedom. One outcome has been a routine assumption that the multiple attempts to pass printing legislation in the decade after 1695 tried to restore press licensing, and so censorship. Recent accounts have reinforced this view in tracing a pathway to the 1710 Copyright Act, assuming censorship as a cause of Church and state while focusing on literary property as the cause of print trade and authors. Yet a close reading of the evidence overturns the view that the lapse of censorship in 1695 was followed by a series of licensing bills. Instead, press bills sought compulsory imprints, as Milton's *Areopagitica* had recommended in 1644 and Locke's circle advocated in 1695. This became, *via* Defoe, a connecting-point between religious politics and copyright. This article shows how working from 1695 towards 1710 as the year of the Sacheverell trial provides a new perspective on 'the end of censorship', tied to acute post-revolution division in the Church over toleration and the suppression of heresy. From this perspective, the abandonment of licensing *was* a Church cause, orchestrated, in part, by the archbishop of Canterbury to outflank high church opponents.

Keywords: censorship; toleration; print culture; political discourse; copyright; William III; Anne

1

The trial of Dr Henry Sacheverell concluded on 27 March 1710 with the burning of the printed sermons for which parliament had pronounced him guilty of high crimes and misdemeanours, a libeller of Church and state.[1] Little more than a week later, at the prorogation on 5 April, the world's first copyright statute was enacted.[2] The two parliamentary episodes were formally unconnected and have remained so in the historical account, yet in their differing ways each concerns the freedom and control of the press. Historians have, increasingly of late, viewed efforts to legislate on the press following the lapse of pre-publication licensing in 1695 – a dozen bills over the next 15

[1] *The Tryal of Dr. Henry Sacheverell* (1710) [ESTC T051985], 333–5. I use the first quarto edition printed by Henry Clements.
[2] 8 Anne, c. 19; *LJ*, xix, 144.

years[3] – through the lens of the unfolding story of copyright, working towards the 1710 act.[4] However, as Geoffrey Holmes observed, not only would Sacheverell's trial be unthinkable if his sermons had not been printed but the pamphlets marked the 'shrill crescendo' of a high church campaign to suppress heterodox opinion whose target was 'particularly the peril of the printed word'.[5] Silencing Sacheverell was, ironically, an imperative born, in part, of high church failure to secure the censorship of others, through legislation or other means.

When the Licensing Act[6] came up for renewal in 1695, John Locke's political associates, John Freke and the MP Edward Clarke, known as 'the College' circle, identified three groups of people who had a particular interest in the fate of the legislation, alongside writers and readers – the print trade, the government, and the Church of England.[7] This trio, while externally and internally divided, suggests three overlapping strands of the press regulation story in 1695 and after, centred on the print trade, on civil politics and on religious politics. For the print trade, a lingering impulse behind regulation was concluded in 1710 by the Copyright Act, imperfect as it was. Meanwhile, the political strand, as traced by Alan Downie, saw pragmatic government turn from censorship to information management and strategic post-publication punishment through Robert Harley's initiative and Daniel Defoe's pen.[8] But leaving the corridors of ministerial power and working towards 1710 as the year of Sacheverell more than the year of copyright gives a different view of the path after 1695, highlighting a crucial third strand tied to the trauma of post-revolution religious politics and, in particular, the relationship between censorship and toleration.[9]

This article traces this neglected strand, working within a context of Church conflict rather than copyright or a more secular arena of political manœuvring, while recognizing the religious context as a key dimension of contemporary political culture, in turn partly shaped by commercial publishing priorities. Central figures in this account will include Locke and other political writers but also Thomas Tenison, who became archbishop of Canterbury at the start of 1695. Tenison would later profess to having 'offered several bills' on the press to parliament – a level of involvement so far unrecognized – yet to

[3] The 12 are: two reviving bills for the 1662 act (1695 and 1696) plus press-related bills in 1695 (March), 1695–6, 1696–7, 1697 (news), 1698 (Blasphemy Act), 1698–9, 1702, 1703–4, 1707, 1710; cf. John Feather, *Publishing, Piracy and Politics* (1994), 51.

[4] Ronan Deazley, *On the Origin of the Right to Copy* (Oxford, 2004), 1–50; Michael Treadwell, 'The Stationers and the Printing Acts at the End of the Seventeenth Century', in *The Cambridge History of the Book in Britain* (5 vols so far, Cambridge, 1999–2009), iv, 755–76; John Feather, 'The Book Trade in Politics: The Making of the Copyright Act of 1710', *Publishing History*, viii (1980), 19–44; Feather, *Publishing*, 50–63; Mark Rose, *Authors and Owners: The Invention of Copyright* (Cambridge, 1993), 31–48.

[5] Geoffrey Holmes, *The Trial of Doctor Sacheverell* (1973), 55, 72.

[6] The legislation's long title now tends to be truncated to 'Printing Act' but present purposes justify a return to the formerly favoured term 'Licensing Act', which seems to have been coined by Matthew Tindal, grew in popularity later in the 18th century and became the standard term up to the 1980s: Matthew Tindal, *A Defence of the Rights of the Christian Church* (1709), 163.

[7] More specifically, the court, the bishops and the Stationers' Company: *The Correspondence of John Locke*, ed. E.S. De Beer (8 vols, Oxford, 1976–89), v, 291–2, letter 1860 (14 Mar. 1695).

[8] J.A. Downie, *Robert Harley and the Press* (Cambridge, 1979).

[9] On press regulation responding to religious and moral imperatives: Geoff Kemp, 'Introduction', in *Censorship and the Press, 1580–1720*, gen. ed. Geoff Kemp and Jason McElligott (4 vols, 2009), iii, pp. ix–xxvii (this volume edited by Geoff Kemp); David Hayton, 'Moral Reform and Country Politics in the Late Seventeenth-Century House of Commons', *Past & Present*, No. 128 (1990), 70.

Sacheverell he remained a 'perfidious prelate' obstructing the suppression of printed heresy.[10] Part of the explanation for this seeming anomaly overturns routine assumptions that the period after 1695 was marked by a 'succession of Licensing Bills', a view as old as Blackstone's *Commentaries*.[11] To put the case boldly, there is no certain evidence that any new legislative proposals between the expiry of the Licensing Act and the Copyright Act tried to impose compulsory licensing of books and pamphlets. Two bills whose content is unknown *may* have done so, and another proposed licensing news, but no surviving draft legislation proposes the pre-publication censorship of printed works as such. In the main, these draft bills instead focused on making printers, publishers and, indirectly, authors, answerable to post-publication laws, primarily through compulsory imprints. This was to propose legal compulsion but it was the compulsion advocated by John Milton's *Areopagitica*, not proscriptive pre-publication licensing. The aim, in Tenison's case, as for Locke's circle, was primarily to divert high church repressive ambition directed against the religious latitude associated with the 1689 Toleration Act.

2

The Licensing Act was ecclesiastical at heart, wrote Locke in manuscript criticisms that contributed to its demise in 1695.[12] While it was other things too, the legislation shared a birthday and motivation with the Act of Uniformity, both having been granted royal assent on 19 May 1662 as weapons in the Restoration armoury against the threat of dissent and division to church and state.[13] Charles II urged MPs to curb the liberty of the press as a cause of both rebellion and religious schism and parliament obliged with a statute initially restricted to a term of two years (13 & 14 Car. II, c. 33), followed by a one-year extension.[14] The legislation was then granted a longer term which saw licensing lapse in the political turmoil of 1679.[15] The act was revived under James II in 1685, wavered in application but continued through the revolution of 1688, and was renewed for a fourth and last time in 1693, again for a short period.[16] The act expired with the prorogation on 3 May 1695, renewal having been rejected, as it would be again in March 1696 – the last attempt to revive the 1662 Licensing Act.

---

[10] *Records of Convocation*, ed. Gerald Bray (20 vols, Woodbridge, 2006), ix, 220–1. Tenison's role in press legislation has been largely ignored, apart from mention of his contact with the Locke circle in 1695 and Harley in 1702. The latter furnishes the only discussion in the standard biography, and even then an incorrect reference is given for Harley's letter: Edward Carpenter, *Thomas Tenison* (1948), 288.

[11] Feather, 'Book Trade', 25; William Blackstone, *Commentaries on the Laws of England* (4 vols, Oxford, 1769), iv, 152. For similar views see Downie, *Robert Harley*, 3; Deazley, *Origin*, 2; Rose, *Authors*, 34.

[12] The criticisms survive in two manuscript copies, one in the Bodleian Library, Oxford, at MS Locke, b. 4, 75–6, the other, in Locke's hand, among the Shaftesbury Papers at The National Archives, Kew, PRO30/24/30/30, Part 1, 88–9v. The first is printed in *Locke Correspondence*, ed. De Beer, v, 785–91; also in John Locke, *Political Essays*, ed. Mark Goldie (Cambridge, 1997), 330–7. The TNA variant is printed in *Censorship*, gen. ed. Kemp and McElligott, iii, 417–21.

[13] 13 & 14 Car. II, c. 4 (Act of Uniformity); *CJ*, viii, 434–6; *LJ*, xi, 471–2.

[14] 16 Car. II, c. 8. On the king's injunction to parliament: *CJ*, viii, 425: 10 May 1662.

[15] 16 & 17 Car. II, c. 4; *CJ*, ix, 582, 600, 634.

[16] 1 James II, c. 17; 4 Wm & Mary, c. 24; Raymond Astbury, 'The Renewal of the Licensing Act in 1693 and its Lapse in 1695', *Library*, 5th ser., xxxiii (1978), 296–322.

A summary of the act from an ecclesiastical standpoint is provided in the *Codex* compiled by Tenison's disciple, Edmund Gibson, after the Sacheverell affair, where it was categorised as a measure against protestant heresy: 'The late Times produced many Heretical, Schismatical, and Blasphemous Books. Enacted, that, no Person shall Print any Books, against the Doctrine and Government of the Church of England, nor import, or sell such.' Alongside were the act's opening lines, elaborating the ban on any publication expressing doctrine or opinion 'contrary to the Christian Faith, or the Doctrine or Discipline of the Church of England'.[17]

Gibson's abridgement of the expired act, not insignificantly, omitted details of the pre-publication mechanisms to effect these ends, sections in which the episcopal authorities were mentioned 29 times.[18] The act required the registration of presses, with master printers subject to approval by the archbishop of Canterbury or bishop of London. Importing printed works also needed their approval, and while the civil authorities reserved powers to seize works, those deemed heretical or blasphemous were delivered to the archbishop and bishop to take 'further course for the suppressing thereof'. Most importantly, the 1662 act required all works to be licensed before publication, with authority over divinity, philosophy and science in the hands of the archbishop and the bishop of London.[19] Other categories had other licensers, notably the secretaries of state for political books, although for much of the act's life this, too, was a sword wielded against religious dissenters, adjudged enemies of the state by the chief licenser, Roger L'Estrange.[20] The *Codex*'s omission of the apparatus of control is suggestive because the archiepiscopal position under Tenison was broadly to maintain opposition to irreligion without proscriptive pre-publication licensing, a low church attempt to steer between high church persecution and no-church licentiousness.

The essential background was the legislation entered in the *Codex* under 'Toleration of Dissenters' – the 1689 statute easing penalties on nonconformists but fatefully drawing the line at preaching or writing against the doctrine of the trinity or denying scripture's divine inspiration.[21] The Toleration Act actually owed an indirect debt to the Licensing Act, for in James II's reign ecclesiastical licences had authorised and protected the publishing campaign led by Tenison and other London divines against Roman catholic treatises printed on the king's authority.[22] This had advanced Tenison's reputation – even opponents like Swift could admire publishing 'in those dangerous times' – while also helping forge the anti-papal whig alliance of 'moderate protestants' which he saw as fundamental to the anglican church's deliverance and post-revolution security, making a

[17] Edmund Gibson, *Codex Juris Ecclesiastici Anglicani* (2 vols, 1713), i, 426. On Gibson and Tenison, see Stephen Taylor, ' "Dr Codex" and the Whig "Pope": Edmund Gibson, Bishop of Lincoln and London, 1716–1748', in *Lords of Parliament: Studies, 1714–1914*, ed. R.W. Davis (Stanford, CA, 1995), 9–28.

[18] Including references to the archbishop of York and diocesan bishops other than the bishop of London.

[19] *The Statutes of the Realm* (11 vols, 1810–28), v, 428–35.

[20] Geoff Kemp, 'L'Estrange and the Publishing Sphere', in *Fear, Exclusion and Revolution: Roger Morrice and Britain in the 1680s*, ed. Jason McElligott (Aldershot, 2006), 67–90.

[21] Gibson, *Codex*, 616.

[22] Thomas Tenison and William Clagett, *The Present State of the Controversie Between the Church of England and the Church of Rome* (1687); Thomas Tenison et al., *A Collection of Cases and Other Discourses Lately Written to Recover Dissenters to the Communion of the Church of England* (1685).

priority their comprehension within a broadened Church, supplemented by duly circumscribed toleration.[23]

Press freedom was not embraced in 1689 as a core 'revolution principle' but identifying post-revolution political and religious orthodoxy quickly made books battlelines and press control precarious and open to criticism. A political example was the licenser, Edmund Bohun, approving *King William and Mary Conquerors* only for parliament to burn the book as a work of non-resistance (Bohun believed), only for Sacheverell to later claim that the tract's burning showed parliament's support *for* non-resistance.[24] The religious settlement raised further questions about policing the press for orthodoxy. When, in 1689, parliament invited the newly-assembled Church of England convocation to consider comprehension measures to accompany the recently-passed Toleration Act, the high church clergy in the lower House manifested their opposition to both by attacking twin printed targets, urging action against the anti-trinitarian *Brief Notes on the Creed of St Athanasius* and the low church comprehensionist *Letter to a Friend*. The upper house of bishops, bolstered by recent whig appointees, declared that convocation could not assume an independent power to condemn books and doctrines without encroaching on civil authority under the Act of Supremacy, thereby foiling suppression, although in the event failing to save comprehension.[25]

The path of press control after 1689 was to be dominated by high churchmen pressuring proxies in pursuit of repression – bishops, parliament, or crown – while insisting on the Church's independent power to condemn. It was also shaped by toleration's trinitarian limits yielding heresy-hunting of error inside as well as outside the Church, while episcopal moderation towards printed opinion was denounced by opponents as comprehension by stealth and a vote to 'Cherish such Monsters' rather than tolerate them, as Sacheverell later contended.[26] The 'trinitarian controversy' and 'socinian controversy' of the 1690s, and later the 'Church in danger' crisis, were played out through the problematic politics of policing print. The fate of press regulation cannot be divorced from the politics of religious authority and toleration that followed, and indeed preceded, the revolution; both the toleration of 1689 and licensing's lapse in 1695 redressed statutory repressive powers granted at the Restoration.

Religion shaped the demise of the Licensing Act in 1695, its lapse far from the ideology-free accident suggested by historians since Macaulay.[27] At the start of the year a Commons' committee recommended renewing the act but, instead, a new printing bill was ordered, which was introduced by Edward Clarke in March.[28] The Lords, meanwhile, added the Licensing Act to a reviving bill, but on 18 April agreed to its removal after hearing reasons delivered on behalf of the Commons by Clarke, partly inspired by

[23] *Examiner*, no. 22: 21–8 Dec. 1710; Taylor, 'Dr Codex', 21; Carpenter, *Tenison*, 440–2.

[24] Charles Blount, *King William and Queen Mary Conquerors* (1693); Edmund Bohun, *Diary and Autobiography* (Beccles, 1853), 109–10; *CJ*, x, 785; *Tryal*, 51–2, 262.

[25] Thomas Lathbury, *A History of the Convocation of the Church of England* (1853), 332; White Kennett, *The History of the Convocation of the Prelates and Clergy of the Province of Canterbury* (1702), 112–13.

[26] Henry Sacheverell, *The Perils of False Brethren* (1709) [Madan 57], 25.

[27] Lord Macaulay, *History of England* (4 vols, 1967), iv, 126. For primary sources and commentary: *Censorship*, gen. ed. Kemp and McElligott, iii, 413–36.

[28] *CJ*, xi, 200, 228, 254, 287–8.

the criticisms which Locke had drafted late in 1694.[29] Freke's remark that the bishops 'think property a very popular word, which Licencer is not' suggests not only how licensing already lacked support but that religious motives may be under-represented in the record.[30] None the less, both Locke's criticisms and Clarke's reasons raised the subject, broadly aligning with the spirit, if hardly matching the substance, of Locke's *Letters* on toleration.[31] As well as counting up the cost to learning and trade of protecting 'mother church', Locke complained that licensing made judgment of heresy subject to the 'humours' of current ecclesiastical interpretation, comparing this to catholic condemnation of Copernican astronomy.[32] Clarke observed that the act left open not only what counted as heretical and seditious but 'offensive', which he suggested authorised James II to ban books against popery (an ironic example).[33] Amongst other comments, Locke echoed Charles Blount, who adapted Spinoza, who followed Tacitus, in urging that a man should 'have liberty to print whatever he would speak', being 'answerable for the one just as he is for the other', but not 'gagging a man for fear he should talk heresie or sedition'.[34] The College allies, in effect, opposed licensing as arbitrary private judgment, albeit legally empowered, contrasted with answerability to the public judgment of law.

The nature of the College's concern is illuminated by the example of Locke's own *Reasonableness of Christianity*, which he wrote as parliament considered licensing, travelling to London soon after the act's expiry on 3 May to arrange publication.[35] The significant point for present purposes is that the work did not *oppose* the trinity, it did not *mention* the trinity, hence Locke's remark in response to critics that 'Mine it seems in this Book, are all sins of Omission'.[36] Interpreters then, and now, disagree on whether a heretic unitarian or an eirenic trinitarian lies behind Locke's focus on belief in Christ as the sole requirement for being a tolerated christian.[37] But this is the point, because an omission may be hard to prove a crime whereas ecclesiastical licensers would have had power and discretion to punish the 'sin' by refusing to authorise the book. One adversary

---

[29] *LJ*, xv, 545–6; *Censorship*, gen. ed. Kemp and McElligott, iii, 414.

[30] *Locke Correspondence*, v, 291: 14 Mar. 1695.

[31] John Locke, *A Letter Concerning Toleration* (1689), and its sequels. Detailed comparison of Locke's views on toleration and on free expression is beyond the scope of this article, and will be developed in another; for an early essay see Geoff Kemp, 'Ideas of Liberty of the Press, 1640–1700', University of Cambridge PhD, 2000, pp. 223–32.

[32] *Locke Correspondence*, v, 785–91.

[33] *LJ*, xv, 545–6.

[34] Locke, *Political Essays*, 331, 337. Charles Blount, *A Just Vindication of Learning, and of the Liberty of the Press* (1679), 12; Benedictis de Spinoza, *Tractatus Theologico-Politicus* (Amsterdam, 1670), in translation *A Treatise Partly Theological and Partly Political* (1689), 435; Tacitus, *The Histories* (2009), 1. Locke owned Blount's tract, repr. in 1695.

[35] Locke travelled to London on 20 May, obtained a contract dated 12 June and the book appeared in August: John Locke, *The Reasonableness of Christianity*, ed. John C. Higgins-Biddle (Oxford, 1999), p. xli. He had started work on the project at the beginning of 1695: John Locke, *A Second Vindication of the Reasonableness of Christianity* (1697), 'To Mr. Bold'.

[36] John Locke, *A Vindication of the Reasonableness of Christianity* (1695), 9–10.

[37] Astbury remarks that Locke would not have relished presenting the manuscript to the censor: Astbury, 'Renewal', 313; Locke, *Reasonableness*, p. lxviii; John Marshall, *John Locke: Resistance, Religion and Responsibility* (Cambridge, 1994), 413–14; John Marshall, *John Locke, Toleration and Early Enlightenment Culture* (Cambridge, 2006), 671.

went so far as to claim that Locke's silences were 'publishing to the World' his heresy, drawing the retort that condemnation could not extend to 'any thing more than what the Author has Published'.[38]

These concerns form the background to the bill 'for the better regulating of Printing, and Printing Presses' introduced by Clarke in March. Its contents are mainly known from a transcript sent to Locke by Freke, although an earlier version survives in the papers of another of Locke's correspondents, William Brockman, who sat on the drafting committee with Clarke.[39] As well as removing episcopal oversight of printer numbers and imported books, the bill deleted the 1662 preamble's elaboration of the dangers of heretical and seditious books, and demoted and reworded the declaration banning opinions 'contrary to the Christian Faith, or the Doctrine or Discipline of the Church of England', which became 'Contrary to the Christian Religion as it is Establisht by Law in this Realm'. Freke assured Locke that these were 'some of the best words in the Bill' (they are underlined in the Brockman draft), because they subordinated ecclesiastical interpretation to adjudication under civil authority and rendered needless Locke's concern at retaining the word 'hereticall' at another point.[40]

Equally importantly, however, the bill removed licensing. The drafts carry no reference to compulsory, proscriptive licensing, or, indeed, to 'licensing' at all, apart from a fleeting mention of past licences. Raymond Astbury's classic account of these events was simply wrong in claiming that the College-backed proposals reasserted 'the Stuart system of preprinting censorship' in the key areas of politics, divinity and law, a misreading widely shared and followed.[41] The bill required printers to notify erecting a press and to deliver a copy of each work as it was printed to government, legal or Church authorities.[42] It also required an imprint with the names of printer and publisher so that they would be answerable for the work, as would the author they identified. However, there was no licence involved. To equate compulsory imprints with licences entirely misses the point.[43] Milton's *Areopagitica*, soon to be reprinted for the first time since 1644, opposed licensing and proposed 'that no book be Printed, unlesse the Printers and the Authors name, or at least the Printers be register'd', allowing for post-publication remedy.[44] To early-modern minds, the end of licensing *was* liberty of the press.

If the opacity of the bill's wording was intended to obscure the removal of licensing, modern interpreters were fooled more than were contemporaries. Tenison, closely following events, invited comment from Oxford and Cambridge universities and

---

[38] John Edwards, *Socinianism Unmask'd* (1696), 37; Locke, *Second Vindication*, 405–6.

[39] Bodl., MS. Locke b. 4, 77–8, repr. in *Locke Correspondence*, v, 791–5; BL, Add. MS 42592, f. 203. The Brockman copy has a note about adding the lord chancellor and lord keeper to one clause, effected in the Freke version. Brockman joined the committee on 27 February: *CJ*, xi, 250.

[40] *Locke Correspondence*, v, 294–5, letter 1862: 21 Mar. 1695. In the Brockman copy the relevant phrases are underlined, the only lines so emphasized.

[41] Astbury, 'Renewal', 311; Feather, 'Book Trade', 23; Deazley, *Origin*, 7; Rose, *Authors*, 33; Treadwell, 'Stationers and Printing Acts', 770–1. The legislation is entitled 'The Licensing Bill' in the *Locke Correspondence*. Mark Goldie correctly points out that the intention was to avoid licensing: Locke, *Political Essays*, 329.

[42] The bill extended this authority to diocesan bishops, another clause having permitted presses outside the 1662 limits of London, Cambridge and Oxford.

[43] Downie makes this equation: J.A. Downie, 'The Development of the Political Press', in *Britain in the Age of Party, 1680–1750: Essays Presented to Geoffrey Holmes*, ed. Clyve Jones (1987), 117.

[44] John Milton, *Areopagitica: A Speech of Mr. John Milton for the Liberty of Unlicenc'd Printing* (1644).

received protests that, although printers had to deliver copies ahead of publication, there was no provision to refuse permission, allowing freedom 'to Print and Publish what they Please without any leave and Lycence'.[45] It was objected that this conferred a 'like liberty' to publish for or against religion and government.[46]

In the event, the March bill lapsed at the end of the session in May, along with the 1662 Licensing Act.[47] When the next session commenced, Clarke and Robert Harley were ordered to bring in another bill, which received a second reading on 3 December 1695.[48] A draft of the bill, found among Tenison's papers at Lambeth Palace, shows that it revised the March bill by reintroducing the word but not the previous proscriptive form of licensing, by providing that books '*may* be Licensed', the authority of an imprimatur substituting prior approval for prior restraint.[49] The university critics, again, complained that tracts 'may be printed without such License' while a marginal comment on another draft, held at Cambridge University, noted that if a licence was requested the licenser had no 'power to make any Alteration'.[50]

In the second week of December, Tenison conveyed a request to Clarke that the bill might better protect the Church, speaking for worried bishops but also seeking to allay the pressure from the universities over heretical publishing. Oxford's warnings of the bill's religious impact the previous week came just days after the university convocation issued a decree against the tritheist heresy it found in William Sherlock's tracts on the trinity, perhaps stirring memories of the university's notorious book-burning decree of 1683. Freke observed to Locke, of the archbishop's intervention, that amendments proposed by 'soe reasonable and fair a man' were likely to be acceptable although unlikely to satisfy the bulk of the clergy.[51] The nature of Tenison's proposals is uncertain but if 'reasonable' to the College, clearly did not feature compulsory licensing. It is possible that they concerned imprints, perhaps connecting with the bishops' reference to 'property' which had puzzled Freke. The voluntary licensing provision probably predated the archbishop's intervention, as do amendments in the draft he possessed. One deleted the word 'heretical' which had earlier worried Locke. Another may have reflected contact between Clarke and dissenters, adding voluntary licensing by 'five or more persons of Credit of the Congregacon to which the said Author does in point of perswason

[45] Lambeth Palace Library, MS 640, item 20, p. 249. The point is reiterated in a later university commentary: Lambeth Palace Library, MS 939, p. 10. The first manuscript is in Tenison's papers, the second endorsed in Tenison's hand 'Oxf. obj. ag. scheme of Printing Act'. The latter discusses March and December bills. Both manuscripts are printed in *Censorship*, gen. ed. Kemp and McElligott, iii, 431–6.

[46] *Censorship*, gen. ed. Kemp and McElligott, iii, 433.

[47] *CJ*, xi, 333.

[48] *CJ*, xi, 341, 345.

[49] Lambeth Palace Library, Cod. Tenison, MS 640, item 17, pp. 207–35 (italics added): 'A Bill for the Regulation of Printing and Printing Presses'; a slightly earlier draft is in Cambridge University Library, MS Oo.6.93, item 6, 39–47. The Tenison manuscript is printed, and compared with the Cambridge draft, in *Censorship*, gen. ed. Kemp and McElligott, iii, 425–30. Astbury notes that this bill made licensing optional: Astbury, 'Renewal', 318. The bill also reintroduced reference to imported books, including the seizure of seditious or atheistic works, although episcopal oversight was not restored.

[50] See *Censorship*, gen. ed. Kemp and McElligott, iii, 435, 503–4 n. 15.

[51] *Locke Correspondence*, v, 482, letter 1978: 14 Dec. 1695; Lambeth Palace Library, MS 939, item 10; *An Account of the Decree of the University of Oxford, against some Heretical Tenets* (1695). The decree as published at Oxford did not name its targets (which included a sermon by Joseph Bingham) but the London republication made explicit the application to Sherlock's pamphlets.

belong'.[52] To the main advocates of press control, this recognition of dissent was probably worse than no licensing at all.

With the bill buried in committee, the year 1695 ended without new press regulation and without licensing, Freke expressing confidence that 'young members' would not countenance the earlier act's revival.[53] The corollary was that other MPs were less opposed, most obviously high church tories but also some government whigs and country members less favourable towards the emerging cause of liberty of the press than to the reviving cause of moral reform.[54] It is widely recognized that the 'end of censorship' in 1695 was not a watershed immediately apparent to contemporaries, who shared neither our hindsight nor terminology. Indeed, support for press control was partly sustained by the upsurge in publishing following licensing's lapse, whether the quotidian *Flying-Post* or the controversial appearance of John Toland's *Christianity Not Mysterious* at the end of 1695.[55] At the same time, however, licensing's support should not be exaggerated: there were practical and principled objections, high church zeal created its own opposition, and enforced attention to alternative measures, including search warrants as well as post-publication punishments, were making press restraint without licensing a reality.

The Church's continuing support for censorship has tended to be taken as read but, as already suggested, the abandonment of licensing was becoming a Church cause – a strategic cause in a divided institution. For the anglican leadership, a licensing system intended to secure the quiet hum of uniformity had become a focus for noisy internal conflict. Disagreement over the basic principle was less the issue than was the imprimatur as a disputed badge of orthodoxy. Earlier in 1695, for example, the high churchman, Robert South, had justified his latest salvo on the trinity as a riposte to the single word 'Licens'd' on a Sherlock tract, declaring that 10,000 imprimaturs were incapable of 'Licensing Heresy into Truth', and that the author having this 'Stamp of Publick Licence' rather than being disowned by the Church was more 'monstrous, and astonishing than all his detestable Heresies'.[56] In April, the two licensing bishops – the whig Tenison and tory Henry Compton – heard the recantation of Compton's chaplain, who had licensed criticisms of bishop Gilbert Burnet's account of Christ's divinity.[57] Tenison agreed with Burnet that the Church's adversaries were 'the gainers by every dispute' and he avoided granting his own imprimatur – only Compton's is evident in 1695 – although this, too, could be a source of dispute.[58] To worried allies, heresy could appear 'connived at', while an opponent complained shortly before licensing's lapse that the archbishop prevented

[52] *Censorship*, gen. ed. Kemp and McElligott, iii, 426. Freke refers to planned contact between Clarke and a 'Godly Deputy': *Locke Correspondence*, v, 483, letter 1978: 14 Dec. 1695.

[53] *Locke Correspondence*, v, 476, letter 1974: 5 Dec. 1695.

[54] Hayton, 'Moral Reform'.

[55] Toland's book was advertised from Dec. 1695: Justin A.I. Champion, *Republican Learning: John Toland and the Crisis of Christian Culture, 1696–1722* (Manchester, 2003), 70–1.

[56] Robert South, *Tritheism Charged Upon Dr Sherlock's New Notion of the Trinity* (1695), 151, 267; responding to William Sherlock, *A Defence of Dr Sherlock's Notion of a Trinity in Unity* (1693). The source of Sherlock's licence was not clear.

[57] Roger Altham, *A True Copy of Mr. Roger Altham's Recantation, for Licensing Mr. Hill's Books against the Bishop of Salisbury* (1695).

[58] Tenison only seems to have licensed his predecessor's sermons: John Tillotson, *Of Sincerity and Constancy in the Faith and Profession of the True Religion* (1695).

clergy writing against the 'latitudinarian leven', adding: 'no one labours more industriously than your self, to debar them the liberty of the Press'.[59]

Tenison feared conflict, feared giving opponents ammunition and feared the deeper implications of attempting to define heresy and to license orthodoxy in intractable disputes like that over the trinity.[60] When the university of Oxford did so by issuing its decree, he privately blasted the vice-chancellor for this 'high usurpation' on royal prerogative and 'manifest violation' of the law, while also discountenancing public replies.[61] The archbishop, instead, supported the king's *Directions* to the clergy in February 1696 that ordered an end to disputes about the trinity, with lay offenders who wrote and published warned of punishment by the civil authorities for causing public discord.[62] Tenison's contribution to ending licensing would continue to be guided by a desire for the peace of silence not enthusiasm for open debate, with an emphasis on the stability and public authority of the Church rather than on its soul-searching. His staunch defence of the royal supremacy led to frequent accusations of the Erastianism he had criticized in *The Creed of Mr. Hobbes Examined* (1670), but he deferred to the state to preserve the Church, as he saw it, against divisive high church rigour diverting it from its main tasks of opposing popery and lay irreligion and immorality. Put another way, Tenison was more concerned about blasphemy than about heresy.

3

On 19 March 1696, a final attempt to revive the original Licensing Act was swiftly rejected in the Commons, while the bill of the previous December failed to progress by the end of the session in April.[63] In October 1696, in the next session, Harley and Edmund Waller were asked to prepare new legislation and on 2 February 1697 Clarke's neighbouring MP, Thomas Bere, presented a press bill which went to committee.[64] By this time, the high church attack on heresy and moderation had taken a new turn under the banner of the campaign to reconvene convocation, led by Francis Atterbury's *Letter to a Convocation Man* at the end of 1696.[65] Atterbury announced the spark for the campaign as being books 'Published without controul' by 'Deists, Socinians, Latitudinarians, Deniers of Mysteries, and pretending Explainers of them', targeting works by Sherlock and Burnet as well as Locke and Toland. The blanket ban of the *Directions* was seen as favouring the heterodox, he

---

[59] Lambeth Palace Library, MS 930, item 29: Payne to Tenison; *A Letter to the Author of a Sermon, Entitled, A Sermon Preach'd at the Funeral Of Her Late Majesty Queen Mary, Of ever Blessed Memory* (1695), 7–8. This tract is sometimes (mis)attributed to the nonjuring bishop, Thomas Ken.

[60] Gilbert Burnet, *History of his Own Time* (1883), 650.

[61] BL, Stowe MS 799, f. 149; Lambeth Palace Library, MS 930, item 29.

[62] William III, *Directions To Our Arch-Bishops and Bishops, For the Preserving of Unity in the Church, Concerning the Holy Trinity* (1696); *Memoirs of the Life and Times Of the most Reverend Father in God, Dr. Thomas Tennison* (1716), 49–50.

[63] *CJ*, xi, 523.

[64] *CJ*, xi, 567, 686; *Locke Correspondence*, vii, 240–1. Deazley corrects Feather's claim that the October order and February presentation involved different bills, although Deazley's view that the bill 'in effect, advocated the reinstatement of the Licensing Act' is supposition: Feather, 'Book Trade', 22; Deazley, *Origin*, 17 n. 67.

[65] Francis Atterbury, *A Letter to a Convocation-Man Concerning the Rights, Powers, and Priviledges of that Body* (1697).

complained, and the Church's failure to censor or censure left the laity defenceless against error.[66]

The high church campaign canvassed as means of suppression the greater use of ecclesiastical courts and greater use of the bishops' influence in parliament to secure press legislation, although the key was held to be the independent power of a reassembled national convocation to condemn heretical books and authors. Atterbury praised Bishop Trelawney for having excommunicated Arthur Bury in 1690 for the 'heresy' of his *Naked Gospel*, and argued that parliament must be guided by convocation because 'country gentlemen, lawyers and merchants' could not judge orthodoxy.[67] But he also argued that England's religion was not 'meerly parliamentary' and the Church's spiritual power made convocation a court with jurisdiction over 'Crime Ecclesiastical', its business the 'preventing, or suppressing Heresies and Schisms'.[68]

Tenison's fears of a book-burning heresy hunt were growing. He encouraged, in reply, William Wake's *Authority of Christian Princes*, which reprised the bishops' position that convocation could not act without the king's 'licence' (i.e., summons and approval) and that it was dangerous for the Church to take sides in disputes or allow discontents to claim power such that books 'publish'd by Men, whom they did not like, should be censured; and executed as Heretical'.[69] Atterbury's insistence on convocation's independent power tended to cut across high church calls for statutory licensing, a 'contradiction' Matthew Tindal pinpointed and one that Wake tried to exploit.[70] He argued that a more effective remedy than 'ten thousand Canons made by the Convocation' would be an act in Atterbury's 'own words' to require an episcopal licence for all books on religion.[71] The invitation's purpose as a diversion towards more controllable and constitutional channels, if not simply an attempt to play on Atterbury's mistrust of the leadership, would become clearer in Tenison's response to convocation finally meeting in 1701.

The contents of the printing bill of February 1697 are unknown. Wake's proposal, published in mid-March, showed no awareness of it.[72] It seems very unlikely that the proposals involved licensing, however. This would have rendered redundant a bill aimed specifically against publishing news 'without Licence' introduced and swiftly rejected while the general bill was in committee.[73] Moreover, the printing bill appears to have shared the title of the College legislation and its sponsor, Bere, was a political ally of Clarke.[74] The news bill is, in fact, the only legislation drafted between 1695 and 1710

[66] Atterbury, *Letter*, 6, 8–9.

[67] Atterbury, *Letter*, 10. Bury's punishment was actually for contumacy. Locke referred in his criticisms of licensing to the condemnation of Bury's book, *The Naked Gospel* (1690).

[68] Atterbury, *Letter*, 14–15, 21, 36.

[69] William Wake, *The Authority of Christian Princes Over their Ecclesiastical Synods Asserted* (1697), 282, 329, 337.

[70] Matthew Tindal, *An Essay Concerning the Power of the Magistrate* (1697), 'Postscript', 184–6. Convocation's upper House also alleged this inconsistency: Kennett, *History of the Convocation*, 130.

[71] Wake, *Authority*, 341–2.

[72] The work was advertised in the *Post-Boy*: 13–16 Mar. 1697.

[73] *CJ*, xi, 765, 766–7; Feather, 'Book Trade', 25.

[74] It is even possible that the bill was one of Tenison's 'several' bills, which he said involved 'both houses': see below, p. 60. On Bere being part of the Somerset 'College' connection: William Gibson, *Religion and the Enlightenment, 1600–1800: Conflict and the Rise of Civic Humanism in Taunton* (Bern, 2007), 171; *The History of Parliament: The House of Commons, 1690–1715*, ed. Eveline Cruickshanks, Stuart Handley and D.W. Hayton (5 vols, Cambridge, 2002) [hereafter cited as *HPC, 1690–1715*], i, 526.

undeniably to propose licensing and, not insignificantly, the only one prior to the 1707 Copyright Bill unconnected to religious disputes and the circles of Locke or Tenison. Whether the provisions of the press regulation bill were stronger or weaker than earlier bills, its failure to emerge from committee is, perhaps, unsurprising given that the committee's membership pitted tory MPs with a frequent interest in press regulation, such as Gilbert Dolben and Simon Harcourt, against an imposing set of whig counterparts in Robert Molesworth, Walter Moyle and Anthony Ashley Cooper, the future 3rd earl of Shaftesbury.[75] Opposition to the return of licensing thereby linked the College circle with radical whigs and the country-commonwealth campaign against a standing army that developed during 1697, as part of a previously unappreciated spectrum of 'anti-censorship' strategising that stretched from anglican prelate to republican dissenter.[76]

This was anti-censorship in early modern terms, however, and the prelate's concern at published blasphemy was made evident in the next parliamentary session, which opened with the king's speech stressing the threat of 'profaneness and immorality' and concluded with the 1698 Blasphemy Act.[77] At the same time, arguments for liberty of the press were also now coming to the fore. Addresses between Commons and king in mid-February 1698 complained of books and pamphlets against the trinity or otherwise subversive, while 16 February saw the immediate rejection of another bill for regulating printing.[78] The contents of this bill are also unknown, although fears of licensing's revival were reflected in Matthew Tindal's important pamphlet *A Letter to a Member of Parliament, Shewing, that a Restraint On the Press is Inconsistent with the Protestant Religion, and dangerous to the Liberties of the Nation*, which appeared in the first week of March.[79] Tindal showed no knowledge of the bill's details but conjectured that the conjunction in the Commons of its 'unanimous' rejection and the address to the king against blasphemy showed that MPs made a crucial distinction between pre-publication censorship's violation of conscientious expression and the justified post-publication punishment of truly immoral works.[80] Tindal's tract combined extensive quotation from *Areopagitica* – republished in 1697 and again with Toland's input in 1698[81] – with a debt to Locke and a broad attack on high church priestcraft to produce landmark claims for liberty of the press as a natural right and the 'bulwark' of all other liberties, meriting belated entry into the canon of revolution principles.[82] An intriguing report by Defoe, apparently previously unnoticed, alluded to Tindal's *Letter* as

[75] Hayton, 'Moral Reform', 71; *HPC, 1690–1715*, i, 356. Shaftesbury joined the committee on 6 April.

[76] Champion, *Republican Learning*, 98; Lois G. Schwoerer, 'The Literature of the Standing Army Controversy, 1697–1699', *Huntington Library Quarterly*, xxviii (1965), 190–2.

[77] *CJ*, xii, 1–2.

[78] *CJ*, xii, 2, 93, 99, 104. The bill was introduced by the 'church whig', John Pocklington: *HPC, 1690–1715*, v, 163–4.

[79] The pamphlet was advertised as 'This day is published' in the *Post Man*, 3–5 Mar. 1698.

[80] Matthew Tindal, *A Letter to a Member of Parliament* . . . (1698), 18–19. The tract is reprinted in *Censorship*, gen. ed. Kemp and McElligott, iv, 32–51 (this volume edited by Mark Goldie and Geoff Kemp).

[81] *The Works of Mr. John Milton* (1697); *A Complete Collection of the Historical, Political, and Miscellaneous Works of John Milton* ('Amsterdam', 1698).

[82] Tindal, *Letter*; see also Ernest Sirluck, '*Areopagitica* and a Forgotten Licensing Controversy', *Review of English Studies*, new ser., xi (1960). There is no doubt that Tindal was the author, although D. Wing, *A Short-Title Catalogue of Books Printed in England* . . . (3 vols, New York, 1972–82), lists the tract as anonymous (L1680) and Early English Books Online (EEBO) (*http://eebo.chadwyke.com*) credits Toland. Apart from internal and other evidence, it was reprinted in a collection of Tindal's tracts in 1709: Matthew Tindal, *Four Discourses* (1709).

itself being a bulwark intended to protect the commonwealth publishing campaign of 1698–9, which, along with the standing army controversialists led by John Trenchard, saw a republican canon of Milton, Sidney, Harrington and Ludlow appear in print.[83] Like Milton, Tindal argued that a compulsory imprint identifying the printer or bookseller could have a beneficial deterrent effect on atheism and sedition (unlike Milton, he excluded authors).[84] The *Letter* would see further service as an attack on high church licensing ambitions, its arguments reprinted in 1700, 1704, 1705 and 1709, drawing a number of replies.[85]

In the house of lords, meanwhile, Narcissus Luttrell recorded that on 24 February 1698, 'a bill was brought in by the archbishop of Canterbury against atheism, blasphemy, &c, and to punish the printers of scandalous books and pamphlets against our religion and government'.[86] In fact, one bill was introduced and another ordered that day, both involving Tenison. A judge, Sir John Powell, was asked to prepare legislation restraining the press, resulting in a bill devised with Tenison that took almost a year to appear.[87] The earlier bill brought in by the archbishop opposed blasphemy and immorality, including anyone who 'by writing, printing, teaching, or advised speaking' denied god, the trinity, christianity, or scripture's divine inspiration.[88] This was subsequently merged into a similar Commons' measure which became the Blasphemy Act, incorporating the threat of punishment for irreligious publication, although not strictly a press bill and insufficiently effective to satisfy critics.[89]

On 4 January 1699, the Lords received the bill drafted by Powell for 'better regulating' the press, which did not mention licensing but proposed compulsory imprints and registration of presses. The bill went to committee and amendments were reported by Burnet on 23 January.[90] A heavily scored-through draft in the Parliamentary Archives shows rather dramatically the changes involved, which stripped the bill down to terse clauses (by legislative standards) requiring that the printer notify the siting and ownership of a press; that printer and publisher identify themselves in the imprint; and that they identify the author on demand by government, court or university authorities or be punished as the author.[91] The deletions, which included the preamble, excised all reference

---

[83] Daniel Defoe, *A Brief Reply to the History of Standing Armies in England* (1698), 24. Defoe mistakenly attributed the rejection of the February bill to Tindal's *Letter*.

[84] Tindal, *Letter*, 18–19.

[85] The 1704 appearance was Tindal's adapted version *Reasons Against Restraining the Press*. The 1705 appearance was in *A Collection of State Tracts* (3 vols, 1705–7), ii, 614–26, accompanied by two of Tindal's political treatises and several Commonwealth tracts. Locke owned the 1698 edition: John Harrison, *The Library of John Locke* (Oxford, 1965), 214, 249.

[86] Narcissus Luttrell, *A Brief Relation of State Affairs* (6 vols, Oxford, 1857), iv, 347.

[87] *LJ*, xvi, 217. Deazley contends that the bill was never brought before the house: Deazley, *Origin*, 20. However, no other order was made ahead of the 1699 bill being introduced in the Lords as drafted by Powell.

[88] HMC, *Lords MSS*, new ser., iii, 112. The word 'printing' was added to the draft.

[89] *CJ*, xii, 138, 160, 177; *LJ*, xvi, 343. An amendment added polytheism to the list of proscribed beliefs but a Lords' amendment was rejected because it would have inadvertently targeted jews: *CJ*, xii, 183, 280, 295; *LJ*, xvi, 271. Wake later complained that few prosecutions were pursued under the act: J.C.D. Clark, *English Society 1688–1832* (Cambridge, 1985), 286.

[90] *LJ*, xvi, 358, 364.

[91] Parliamentary Archives [hereafter cited as PA], HL/PO/JO/10/1/510/1339: 'A Bill for the better regulating of Printing & Printing Presses'. The bill is printed in HMC, *Lords MSS*, new ser., iv, 420, and in *Censorship*, gen. ed. Kemp and McElligott, iv, 125–31.

to heresy, blasphemy, or religion generally, as well as sedition. The requirement that anyone who printed or published anything 'Atheisticall or hereticall' had to identify the author, became simply a requirement to identify the author on demand. Clearly this was not intended to permit atheism but presumably to sidestep issues such as defining heresy and make the provisions sufficiently uncontroversial for acceptance. If so, the tactic failed. The amended bill passed the Lords but was rejected in the Commons on a first reading, and 'by a great majority', according to the whig MP, William Cowper (who later presided at Sacheverell's trial as lord chancellor). Cowper's account of the debate is brief but important in indicating how the idea of press freedom was gaining ground. On the general principle, he reported, MPs took the view that 'to make any one judge of reason, what was fit to be published and what to be suppressed, was contrary to the Libertys of a free people – that the Liberty of the press had greatly promoted the true notions of government and scattered the seeds of liberty which had otherwise been oppressed'. Given this, the bill's alternative of imprints and registration was futile, since anyone risking content likely to incur post-publication punishment would certainly risk ignoring this law, and the dignity of parliament precluded passing 'insignificant laws'.[92] Tindal's influence seems apparent.

The 1699 bill lived on, however, with its provisions and wording as amended being duplicated in further draft bills in early 1702 and late 1703, which Tenison said he had framed with a judge's advice, confirming his close involvement with Powell's draft.[93] In 1702, a report approved by Tenison recorded that: 'the Archbishop and Bishops have several times endeavour'd to procure the passing of a Law to regulate the Press', referring to his part in the 1699 bill and 1702 successor, and probably the Blasphemy Act, if not others.[94] In this way, ironically, the parliamentary path of press proposals from 1699 became dominated by Church-inspired legislation that avoided mention of religion.

The background to Tenison's endeavours in 1702 was convocation having met the previous year. The lower House had immediately set up a committee to examine heretical and atheistic books, delivering *Christianity Not Mysterious* to the bishops with a demand for the suppression of all books of 'like mischievous Nature and Tendency'. The upper House, as in 1689, insisted that convocation had no authority to judicially censure books and to declare heresy risked breaching the supremacy.[95] The more hardened clergy refused to accept this conclusion or Tenison's attempts at prorogation, accusing the bishops of failing even 'to express any Mark of dislike to so ill a Book' (which was untrue).[96] Rumours spread that Toland was spared because of fears that Burnet must be next, a claim repeated by Sacheverell.[97] The lower House played a final card by referring upwards Burnet's *Exposition of the Thirty Nine Articles*, the publication of which Tenison

---

[92] Hertfordshire Archives and Local Studies, Panshanger MS, DE/P/F98, 30 (contractions have been expanded). Cowper's parliamentary diary is printed in 'Debates in the House of Commons 1697–1699', ed. D.W. Hayton, *Camden Miscellany XXIX* (Camden, 4th ser., xxxiv, 1987).

[93] *Records of Convocation*, ed. Bray, ix, 220–1. This may also explain the management of the amendments by Tenison's whig ally, Burnet.

[94] Kennett, *History of the Convocation*, 152.

[95] Kennett, *History of the Convocation*, 72–4, 112–14; Edmund Gibson, *Synodus Anglicana: Or, The Constitution and Proceedings of an English Convocation* (1702), 140–6.

[96] Kennett, *History of the Convocation*, 119–20, 129–31; Lathbury, *History*, 346–7.

[97] William Binckes, *An Expedient Propos'd* (1701), 20–1.

had encouraged.[98] The meeting was then prorogued on the king's instruction, although convocation's repressive rumblings in subsequent meetings continued as a backdrop to debate on the press.[99]

In demanding Toland's suppression, the lower House had called on the bishops to 'think of some Methods, whereby the daring Licentiousness of the Press, in such cases, might be restrain'd' and the clergy would blame the continuing lack of press regulation on episcopal inaction.[100] This was far from the truth, although Tenison's efforts continued to be directed towards mollifying and diverting, more than satisfying, high church demands. His role in the 1702 bill is mainly known because of a letter from Robert Harley on 8 January, in which the new Speaker of the Commons returned a draft bill with his opinion that the archbishop might introduce it in the Lords.[101] In the view of Downie and others, Harley was unenthusiastic but accepted that Tenison could introduce the bill if he chose, implying diverging paths for government and Church on press control.[102] However, the letter is better interpreted as confirming both men's interest in achieving a moderate bill with some chance of acceptance, enacting 'very good methods to have a Printer or Author answerable', with a view to a 'severer course' after publication. The aim was a brief bill to which 'if either House are inclined to make it stronger it is easy for them to make additions'.[103]

A draft of the bill in the Parliamentary Archives is, indeed, brief, as is a later copy at Lambeth Palace, being identical to the amended 1699 bill, so again making no specific reference to religious publishing or episcopal oversight, despite being advanced by the archbishop of Canterbury.[104] This time, the bill did not even pass the Lords, being given a first reading on 22 January but rejected two days later as the only item of business at a Saturday sitting, where less than two dozen attendees included Tenison and Shaftesbury.[105]

4

The proclamation of 26 March 1702 which accompanied Queen Anne's accession, later used as evidence of her defence of the Church at Sacheverell's trial, traced a rise in

---

[98] Burnet, *History of his Own Time*, 658.

[99] Lathbury, *History*, 354–9; George Every, *High Church Party, 1688–1718* (1956), 96. According to Burnet, upper House dissentients were Compton, Trelawney and Sprat: Burnet, *History of his Own Time*, 691.

[100] Francis Atterbury, *Some Proceedings in the Convocation* (1708), Sig. a1r.

[101] Lambeth Palace Library, MS 930, item 25: Harley to Tenison, endorsed 'Mr. Harley abt the press', 8 Jan. 1702; printed in *Censorship*, gen. ed. Kemp and McElligott, iv, 132.

[102] Downie, *Robert Harley*, 55; Deazley, *Origin*, 23; Feather, 'Book Trade', 28. Carpenter agrees that Harley backed the bill but adds a quoted line of support, seemingly from Harley, which has proved untraceable: Carpenter, *Tenison*, 288.

[103] *Censorship*, gen. ed. Kemp and McElligott, iv, 132.

[104] PA, HL/PO/JO/10/6/19/1706, printed in HMC, *Lords MSS*, new ser., iv, item no. 1706. For the Lambeth Palace draft, see below, pp. 62–3.

[105] *LJ*, xvii, 23. The Shaftesbury papers include, alongside a copy of Locke's 1695 criticisms, a clause apparently intended as an anti-jacobite amendment to the 1702 bill, out of keeping with its unspecific spirit: TNA, PRO 30/24/30/30 Part 1, printed in *Censorship*, gen. ed. Kemp and McElligott, iv, 283.

heretical, irreligious and seditious publishing to the Licensing Act's fall.[106] However, it would be nearly two years before another attempt at press legislation in parliament, although both Houses continued to censure individual publications. One included the claim, satirical but not untrue, that an 'Old Whig' commitment to liberty of the press had benefited the tory cause under whig government.[107] In the month of Anne's accession, with high church hopes high, Sacheverell's print debut *The Political Union* called for defence of the Church in pulpit and press and, notoriously, for hanging out 'the Bloody Flag' against its dissenting enemies and 'Treacherous False-Friends'.[108] In *The Character of a Low-Church-man* soon afterwards, he complained that convocation's campaign against the 'Unlimited License of the Press' had been stifled by a prelate afraid for his friends, forcing the high church clergy to 'make their Appeal to the Press'. The upper House condemned such appeals as an 'insolent liberty' of promulgating synodical affairs without a royal licence.[109] At the time of the next press bill, in 1704, Defoe would capture Tenison's worst nightmare with the suggestion that, with the bishops tainted by moderation, only 'a Loyal and True Church Licencer' would gain the support of the lower house of convocation, so that 'Sacheverel may hoist his Bloody Flag against the Dissenters'.[110]

The 1704 bill was introduced in the Commons on 13 January by Harcourt as solicitor-general, having been ordered on 15 December, the day that parliament censured John Tutchin for comments in the *Observator* on the defeated Occasional Conformity Bill.[111] This was also the day that Tenison reported his parliamentary efforts in a speech to convocation, revealing that he had another draft press bill in hand. Having admitted the failure of diocesan proceedings against William Coward's mortalist writings, Tenison said that the broader 'evil' required regulation of the press but he had 'offered several bills in which I have been so unfortunate as to be disappointed in one place or other, not because they were faulty in matter, form or temper, but because they were bills of restraint'. He added that the bills were drafted with the advice of one of the judges but he was unwilling to offer the latest without knowing whether there was a disposition to receive it. He also promised that given 'sufficient synodical power' it would become clear that 'the bishops have a just zeal against all pestilent and wicked scribbles, such a zeal as is neither palled (if I may speak) with lukewarmness or overheated with indiscreet and unnecessary fierceness'.[112] It is hard to avoid feeling that the archbishop was trying to pull the wool over the eyes of his high church flock.

[106] *By the Queen, a Proclamation for Restraining the Spreading and Printing and Publishing of Irreligious and Seditious Papers* (1702); *Tryal*, 243–4.

[107] Charles Davenant, *Tom Double Return'd Out of the Country* (1702).

[108] Henry Sacheverell, *The Political Union* (1702) [Madan 1–2], preface, 59.

[109] Henry Sacheverell, *The Character of a Low-Church-man* (1702) [Madan 7–11], 9–11; Kennett, *History of the Convocation*, pp. iv–v.

[110] Daniel Defoe, 'To the Honourable the C – s of England . . . Relating to the Bill for Restraining the Press', in *The Political and Economic Writings of Daniel Defoe*, ed. W.R. Owens and P.N. Furbank (8 vols, 2000), viii, 163–6; J.A. Downie, 'An Unknown Defoe Broadsheet on the Regulation of the Press?', *Library*, 5th ser., xxxiii (1978), 51–8.

[111] *CJ*, xiv, 249, 278.

[112] *Records of Convocation*, ed. Bray, ix, 220–1.

A copy of Tenison's bill is in Cowper's papers, endorsed 'My draught of an Act for restraining of the Press. 1703/4. This deld to me by ArchB. of Cant. Tenis.'[113] This draft, recently printed for the first time, appears to be based on the copy made of the 1702 bill held amongst Tenison's papers at Lambeth Palace, which has the date '22 Nov 1703'.[114] The version in Cowper's papers differs only in references to queen rather than king, plus mention of university register-books. In other words, it maintains the silence on licensing and religion. Tenison probably aimed to introduce the bill in the Commons through Cowper, although it is unclear whether it constituted the bill brought in by Harcourt, which was sent to committee by 127 votes to 90 but did not reappear.[115] Harcourt's bill was described as aiming 'to prevent the Licentiousness of the Press', whereas the Tenison-Cowper bill was titled 'for regulating of printing', and both a printers' petition and Defoe's *Essay on the Regulation of the Press* assumed it reintroduced licensing; indeed, the petition referred to a clause preventing any book or pamphlet being printed 'until licensed'.[116] But there is still room for doubt: the Tenison-Cowper manuscript is the only candidate, Luttrell described Harcourt's legislation as the 'bill for regulating printing', and, perhaps most tellingly, Gibson wrote in 1704–5 of Tenison having recently twice attempted to have the 'Two Houses of Parliament' pass a bill against 'the licentiousness of the press', implying the 1702 and 1704 bills.[117] Perhaps the printers mistook registering presses and providing imprints as 'licensing'. Or perhaps there was no disposition to receive Tenison's bill.[118] It is hard to say. One recent account claims that the 1704 bill 'clearly advocated a return to a system of pre-publication licensing' but this is not clear at all.[119]

Whether or not Defoe was mistaken in assuming that the intention was licensing, his *Essay* on the press marked a key transition in the debate. The tract argued against licensing as making 'the Press a slave to a Party' and tool of arbitrary government, as had Tindal, but also advanced some interestingly specific proposals.[120] The first was a recklessly hopeful plan to specify the points relating to the Church that were not to be debated. The second was a proposal that the name of printer, publisher or author must be imprinted or anyone found selling the work would be held accountable as the author.[121] This was a conclusion not too far from Tenison's proposal of compulsory imprints. However, Defoe presented his proposal as having the added value of securing copyright for authors, devoting his final pages to the benefits of authors both owning their labours and owning their crimes – if the law was going to punish them for bad

---

[113] Hertfordshire Archives and Local Studies, Panshanger MS, D/EP F136; printed in *Censorship*, gen. ed. Kemp and McElligott, iv, 133–8.

[114] Lambeth Palace Library, MS 640, item 19. It also has the date 'Jan 1701' (i.e., 1702).

[115] *HPC, 1690–1715*, ii, 770; *CJ*, xiv, 278, 287. Clarke reported to Locke on 13 January that the bill had been brought in, and expressed confidence that 'it will bee thrown out againe': *Locke Correspondence*, viii, 162–3.

[116] *CJ*, xiv, 338: 'A Petition of the Free Workmen Printers'; Daniel Defoe, *An Essay on the Regulation of the Press* (1704). An undated quaker pamphlet probably appeared around this time: *Some Considerations Humbly Offered By the People called Quakers, Relating to the Bill for the restraining the Licentiousness of the Press* ([1703/4]).

[117] Luttrell, *Relation of State Affairs*, v, 381, 392; Edmund Gibson, *The Complainer Further Reprov'd* (1705), 3–6, 24.

[118] As well as Harcourt, the first-named MP among those ordered to present the bill, Francis Gwyn, was a high church tory, as was the committee chairman, Gilbert Dolben: *CJ*, xiv, 249, 347.

[119] Deazley, *Origin*, 26.

[120] Defoe, *Essay*, 4.

[121] Defoe, *Essay*, 14–17.

books, it should ensure that they benefited from their good works. He subsequently continued his campaign in the *Review*, arguing that the press could be regulated without 'the Tyranny of a Licenser' by obliging authors to set their names to their books, to secure 'Property of Copies' and end 'Nameless Trumpery'.[122] The move to identifying authors in the imprint, and to greater security of property, were key variations on Tenison's theme, but Defoe's plan diverged rather than departed from the measures inspired by Church concerns, on a path from toleration to copyright.[123]

5

Although Defoe's *Review* urged parliament to adopt his scheme in November 1705, it would be 1707 before another printing bill emerged. At the end of 1704, convocation's lower house issued a 'Representation' urging Tenison and the bishops 'to use your Interest in the Parliament for the passing a Bill against the Licentiousness of the Press'.[124] On Tenison's behalf, Gibson offered the retort, previously noted, that the archbishop had sent a bill against the 'licentiousness of the press' to members of the lower House, along with one on Church rates, but they were 'return'd without any Intimation that they had been at all consider'd'. He added that a copy of the Press Bill remained available for perusal and comment. Gibson also criticized the liberty taken by high churchmen 'to Print and Publish the Grievances of the Clergy'.[125] This latter issue escalated in 1705 after the *Memorial of the Church of England* proclaimed 'supine' negligence in Church and state, sparking book-burning, prosecution, and in December a ban on claims of 'the Church in danger'.[126] The possibility of legislation to restrain the press continued to fade, however. Defoe reflected that licensing was 'so many Years being laid aside' that it was no longer a feasible option.[127] Time also encouraged the myth that press freedom was, indeed, a 'revolution principle', Tindal telescoping removal of 'the Penal Laws, and the Restraint of the Press, the Badges of Popery' in his *Rights of the Christian Church*, itself a focus for high church fury.[128] The post-publication assault on the *Memorial* also led its tory defender, William Pittis, to urge that the Licensing Act, now 'fast asleep', should not be roused.[129]

[122] *Review*, ii, no. 106, pp. 421–4: 8 Nov. 1705; no. 107, pp. 427–8: 10 Nov. 1705.

[123] Defoe's relationship to press legislation in other regards has been extensively documented by Downie, Deazley, Feather and others.

[124] *A Representation Made By the Lower House of Convocation . . . Shewing The Diligence of the Lower, and Remissness of the Upper-House, in suppressing Books published against the Truth of Christianity* (1705). Relevant excerpts are reprinted in *Censorship*, gen. ed. Kemp and McElligott, iv, 136–8.

[125] Gibson, *Complainer Further Reprov'd*, 13–16.

[126] [James Drake], *The Memorial of the Church of England* (1705); Downie, *Robert Harley*, 80–100; *Censorship*, gen. ed. Kemp and McElligott, iv, 143–5.

[127] Defoe, *Essay*, 6–7.

[128] Matthew Tindal, *The Rights of the Christian Church* (1706), 409–11; Matthew Tindal, *A Second Defence of the Rights of the Christian Church* (1709), 73. Tindal incurred low church wrath too but Burnet warned Tenison that answering him would involve concessions that would be seized on by their opponents: Lambeth Palace Library, MS 930, item 12; MS 931, item 18.

[129] William Pittis, *The Case of the Church of England's Memorial Fairly Stated* (1705), 44–51. Pittis was pilloried for his book: Abel Boyer, *The History of the Reign of Queen Anne . . . Year the Fifth* (1707), 486.

That the character of legislation was moving away from restraint is confirmed by the 1707 bill's appearance under the rubric of 'Copy Right' not regulation in the *Commons Journal*.[130] The bill's precise contents are not known but may have been close to the Copyright Act, since the printer, John How, claimed that the bill failed because of concerns about inflated prices for books, an objection specifically addressed in the 1710 act. It would, however, be wrong to suppose that the Church connection had simply dropped out of the picture entirely. Tenison sought discussions on the bill and the objection reported by How, that the poor would be deprived of access to the Bible and devotional works, also had a Tenisonian flavour. Moreover, Defoe suggested that the 'High Party' had obstructed the bill.[131] Defoe's support for the legislation may also have hinted that the bill included compulsory imprints, absent in 1710.[132]

In the week of Sacheverell's outburst against the 'Perils of False Brethren' of 5 November 1709, and with the new session of parliament days away, Defoe returned to his campaign, insisting that whigs and tories could find common cause on press legislation. Later in the month he, again, advocated a single measure 'both to restrain a licentious Liberty of the Press, and to secure to the Authors of Books their Right of Property', alleging a socinian and deist 'Plague' within the Church. Even high church tories knew 'a Licenser of the Press will not go down with a Nation of Liberty', he argued.[133] In the event, as John Feather observed, 'there was to be none of Defoe's scheme for *compulsory* imprints' in the 'Act for the Encouragement of Learning'.[134] A new bill was introduced on 11 January 1710, providing for the *voluntary* entry of works in the Stationers' Company register-books, and after some expansion and amendment the act's provisions went into operation on 10 April. Authorial copyright was confirmed in new works, while later clauses exempted imported books and allowed for appeal against high prices to officers of government, university, court and Church. Ironically, this meant that one of the few printing bills without Tenison's close involvement restored a role for the archbishop of Canterbury.

As the Copyright Bill progressed, the Sacheverell impeachment advanced in parallel, printing legislation and religious dispute now disconnected. Defoe abandoned mention of restraint, while the *Observator* declared the bill to be advancing freedom of the press by fostering writers' labours.[135] Attention to the Sacheverell trial is, none the less, instructive as a coda to the toleration narrative, as well as its telos in this article. The trial had multiple causes, concerns and consequences but at root was a prosecution for published opinion, building to a book-burning finale. Moreover, Sacheverell's censured sermons are suggestive of both the persistence and frustration of high church

---

[130] *CJ*, xv, 313, 316; Feather, 'Book Trade', 30–3.

[131] E.H. Pearce, *Sion College and Library* (Cambridge, 1913), 281; *Review*, vi, no. 91, p. 363: 3 Nov. 1709. Tenison may have proposed an amendment adding Sion College to the legal deposit libraries: Pearce, *Sion College*, 281; *CJ*, xv, 322.

[132] Defoe urged Harley to rescue the 'stopt' bill: Daniel Defoe, *The Letters of Daniel Defoe*, ed. G.H. Healey (Oxford, 1955), 212.

[133] *Review*, vi, no. 91, p. 363: 3 Nov. 1709; no.101, p. 403: 26 Nov. 1709.

[134] Feather, 'Book Trade', 34–7.

[135] *Review*, vi, no. 133, pp. 531–2: 11 Feb. 1710; *Observator*: 1–4 Feb. 1710.

censorship hopes, his entire platform based on opposition to the 'communication of sin' through press and pulpit, 'those Mints of Atheism, and Irreligion'.[136] The core claim of the *Communication of Sin* was that publishing and propagating heresy and error extended their evil beyond mere crime and death: Arrius, Socinus and the 'Atheistical Monsters' Hobbes and Spinoza, though 'Rotten in their Graves, still stink above Ground'. Moreover, a parallel 'Communication of Guilt' was held to extend to governors who authorised offending works or gave 'Tacit Approbation' through 'Cowardly Forbearance'.[137] Those who printed and published their sinful errors, he declared in *The Perils of False Brethren*, merited censure by convocation and correction by the state, but the latter was a sword borne in vain, leaving him appealing to the 'Popular Tribunal' – a recourse his politics could barely admit to, of course.[138]

The prosecution declared it an act of the 'highest aggravation' that Sacheverell not only delivered the sermons but 'thought fit to Print and Disperse about Forty Thousand of them over the Kingdom', his position as churchman not hackney pen justifying parliament's direct intervention in the 'great Licentiousness of the Press'.[139] Sacheverell, as well as claiming the encouragement of the lord mayor and Derbyshire grand jury as his licence, insisted that his attacks were not on governors but on the 'Heterodox Opinions, and damnable Heresies, which are daily publish'd', these being the true source of danger to the Church.[140] In Burnet's summary, Sacheverell's defence was that he did not reflect on what toleration was allowed by law but on the failure to prevent or punish 'impious and blasphemous books'.[141] The effect was both to insinuate and deny that his reference to the 'perfidious prelate', Grindal, was to the perfidious Tenison, Wake observing that the 'Application is plain, and Home'.[142] The gout-afflicted Tenison was not present to witness.

While Sacheverell's defence, unsurprisingly, did not proceed on free speech grounds, an intriguing argument emerged as he elaborated on toleration. He contended that the clergy retained a power and, indeed, a duty to denounce nonconformists, regardless of the protection of the Toleration Act. The coercive power of ecclesiastical courts could be vetoed by the civil courts but the pastor's power of 'pronouncing Censures purely Spiritual' was *jure divino*, and exempting nonconformists from legal penalties did not alter the fact that they were nonconformists and open to 'the censuring of Notorious Offenders'. Sacheverell did not specify the form of censure but the justification, being offered in defence of his sermons, would presumably extend to his continued appearance in print: a God-given right to (his) liberty of the press.[143] The claim was also applied to the duty of Church superiors to anathematise heterodox opinions, which were helpfully

---

[136] Henry Sacheverell, *The Communication of Sin* (1709) [Madan 48], 35.

[137] Sacheverell, *Communication*, 31–4.

[138] Sacheverell, *Perils of False Brethren*, 13.

[139] *Tryal*, 60, 99. Later estimates suggest around 100,000 copies of the sermons were in circulation by the end of the trial: Holmes, *Trial of Doctor Sacheverell*, 75.

[140] *Tryal*, 28–32, 250.

[141] Burnet, *History of his Own Time*, 849.

[142] *The Bishop of Lincoln's and Bishop of Norwich's speeches in the House of Lords, March the 17th* (1710) [Madan 338], 14.

[143] *Tryal*, 206.

laid out by the defence in a 'black Catalogue', published as *Collections of Passages*. Sacheverell's accusers observed that this was to republish forgotten blasphemies in order to oppose publishing blasphemy.[144]

Sacheverell's speech was already in print by the time that the Lords began its deliberations, with copies intercepted in letters leaving London.[145] His punishment included the order that the two printed sermons be burnt, with the lord mayor reportedly 'not a little mortify'd' at being expected to assist in burning publications he encouraged.[146] The bonfire grew. The Lords added Oxford University's 1683 decree, used in Sacheverell's defence and lately reprinted as ostensibly 'Published by Authority', in fact only the authority of 1683. The Commons ordered the *Collections of Passages* to be burned, and also Tindal's *Rights of the Christian Church* and its *Defence*. According to Abel Boyer's account, not only the *Collections* but the many tracts it listed were burned on 25 March, while two days later Sacheverell's sermons and the Oxford decree followed.[147] Boyer added that anyone who thought the matter would die with the flames soon found it rekindled with addresses and pamphlets. As Holmes later put it: 'the whole country had caught fire'.[148]

Neither printed debate nor calls for press control were doused in 1710. In 1711, convocation's lower House issued another *Representation* tracing licentiousness to the revolution, toleration and the 'Removal of that Restraint, which the Wisdom of former Times had laid upon the Press', calling for a new act against the 'Liberty of Printing'.[149] The queen's speech in 1712 urged press legislation, prompting an order for a bill on 'publication of libels'. When the bill appeared it was under the rubric of 'ways and means' and would become the Stamp Act, opposing taxation to cheap political criticism in newspapers and pamphlets by means of compulsory imprints in an unanticipated outcome for the campaign of Tenison and then Defoe (who had opposed taxing print in 1704).[150] In 1711, Tenison took action against the heterodox publishing of William Whiston.[151] In 1713, there was a failed attempt to pass a bill against blasphemous and seditious libels and 'for the better Regulating of the Press'.[152]

It is not my claim that the year 1710 marked the end of support for pre-publication press control. None the less, Sacheverell's trial affected how some of its remaining supporters viewed liberty of the press. In 1711, Swift argued that whigs should recognize the liberty of expression they received from the tories, compared with the 'messengers and warrants' that whigs used when in power.[153] Ahead of the 1714 election, Francis Atterbury, now bishop of Rochester, took the Sacheverell trial to exemplify whig invasions of press freedom, and even listed among the 'Merits of the Church-Party' a

---

[144] *Tryal*, 250; *Collections of Passages Referr'd to by Dr. Henry Sacheverell in his Answer to the Articles of his Impeachment* (1710) [Madan 237–40].

[145] Holmes, *Trial of Doctor Sacheverell*, 215.

[146] Boyer, *History*, 332.

[147] Boyer, *History*, 334–5.

[148] Boyer, *History*, 335; Holmes, *Trial of Doctor Sacheverell*, 234.

[149] *A Representation of the Peresent State of Religion* (1711), 13, 17.

[150] *CJ*, xvii, 77, 185, 195–6.

[151] *A Complete Collection of State Trials*, comp. T.B. Howell (34 vols, 1816–28), xv, 703–4.

[152] *CJ*, xvii, 293, 347, 360.

[153] *Examiner*, no. 26: 18–25 Jan. 1711.

commitment to 'No Restraint of the Liberty of the Press'.[154] Another writer developed Sacheverell's logic by making a case for liberty of the press as the independent means of public censure sought by the clergy, whereas its removal would mean subordination to Erastian 'Court Bishops' and the discretionary power of their licensers. The author claimed that a major reason 'the Church does not now groan under a Whiggish and Republican Army' was Sacheverell's publication of his sermons and speeches, 'and those had never been Printed, if there had been a Restraint on the Press'. The author proposed compulsory imprints to punish crime once committed, opposing licensing as an expedient 'so long exploded by all Parties'.[155]

Licensing was exploded, while the notion of 'freedom of censureship' has added significance, given that a parallel development to Sacheverell's trial was the appearance of 'censorship' as a word applied self-consciously and purposively to the press, interestingly not as suppression but as public oversight. The *Tatler* first suggested its own role as 'censor' of society in the week Sacheverell published *The Perils of False Brethren* and claimed the mantle explicitly in the month of his trial.[156] The conceptual and linguistic history of censorship *by* the press and censorship *of* the press is another story, but the spring of 1710 can be seen as not only helping seal the end of pre-publication press censorship but as marking the beginnings of a terminology of 'censorship'.[157]

---

[154] Francis Atterbury, *English Advice to the Freeholders of England* (1714), 28, 31.

[155] *A Word to the Wise* (1712).

[156] *Tatler*, no. 89: 1–3 Nov. 1709; no. 114: 9–11 Mar. 1710; no. 162: 22 Apr. 1710.

[157] The 'beginning of "censorship" ' was part of the original presentation from which this article arose, and is the subject of my further research.

Sacheverell's Harlots: Non-Resistance on Paper and in Practice

EIRWEN E.C. NICHOLSON

This article's point of entry is Plate 3 of William Hogarth's print sequence *The Harlot's Progress* (1732), specifically Hogarth's deliberate, hostile choice of an unframed, titled, small portrait engraving of the Reverend Dr Henry Sacheverell as a 'pin-up' within the harlot's bedroom furniture. The article reappraises and recontextualises Hogarth's choice of Sacheverell, which makes sense in the context of Hogarth's life and work, but which, with Hogarthian irony, is further informed by the subsequent discovery (1747) of Sacheverell's internment alongside a notorious prostitute, given the association of Sacheverell's celebrity and notoriety with his alleged support from London's 'kind shees' and streetwalkers at the time of his trial. This, together with a strong, nascent material consumerist culture, sees Sacheverell anticipating the 'politics out of doors' associated with John Wilkes by 50 years and is a specifically gendered version that has gone largely unexplored.

Keywords: Hogarth; commercialisation; commodification; material culture; iconography; prostitution; print culture; subculture; high church; gender political satire

1

Plate 3 of Hogarth's *The Harlot's Progress* (1732) (figure 1) is, as with other William Hogarth prints, an image now so familiar that for many it may unconsciously have been their first and only glimpse of the Doctor. It introduces an acknowledged but underexplored aspect of the Sacheverell crisis; namely, the support Sacheverell received from women at all levels of society, but not least, in so far as they were singled out for journalistic prurience, from prostitutes of the lower sort. All women were, of course, disenfranchised from the political world of Westminster, but politics does not get more 'out of doors' than a potentially 'kind shee' in St James's Park 'whispering "Are you for the Dr?" ' before transacting business.[1] As evidence both for Sacheverell's enduring celebrity or notoriety and for the very large quantities of portrait prints of him produced at the time of the trial, Hogarth's choice of the Doctor, alongside the fictitious highwayman, Macheath, as, literally, a harlot's pin-up, is not implausible. It is also an expression of Hogarth's visceral anticlericalism, which, after decades of evasion, has been admitted, indeed celebrated, by Ronald Paulson in his latest (2003) Hogarth

---

[1] *The Officer's Address to the Ladies*, pamphlet, 29 Apr. 1710 [Madan 762].

Figure 1: Detail from Hogarth's *The Harlot's Progress* (Plate 3) showing Moll with a portrait of Sacheverell (1732). Engraving from author's collection.

rescension, *Hogarth's Harlot*.[2] But this does not wholly answer the question, *why Sacheverell*, who, at the time the print was made, had been dead for some eight years? To answer this is to understand Hogarth's print as a *palimpsest* – that is, something made up of overlays of visual, verbal, cultural cognition and recognition, of which the association of Sacheverell and London harlots is one layer.[3] It was an association of which a much younger Hogarth, 13 years old at the time of the trial, and a hostile witness to the 'Night of Fire' within the locality of his childhood,[4] would have been aware through printed news, satire and street discourse. This article will examine interrelated discussions about sexual and religious politics, highlighting how, to his detractors, Sacheverell was thought to prostitute his cause but also have an explicitly sexualised appeal. Situating the Sacheverell trial in a gendered context helps to place the debate that his prosecution stimulated among recent research about prostitution and gender.[5]

Prostitutes enjoyed an ambivalent position within both a true and a Habermasian public sphere: they were seen, read and talked about, becoming, as several recent studies have shown, reified figures in an anxious discourse about capitalism and urbanisation. Literature on, and images of, prostitutes (literally the translation of the word 'pornogra-

[2] Ronald Paulson, *Hogarth's Harlot: Sacred Parody in Enlightenment England* (2003). Twentieth-century Hogarth scholarship is too vast to discuss here, but has, Paulson included, variously placed Hogarth as deist or deist lite a fellow-traveller of Woolston and humanitarian-latitudinarian friend of Hoadly (Ronald Paulson, *Hogarth: The Modern Moral Subject* (1991), 293–300); within older scholarship, from the 19th century onwards, as a simple low churchman conscious of the established Church's presumed pastoral shortcomings. Paulson's final(?) 2003 reading is convincing.

[3] For palimpsest, also 'iconotext', as useful frameworks for viewing Hogarth and other 18th-century satirical/polemic graphics: Peter Wagner, *Reading Iconotexts from Swift to the French Revolution* (1995).

[4] Paulson, *Modern Moral Subject*, 20–1, 298–9.

[5] On prostitution see T. Henderson, *Disorderly Women in Eighteenth-Century London* (1999); Sophie Carter, *Purchasing Power: Representing Prostitution in Eighteenth-Century English Popular Print Culture* (Aldershot, 2004).

phy') were, of course, themselves commodities of consumer culture within this discourse.[6] Such a context helps to stress both how politics was inflected by issues of sexuality – the role of women and a defence of the female sex were actively being debated at the time – and how prostitution was symptomatic of a commercialising society that saw both sex and religio-political controversy as consumables.

Common to Hogarth's harlot and the genteel housewife to whom we are introduced in a key passage in the *Spectator* of May 1711, is the trope of consumerism, both material and carnal. The conceptual frameworks of a 'consumer society' and the commercialisation of politics, together with those of celebrity and iconicity, are central to my forthcoming cultural study of Sacheverell, 'Pulpit Idol'.[7] Whereas previous 18th-century studies have been concerned with individuals and contexts wholly secular, thereby excluding Sacheverell, for whom so much pertinent evidence has survived, my analysis will acknowledge the importance of the religious in consumer behaviour. Sacheverell's, and more broadly religion's, place in the consumer society has been neglected because it does not fit the secular framework erected by previous historians. In particular, Sacheverell consumerism challenges notions of secular forms of politeness, consumerism and public sphere. Addressing Sacheverell is thus important both in its own right and as part of a larger revisioning of 18th-century culture; its specifically gendered aspects are far from being incidental within this.

2

The partisan 'kind shees' referred to above are invoked and cajoled in a pamphlet, *The Officer's Address to the Ladies* (1710). In full, the relevant passage reads:

No love now is to be made without religion and the Doctor. When we accost our kind shees in the park, we are whispered 'are you for the Dr'? 'God bless the Dr', says the stroller in the Strand, who never prayed for herself in her life. And for the great ornament and benefit of religion, the Dr's name is a ticket wch admits you into the best favours of all the Phyillises in Drury Lane. Strange! How the women love a High-flyer.[8]

[6] Carter, *Purchasing Power*; Mark Hallett, *The Spectacle of Difference: Graphic Satire in the Age of Hogarth* (1999), 93–114, 119–29.

[7] Classically, N. McKendrick, John Brewer and J.H. Plumb, *The Birth of a Consumer Society* (Bloomington, IN, 1982). See also John Brewer, *The Pleasures of the Imagination: English Culture in the Eighteenth Century* (1997); *Consumption and the World of Goods*, ed. Roy Porter and John Brewer (1993). For 'the commercialization of politics': John Brewer, *Party Ideology and Popular Politics at the Accession of George III* (Cambridge, 1976); Kathleen Wilson, 'Admiral Vernon and Popular Politics in Mid-Hanoverian Britain', *Past & Present*, No. 121 (1988), 74–109; see also Kate Williams, 'Nelson and Women: Marketing Representations and the Female Consumer', in *Admiral Lord Nelson: Context and Legacy*, ed. David Cannadine (2005), 67–89; Kathleen Wilson, 'Nelson and the People: Manliness, Patriotism and Body Politics', in *Admiral Lord Nelson*, ed. Cannadine, 49–65. The conceptual framework of a (not necessarily 'the') 'public sphere' had long been implicit within the historiography of English print satire: following the translation of J. Habermas, *The Structural Transformation of the Public Sphere: An Enquiry into a Category of Bourgeois Society* (Cambridge, MA, 1989), it has become normative, if nuanced, within 18th-century cultural history: see Brian Cowan, *The Social Life of Coffee* (New Haven, 2005), 255–63.

[8] Madan 762, quoted in Geoffrey Holmes, *The Trial of Doctor Sacheverell* (1973), 119–20.

Elsewhere we find references to such women within the crowds who viewed the Doctor's daily progress (an appropriately Hogarthian word) to Westminster Hall, as recorded in a not very *Impartial view of the two late Parliaments* in which 'the white periwig in flowing curls, with a complexion rendered more florid by a large glass of lachrymae Christi . . . prepared the ladies of the hundreds of Drury in his favour', 'Drury' being, for the 18th century, an enduring London prostitution shorthand.[9] But this progress – Sacheverell's, not the harlot's, and one which would be repeated on a grand provincial scale later in 1710 – brings in to play a larger concept of Sacheverell himself as spectacle;[10] and one which was, moreover, refracted negatively and satirically, by both male critics and whig women such as Sarah Churchill and Ann Clavering, as gendered – attractive to the female gaze.[11] In terms of meretricious visiblility, there is a sense in which his critics – extending, arguably, even to Hogarth in 1732 – interpret Sacheverell himself as a harlot: certainly it is notable how tropes of harlotry recur in commentary that was hostile to Sacheverell. George Ridpath, for example, referred to the Doctor's oratory as being 'as far from good language as a painted strumpet is from a real beauty'.[12]

Sacheverell, as we know, was the focus of extreme urban disorder, when meeting houses were attacked during his trial. As a trope, the London streetwalking harlot similarly embodied disorder, something which sporadic brothel riots only reinforced.[13] By 1710 there existed a literature (and iconography) of the London prostitute that was being explicitly invoked by Sacheverell's critics.

A less sophisticated image than Hogarth's, an anonymous broadsheet, significantly titled *The Modern Idol* (figure 2), brings these strands together, along with the Sacheverellite theme of celebrity.[14] In it, in the context of a genteel public open space, 'the Dr' is the centre of a vortex of female violence: face-scratching, hair-pulling, robe-grabbing.[15] The unseemly behaviour of the modern idol (or, rather his idolaters) occurs very much in public view (twice in public view if we think about it as refracted through print media) and presents a distinctively gendered disruption of the essentially homosocial, aspirationally 'polite' public sphere. It recalls Defoe's 'High Church Termagant', as imagined in the *Review* of 9 May 1710: 'Among the ladies – show me a virago, a

[9] Madan 1045, 149–227. For 'Drury' and 'Covent Garden' in popular usage: Carter, *Purchasing Power*, 16, 174 n. 52.

[10] Holmes, *Trial of Doctor Sacheverell*, 83, uses the term twice; see *'Among the Whores and Thieves': William Hogarth and The Beggar's Opera*, ed. David Bindman and Scott Wilcox (New Haven, 1997), 35, 37.

[11] Holmes, *Trial of Doctor Sacheverell*, 127,129, 135 n, 200–1, 230; Ophelia Field, *The Favourite: Sarah, Duchess of Marlborough* (2002), 239–50, 398.

[12] George Ridpath, *The Peril of being Zealously Affected, but not Well: Or, Reflections on Dr Sacheverell's Sermon* (1709) [Madan 75], 6, quoted in Holmes, *Trial of Doctor Sacheverell*, 50; Holmes refers to party's 'prostitution of the pulpit', 32.

[13] See Tim Harris, 'The Bawdy House Riots of 1668', *Historical Journal*, xxix (1986), 537–56; Tim Harris, *London Crowds in the Reign of Charles II: Propaganda and Politics from the Restoration until the Exclusion Crisis* (Cambridge, 1987), 82–91, 166–88; see Jessica Warner, *Craze: Gin and Debauchery in an Age of Reason* (New York, 2002). As my Pulpit Idol: *Dr Sacheverell, Religion and the Commercialisation of Politics, 1710* (forthcoming), will show, these women had a place in the middle-range print trade (verbal and visual, and, briefly, with Sacheverell, in combination) that was itself recognized as a both a social and topographical phenomenon.

[14] E.E.C. Nicholson, 'The English Political Print and Pictorial Political Argument, c.1640–1840: A Study in Historiography and Methodology', University of Edinburgh PhD, 1994.

[15] F.G. Stephens, *Catalogue of Prints and Drawings in the British Museum. Division I: Political and Personal Satires* (4 vols, 1870–83) [hereafter cited as BM], 1513.

Figure 2: *The Modern Idol or Kiss my A-se is no Swearing* (1710). Engraving. © Trustees of the British Museum.

termagant, a stride-rider, that loves her cold tea and swears at her maid; that plays all night and drinks chocolate in her bed; I'll hold five to one she's for the Doctor'.[16]

Yet, arguably, the harlot could disturb spectatorial polite society more insidiously as consumer than as catfighter, which returns us to the Doctor as a harlot's pin-up. By profession the ultimate economic reductionist, the harlot was suspect as a woman enjoying – or at least with the potential to enjoy – some measure of economic independence, and as an emulative consumer: not for nothing was a recent study of the subject titled *Purchasing Power*. In 1724, Bernard Mandeville would write of the 'poor common harlot [who must] have shoes & Stockings, Gloves, the Stay and Mantua Maker, the Sempstress, the Linnen-draper, all must have something by her'.[17] Where Paulson places great emphasis on Hogarth's harlot as being literally consumed by Walpolean male culture,[18] Hogarth's image transcends its own anti-clerical politics to confirm a print

[16] Field, *The Favourite*, 243; an irony obvious to Defoe here, surely, being that the most media-refracted termagant of the hour – and beyond – was the virulently whig, Sarah Churchill. 'Cold tea' was laced with brandy.

[17] Bernard Mandeville, *A Modest Defence of Publick Stews* (1724), quoted in Paulson, *Modern Moral Subject*, 251–2.

[18] Paulson, *Modern Moral Subject*, 249.

culture (at least in London) which was, as early as 1710, nuancedly affordable.[19] This is an issue compromised by poor survival rates – many such prints were pasted directly onto walls; the harlot's is tacked, unframed – and later curatorial biases.[20] But it must also be remembered that while there were cheap prints and cheap women, not all harlots were cheap, and might enjoy possession of one or both of the mezzotints or finer engravings which were the basis of most other Sacheverell portrait imagery.[21]

It has become fashionable to frame Hogarth in relation to an 'interpretative community' of consumers and spectators of varieties of print culture, varying levels of visual and ordinary literacy sustainable in early- to mid-18th-century London.[22] In 1732 there would have been, like Hogarth, contemporaries of the trial who would have been able to 'read' Hogarth's image through memories of the anti-Sacheverell press's jibes at the idolisation of Sacheverell by London whores. But for later viewers, and within Hogarth's own lifetime, *The Harlot's Progress* (figure 1) becomes more palimpsestic than Hogarth could ever have anticipated, showing that the artist had an intuitive grasp of the original association of Sacheverell with prostitutes. In 1747, 15 years after publication, the opening of the vault in St Andrew's, Holborn disclosed that Sacheverell was interred alongside the notorious figure of the high-class harlot, Sally Salisbury (c.1692–1724), an accepted source for cross references in *The Harlot's Progress* series.[23] As a consequence, the Doctor was, as it were, resurrected in whig wit with, as Geoffrey Holmes puts it, 'epitaphs suitable to their respective reputations', and the satirical godsend of the political-sexual innuendo of non-resistance:

> Lo! To one grave consigned, of rival fame,
> A reverend Doctor and a wanton dame.
> Well for the world both did to rest retire,
> For each, while living, set mankind on fire.

[19] Eirwen E.C. Nicholson, 'Consumers and Spectators: The Public of the Political Print in Eighteenth-Century England', *History*, lxxxi (1996), 5–21; Timothy Clayton, *The English Print 1688–1802* (1997). Hallett, *Spectacle of Difference*, 30, while focused on the satirical corpus in context, acknowledges Sacheverell as a domestic icon through the portrait print. It is worth noting that Hogarth makes no distinction of age or condition between the harlot's Sacheverell and Macheath prints; it is not impossible that the harlot's Sacheverell is contemporary with the Macheath and hence a later (re)publication; as frontispiece for J.C.D. Clark's, *English Society 1660–1832* (Cambridge, 2000), the author uses a c.1740 reprint of an iconic 1688 image of the seven bishops which was, in fact, itself a source for the Sacheverell handkerchief discussed here.

[20] For institutional collecting and curatorial prejudices and lacunae now difficult to remedy, in this case at the British Museum, see Sheila O'Connell, *The Popular Print in England 1550–1850* (1999); Antony Griffiths, *The Print in Stuart Britain 1603–1689* (1998) (note the cut-off date).

[21] Sacheverell iconicity via portrait prints is central to Pulpit Idol. The two mezzotint models from which most engravings, the medal, handkerchief and fan representations and some print satires derive are: J. Smith after A. Russell, and A. Johnston after T. Gibson: John Chaloner Smith, *British Mezzotinto Portraits from the Introduction of the Art to the Early Part of the Present Century* (4 vols, 1883), 219.I, 4.II.

[22] Paulson, *Modern Moral Subject*, 247, 248; Hallett, *Spectacle of Difference*, 1–55.

[23] Through both her early patronage by Col. Francis Charteris and later by bawd Mother Needham, similarly her criminal record, including Bridewell, and ultimately, although this is not incorporated into Hogarth's *The Harlot's Progress*, her syphilitic death in Newgate for the 1713 murder of a young peer at a Covent Garden tavern. At this point she already enjoyed celebrity, both elite and popular, and by 1723 portrait-print iconicity. As with Sacheverell, her sentence was light: see Charles Walker, *Authentic Memoirs of the Life, Intrigues and Adventures of the Celebrated Sally Salisbury* (1723), and http://en.wikipedia.org/wiki/Sally-Salisbury. Paulson, *Modern Moral Subject*, 184, 247, has Hogarth placing Sacheverell in Plate 3 in a trinity of relatively successful criminality; quoting *The Free Briton*: 15 July 1731, as demanding to know 'Why was *Sacheverel* distinguished with a royal presentation', 247.

And pithier, and arguably more pertinent:

A fit companion for a high-church priest'
He non-resistance taught, and she profest'.[24]

Hogarth's harlot remains an ambivalent figure. In hostile readings she is meretricious, criminal and ephemeral; encoded as such, she, Sally Salisbury and with them Sacheverell, are interchangeably harlots. That Hogarth's harlot is depicted not walking the pavements of Drury,[25] but in her own (Drury) room, brings us to the second, and more developed, association of Sacheverell and subversive women, only this time at higher levels of society and consumption, and safely (or rather, as we shall see, not so safely) 'within doors' as participants in the distinctive commodification of Sacheverell.

3

In his notorious *A Modest Defence of Publick Stews* (1724), Mandeville rehearsed the classic argument for the social, as well as economic, value of prostitution with the analogy of a spoiling piece of meat: 'by sacrificing a Small Part already Tainted' the butcher 'wisely secures the safety of the Rest'; the services of the prostitute protect 'good' women within doors.[26] The attendance and behaviour of elite women of both parties at the trial is well documented and was predictably satirised, as in the broadsheet *Love and Divinity united. Being a true copy of verses of a young wealthy lady of quality that fell in Love with Dr Sacheverel* [*sic.*] *at his trial in Westminster-hall*.[27] It also allowed for ambivalently psephological satires. The penny pamphlet, *The London Ladies Petition* sexualises the trial in a way impossible to reconcile within any paradigm of politeness. Its full title is *The London Ladies Petition, to have the chusing of able and sufficient members, instead of their husbands, that may stand stiffly by the Church*. In it, the female well-wishers of the Church and Sacheverell ask an unnamed lord to give them the vote, in place of their incompetent and unreliable husbands. More psephological than bawdy, *The Parliament of Women: or, the nation well-manag'd by female politicians* has one member suspended for not possessing a portrait of Sacheverell.[28]

When we move from the semi-public 'space' of Westminster Hall to the private, enclosed space of the domestic interior, as in a pro-Sacheverell print, *Quod Risum Movet*

---

[24] Holmes, *Trial of Doctor Sacheverell*, 267.

[25] John Gay, *Trivia, or the Art of Walking the Streets of London* (1716); the gendered intersections of London's print and street culture are recalled in Sally Salisbury's own earliest and possibly parallel career as a pamphlet-seller in Pope's Head Alley.

[26] Mandeville, quoted in Paulson, *Modern Moral Subject*, 254; Carter, *Purchasing Power*, 52.

[27] Madan 964; Holmes, *Trial of Doctor Sacheverell*, 119–22, 126–7, 200–1; Field, *The Favourite*, 243–5, 247.

[28] *The London Ladies Petition* [Madan 599]; *The Parliament of Women* [Madan 617]: '. . . female politicians: who are to sit and vote till the meeting of the new Parliament: together with a list of the speakers and most considerable members of both houses' [Madan 617]; this said, 'all the members resolved to observe Sacheverell's doctrine of non-resistance whatever the consequences'.

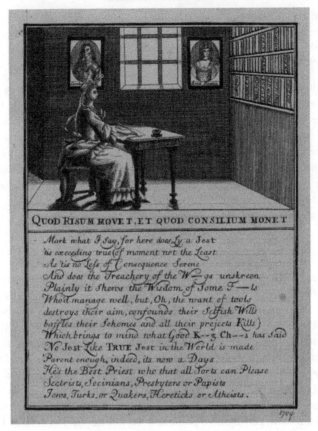

Figure 3: *Quod Risum Movet Et Quod Consilium Monet* (1710). Engraving. © Trustees of the British Museum.

et Quod Consilium Monet, the Doctor's status as a commodified idol becomes more apparent and more threatening to whig (or even tory) patriarchy.[29]

The print (figure 3) resonates with a passage in the *Spectator* in 1711, in which the print-infested closet of another woman is described:[30]

> I remember when Dr Titus Oates was in all his Glory, I accompanied my Friend WILL. HONEYCOMB in a Visit to a Lady of his Acquaintance. We were no sooner sate down, but upon casting my Eyes about the Room, I found in almost every Corner of it a Print that represented the Doctor in all Magnitudes and Dimensions. A little after, as the Lady was discoursing my Friend, and held her Snuff-Box in her Hand, who should I see in the Lid of it but the Doctor. It was not long after this, when she had occasion for her Handkerchief, which upon the first opening discov-

[29] BM, 1504; see also BM, 1514 and *Made and Written by a Youth of 15 Years of Age in the Sight of 3 Pictures which Hung in his Closet* [Madan 959].
[30] *Spectator,* no. 57: 5 May 1711.

ered among the Plaites of it the figure of the Doctor. Upon this my Friend WILL. Who loves Raillery told her, That if he was in Mr Truelove's Place (for that was the Name of her Husband) he should be made as uneasie by a Handkerchief as ever Othello was. I am afraid, said she, Mr Honeycomb, you are a TORY; tell me truly, are you a Friend to the Doctor or not? WILL. Instead of making her a reply, smiled in her Face (for indeed it was very pretty) and told her that one of her Patches was dropping off. She immediately adjusted it, and looking a little seriously, Well, says she, I'll be hanged if you and your silent Friend there are not against the Doctor in your Hearts, I suspected as much by his saying nothing. Upon this she took her Fan into her Hand, and upon the opening of it again displayed to us the Figure of the Doctor, who was placed with great Gravity among the Sticks of it. In a word, I found that the Doctor had taken Possession of her Thoughts, her Discourse, and most of her Furniture.[31]

In this passage the 'Dr' is Dr Titus Oates, and it is true that the consumer culture generated by the Sacheverell trial was, to an extent, prefigured during the Popish Plot of 1678–9; but in the context of 1711 he also stands for Sacheverell. But whereas the Popish Plot was characterised predominantly by an extensive print media, the Sacheverell crisis produced a far richer material culture, including fans, handkerchiefs, ceramics, and portraits.[32] Unlike Oates, however, who had a reputation as homosexual, Sacheverell's reputation was explicitly as heterosexual. Sacheverell thus 'possessed' his female admirers in a way that Oates had not.

This association is supported by *Predictions for the Year 1710* which satirically foresees 'that before the end of this year there will be born within this City and the suburbs thereof great numbers of children in face very much resembling the Revd Dr Sacheverell, which must be esteemed a miracle in favour of the said Dr'.[33] The author goes on to suggest, however, that:

tho this prediction should (and undoubtedly it will) prove true, yet we need not have recourse to a supernatural Power, since the strength of imagination, with the help of those pictures of the Dr which he in his daily visits draws from under his gown, may be sufficient to produce this effect: if therefore Mrs X– should be brought to bed of a child thus stampt, her husband is hereby desired to attribute the cause thereof to the picture which hangs at his bed's feet: and these are further to certifie that for the improvement of the breed of this nation, the said Dr is ready to shew all comers at his house in [blank] and he will attend on persons of quality in their own houses, from noon till midnight if desired.[34]

[31] Joseph Addison and Richard Steele, *The Spectator*, ed. Gregory Smith (4 vols, 1970), i, 175. No. 57's classic criticism of female party rage is remarkably absent from the 'fashioning gender' section of *The Commerce of Everyday Life, Selections from The Tatler and The Spectator*, ed. Erin Mackie (1998).
[32] Handkerchief with Sacheverell portrait: Victoria and Albert Museum, T.351–1960; Fans: Fan Museum, Greenwich, M 973; British Museum, BM, 1525.
[33] The tract is untraced and may exist only within the cross-referential corpus as a satirical tactic.
[34] *Predictions for the Year 1710* [Madan 110]; Samuel Palmer, *A Vindication of the Learning, Loyalty, Morals and Most Christian Behaviour of the Dissenters towards the Church of England* (1705) [Madan 34]; *A Letter from a Member of Parliament Concerning the Occasional Conformity Bill* (1705) [Madan 35].

Returning to our *Spectator* text, and the items with which Mrs Truelove surrounded herself, the decoration of her receiving room might suggest a complaisant or even pro-Sacheverell husband, much in the way that MP Charles Caesar allowed his wife Mary's counter-revolutionary portrait gallery as an assertion of her politics.[35] The implication in the *Spectator*, however, suggests a far from complicit husband, in so far as it turns on the potential of the wife's partisanship as a first step towards adultery: Addison is effectively, and within the controlling courtesies of the *Spectatorial* method, 'red-flagging' her through her dangerous furniture.

It is possible, of course, also to read Mrs Truelove's closet as a shrine with idols and relics. In so doing, and placing Mrs Truelove alongside the second, house-visiting, satire, with its own cross-referent of portrait idolatry, we draw on an older, but relevant trope – that of the literally insinuating papist priest/confessor, as in one 1691 print and which, of course, informs that essential myth of 1688 – the warming-pan baby.[36] Anti-Sacheverell material blurs the lines between idolatry and adultery, and implicates consumption. With *'taking possession'*, Mr Spectator's choice of words is similarly nuanced; if implicitly Sacheverell might take possession of any number of Mrs Trueloves, so Mrs Truelove has herself taken possession of iconic Sacheverell paraphernalia, as a politicised consumer.

4

The harlot's pin-up, Sacheverell as spectacle *en route* to, and in, Westminster Hall, and the more sophisticated icons of Mrs Truelove's closet, blur the lines between the categories of women implicated in Sacheverell idolatry. Female spectatorship of the Doctor took place within and without doors, in the flesh and on paper: if women in both Hogarthian and *Spectatorial* society were ordinarily themselves objects of the male gaze[37] and behavioural regulation, with Sacheverell this is at least temporarily reversed. Commodified, Sacheverell became a public, male, presence within a private female sanctum, with the inference of an independent, or at least quasi-independent, female engagement with London's consumer society on partisan terms. More importantly, he also challenged the larger confessional and dynastic ones on which 1710's partisanship was premised.[38] In writing of the harlot and of Hogarthian England, in terms of 'high' and 'low', 'popular' and 'polite' cultural frameworks, Ronald Paulson has often invoked E.P. Thompson's

---

[35] Valerie Rumbold, 'The Jacobite Vision of Mary Caesar', in *Women, Writing, History, 1640–1740*, ed. I. Grundy and S. Wiseman (1992).

[36] P. Wagner, *Eros Revived: Erotica of the Enlightenment in England and America* (1988), 47–86: *Converte Angliam* (*c*.1716), BM, 1146; Griffiths, *Print in Stuart England*, 261, No.181 (1691); Richard Sharp, *Engraved Record of the Jacobite Movement* (Aldershot, 1996), 82.

[37] Carter, *Purchasing Power*, 66–70.

[38] An important corrective to the whiggism of the 'commercialization' and related conceptual frameworks, and by no means irrelevant to Sacheverell, is jacobite portrait print culture as was clearly sustainable within a London marketplace and semi-public sphere; see Sharp, *Engraved Record*; Paul Monod, *Jacobitism and the English People 1688–1788* (Cambridge, 1989), 70–92; Robin Nicholson, *Bonnie Prince Charlie and the Making of a Myth: A Study in Portraiture 1720–1892* (2002), touches on issues of celebrity and iconicity very relevant to Sacheverell, not least because a female market and sympathy has been implicated. But where Sharp rightly includes portraits of nonjurors, Sacheverell is the first specifically clerical celebrity on a scale that his neglect in relation to Vernon, Wilkes etc. must be questioned in specific relation to the non-secular nature of its subject.

concept of 'subculture'. What, asks Paulson, is this 'popular heretical subculture'? His Thompsonian answer is: something whose base existed inferentially within 'a mass of people beyond the classic reading, property-owning and voting interests'.[39] The problem with this definition is that Sacheverell's harlots, high and low, streetwalking or closeted, were all 'subculture', being, all of them, disenfranchised. What they most certainly were not, in their support of Sacheverell, was 'heretical' or secular. But whereas Paulson can accommodate and hail Wilkes as 'an unusually populist symptom of a Freethinking, anticlerical and anti-establishment tradition',[40] Sacheverell's celebrity within a confessionally orthodox, clerical, counter-revolutionary tradition has been ignored or, as with Hogarth's *The Harlot's Progress* (Plate 3), poorly contextualised.

The marketing and celebrity of Sacheverell 50 years before that of John Wilkes necessitates, in the first place, revision of the chronology of 'the commercialization of politics'. But it is not in merely chronological terms that revision of this concept is required. The conventional contextualisation of the reified 'commercialization of politics' or 'birth of a consumer society' and 'emergence of a/the public sphere' emphasizes the extent to which these phenomena anticipate 'modernity', in the form of an increasingly non-deferential, increasingly *secular* society by appealing to the minds and pockets of those outside the traditional political nation. The non-managed, and as such non-propagandist, market-oriented selling of Sacheverell confounds this. In so far as they were psephologically-challenged, social and economic distinctions between women were irrelevant, their voyeuristic and consumerist interest in the Doctor remarked and satirised; that this had confessional and ideological bases beyond novelty and a general, societal 'rage of party' has been under-explored.[41] But to presume the absence of high church identification on the part of a Covent Garden harlot (consumer as well as consumed) would, indeed, be a 'condescenscion of posterity'. The whisper of the 'kind shees' in St James's Park, '*are you for the Dr?*' is a question that deserves considered answers.

---

[39] Ronald Paulson, *Popular and Polite Art in the Age of Hogarth and Fielding* (South Bend, IN, 1979), pp. ix, x; but see also Wagner, *Reading Iconotexts*, 168.

[40] Paulson, *Popular and Polite Art*, pp. ix, x.

[41] Paulson, *Hogarth's Harlot*, 156; '*Among the Whores and Thieves*', ed. Bindman and Wilcox, 78, 93.

Irish Tories and Victims of Whig Persecution: Sacheverell Fever by Proxy*

D.W. HAYTON

Although the trial of Dr Sacheverell attracted considerable public attention in Ireland, and a great deal of the pamphlet literature generated in England was reprinted in Dublin, there is little explicit evidence of the invocation of Sacheverell's name by Irish tories, in parliament, at elections, or in the indigenous press culture. On the surface, this seems hard to explain, even though Irish protestants were naturally more sensitive than their English counterparts to any challenge to the legitimacy of 'Revolution principles', for at the same time the protestant Irish 'political nation' was bitterly divided by a conflict of parties on the English model, and, indeed, regarded their own struggles as an extension of the warfare of whigs and tories in England. This article seeks to account for the non-appearance of Dr Sacheverell in Irish political discourse by emphasizing the presence in Ireland of two surrogates: Francis Higgins, the roaring anglican controversialist who, like Sacheverell himself, courted 'persecution' by bishops and whig governments, and Sir Constantine Phipps, lord chancellor of Ireland 1710–14, who turned himself into a tory champion in Ireland by using some of Sacheverell's methods of self-promotion. The fact that both were closely associated with the Doctor – Higgins as a chosen replacement for Sacheverell in the pulpit in 1710, Phipps as a defence counsel at the impeachment – infused both with reflected glamour and enabled Irish tories to express their support for Sacheverell indirectly, without calling into question their loyalty to the Williamite settlement.

Keywords: Ireland; toryism; print culture; Church of Ireland; Dr Sacheverell; popular politics

1

The poll for knights of the shire for County Antrim in 1715 was held in the tory stronghold of Lisburn, a small town dominated by the estate of the absentee English proprietor, Lord Conway. The tory candidates, the Hon. John Skeffington, son of Lord Massereene, and Brent Spencer, a former county sheriff who had been active in the persecution of dissenters, were opposed by two presbyterian gentlemen, Clotworthy Upton of Castle Upton, the principal spokesman in Ireland for the dissenting interest, and his cousin, Sir Arthur Langford. The tory Skeffington was returned with the

* For permission to make use of manuscript materials in their ownership or care, I am grateful to the Viscount Midleton; his grace the archbishop of Armagh; the British Library Board; the governing body of Christ Church, Oxford; the comptroller of Her Majesty's Stationery Office; the London Metropolitan Archives; the director, National Library of Ireland; the deputy keeper of the records of Northern Ireland; Staffordshire RO; Surrey History Centre; the Board of Trinity College Dublin; and Worcestershire RO.

presbyterian Upton, but Langford petitioned (encouraged by the result of the general election, which established a whig majority in the Irish house of commons). Among his complaints was the allegation that:

> After the poll . . . there gathered in the street a most tumultuous, riotous and dangerous mob, hallowing and huzzaing, a Skeffington, and Spencer, and Doctor Sacheverell, and down with the Whigs, and no Langford nor Upton, which mob insulted the lodgings of Clotworthy and [his brother] Thomas Upton . . . the said Thomas being employed by the petitioner to represent him in his . . . election, by wounding, knocking down and grievously beating the freeholders, servants and other persons that passed in and out of the . . . house.[1]

What is interesting about this incident is not the use of the party names of whig and tory to distinguish participants in an Irish election, for at the time this was perfectly natural, nor the resort to violence by unruly elements of the populace, which was also far from extraordinary, but the invocation of the hallowed name of Sacheverell by the anti-presbyterian mob. Despite the evidence of some contemporary commentators that the impeachment had set Ireland as well as England 'in a flame',[2] appearances of Sacheverell's name in the Irish sources – public or private – are comparatively rare, and it is whigs rather than tories who are more likely to have made reference to him. One whig satire from 1711 set out to smear Irish tories as hero-worshippers of Sacheverell,[3] while the presbyterian minister of Belfast, John McBride, replying to a high church tormentor who had stigmatised all presbyterians as fundamentally disloyal to the monarchy, responded by citing the high-flying Sacheverell as the embodiment of modern toryism.[4] For their part, the tories alleged that whigs drank such insulting toasts as 'Greg's fate to all Sacheverell's friends', a reference to the clerk in Secretary Harley's office who had been executed in 1708 for spying for the French.[5] Proof of this tendency – if proof were needed – came in the autumn of 1710 when witnesses reported that unruly officers of Sir John Wittewrong's regiment, stationed in Limerick, had been heard carousing under the bedroom window of the high church bishop, Thomas Smyth, drinking 'the litany health' as they called it: 'Confusion, damnation, plague, pestilence and famine, battle, murder and sudden death to Dr Sacheverell and his adherents.'[6] But besides the account of the County Antrim election, I have only been able to discover two other references by Irish tories to Sacheverell: a pamphlet published in 1711 entitled *The Innocency of the Royal*

[1] *CJ Ireland*, iii, 28–9.

[2] *The Observator*, 24 May 1710.

[3] *The Recorder's Speech: with the Principles of the Whigs Defended* ([Dublin], 1711) [Madan, not listed].

[4] John MacBride, *A Sample of Jet-Black Pr—tic Calumny, in Answer to a Pamphlet, Called, A Sample of True-Bleu Presbyterian Loyalty . . .*, (Glasgow, 1713), 113; see also [Joseph Boyse], *Remarks on a Pamphlet Publish'd by William Tisdall, D.D. and Intituled The Case of the Sacramental Test Stated and Argued* (Dublin, 1716), 46.

[5] *Her Majesty's Prerogative in Ireland . . . Asserted and Maintained: In Answer to a Paper Falsly Intituled The Case of the City of Dublin . . .* (1712), 31.

[6] BL, Add. MS 31888, ff. 39–40: abstract of depositions concerning riots committed by army officers at Limerick, [1710] (printed in Maurice Lenihan, *Limerick, its History and Antiquities . . .* (Dublin, 1867), 310–12); T.C. Barnard, 'Athlone 1685; Limerick 1710: Religious Riots or Charivaris', *Studia Hibernica*, xxvii (1993), 72–3.

Martyr . . . Vindicated . . ., which was dedicated to him;[7] and a private letter in 1715 from the whig lord chancellor of Ireland, Alan Brodrick, who noted that a man with whom his relations were embroiled in a legal dispute had refused to drink the duke of Marlborough's health, preferring to toast the Doctor instead.[8]

The absence of specific reference to Sacheverell in Irish tory rhetoric is all the more unusual given that toryism in Ireland was essentially an English importation. There was no indigenous cavalier tradition, the royalist party in the 1640s having consisted of the personal following of the king's Irish lord lieutenant, the marquess (later first duke) of Ormond. Moreover, despite the presence of substantial numbers of protestant noncon-formists in Ireland, and a strong concentration of Scottish presbyterians in Ulster, the sectarian tensions of the Restoration period had failed to stimulate a powerful strain of Stuart loyalism among the anglican clergy and gentry, even during the crisis over exclusion. The experience of a pro-catholic government in 1687–9 confirmed the Williamite loyalties of the protestant landowning elite, so that when the Irish parliament was recalled in 1692, the members appeared to be naturally whiggish in their inclina-tions.[9] Admittedly, further large-scale immigration from the presbyterian south-west of Scotland in the mid 1690s created something approaching a siege mentality among excitable Church of Ireland parsons, and thus provided a distinctively Irish context for the emerging 'high church' element among the political classes. But the appearance of a tory party in the Irish parliament in Queen Anne's reign owed more to the tidal influence of English politics, operating chiefly through the agency of a shared print culture, and the intrigues in Ireland of English-born or English-educated activists. The conflict between self-styled whigs and tories that dominated the political life of Ireland in the first decades of the 18th century was a reflection of the English original. Irish protestants were transfixed by events across the water. Archbishop King of Dublin noted how the talk of London coffee houses was transmitted to Ireland, explaining to a correspondent in England how 'a hint or surmise with you is exemplified here and erected into a certain intelligence'.[10] Party-politicians in Ireland expressed themselves in the same language as did their English counterparts, used the same emblems, debated the same issues and followed the same controversies. At the 1713 election for Dublin City, for example, supporters of the tory candidates, Sir William Fownes and Martin Tucker, bedecked themselves with laurel, just as an English tory mob might have done, and uttered 'loud huzzas for church and queen, Tucker and Fownes; down with faction, spleen etc'.[11] Even the clergy, who would have been most acutely aware of the threat posed to the establishment by the influx of Scottish presbyterians into the north, focused their attention on the specific issues that agitated their English brethren. The grievances embodied in the *Representation of the Present State of Religion in Ireland*, produced by convocation in Dublin in 1711, contained very little with a local flavour, and the only

---

[7] *The Innocency of the Royal Martyr K[ing] Charles the I Vindicated, with His Majesty's Last Speech on the Scaffold . . .* (Dublin, 1711).

[8] Surrey History Centre [hereafter cited as SHC], Brodrick papers, 1248/3, ff. 223–4: endorsement by Brodrick on letter from Katherine Whitfield, 17 Mar. 1714/15.

[9] D.W. Hayton, *Ruling Ireland, 1685–1742: Politics, Politicians and Parties* (Woodbridge, 2004), 36–40.

[10] Trinity College Dublin [hereafter cited as TCD], MS 2531, pp. 238–9, 301: Archbishop King to Francis Annesley, 16 Dec. 1710; to [Samuel] Dopping, 30 Dec. 1710.

[11] *Post Boy*: 26–8 Nov. 1713.

high church cleric to write or preach specifically against Ulster presbyterians, or, indeed, any kind of Irish dissenter, was the vicar of Belfast, William Tisdall, who was animated by bitter personal experience.[12]

Why, then, do we find Irish tories making so little mention of Sacheverell, at least in the surviving record? One possible explanation lies in their sensitivity to the charge of disloyalty which would have been engendered by an overt show of enthusiasm for one whose preaching had allegedly questioned the legitimacy of revolution principles. Irish protestants had so much to lose from the restoration of a catholic monarch that an Irish protestant jacobite was a rare bird indeed. The loyal association of 1696 was subscribed by every member of the Irish parliament bar one, and beyond a handful of enthusiastic undergraduates in Trinity College and the occasional ultra-tory newswriter, the only identifiable protestant jacobites were recent arrivals from England.[13] Susceptibility to guilt by association would account for Irish tories' reluctance to disclose sympathy for Sacheverell, and the contrasting readiness of their opponents to remind the public of the symbolic importance of the Doctor to the high church cause.

At the same time, it would be absurd to say that Irish tories ignored the Sacheverell affair. Besides the letters that passed between Ireland and England, Irish newspapers included reports of the trial and its aftermath,[14] and Irish printers and booksellers bombarded the reading public with printed matter of all kinds relating to Sacheverell. During 1710 alone, 15 such items, originally published in London, were recorded as having been reprinted in Dublin, and a further two items have only a Dublin mark but may well have originated in England.[15] These reprints included the standard account of the *Tryal of Dr Sacheverell* (published by Jacob Tonson at the request of the house of lords), a copy of which we know to have been in the possession of one Irish tory MP, Jeffrey Paul (admittedly in a list of his library dating from 1729).[16] A Dublin reprint of the expensive folio edition was announced early in July 1710, to be sold by subscription, with printers and booksellers acting as agents in Dublin and 16 other towns the length and breadth of provincial Ireland.[17] The existence of this plethora of printed material indicates a healthy market for news of Sacheverell, and while it does not, by itself, provide evidence of widespread support for his cause, it suggests that Irish tories were a good deal more interested in the impeachment, and possibly sympathetic to its victim, than they were prepared to let on.

[12] *A Representation of the Present State of Religion, with Regard to Infidelity, Heresy, Impiety and Popery: Drawn up and Agreed to by Both Houses of Convocation in Ireland . . .* (Dublin, [1711]). For Tisdall, see *ODNB*; *Dictionary of Irish Biography*, ed. James McGuire and James Quinn (9 vols, Cambridge, 2009), ix, 384.

[13] Hayton, *Ruling Ireland*, 37, 145–6; Thomas Doyle, 'Jacobitism, Catholicism and the Irish Protestant Elite, 1700–1710', *Eighteenth-Century Ireland*, xii (1997) 28–59. Cf. Éamonn Ó Ciardha, *Ireland and the Jacobite Cause, 1685–1766, a Fatal Attachment* (Dublin, 2002), ch. 3.

[14] *Dublin Intelligence*: 7 Jan., 25 Feb., 4, 7 Mar. 1709/10, 1 Apr., 30 May, 17 June 1710; *Dublin Gazette*: 14–17, 21–24 Jan., 7–11 Feb., 28 Feb.–4 Mar., 7–11, 11–14 Mar. 1709/10.

[15] See below, Appendix; Falconer Madan, *A Bibliography of Dr Henry Sacheverell* (Oxford, 1884); F.F. Madan, *A Critical Bibliography of Dr Henry Sacheverell*, ed. W.A. Speck (Lawrence, KA, 1978).

[16] *The Tryal of Dr Henry Sacheverell* (1710) [Madan 465]; National Library of Ireland [hereafter cited as NLI], MS 1399: Paul's account book, 1703–31. See also 'The Library of Dennis Molony (1650–1726), an Irish Catholic Lawyer in London', ed. John Bergin and Liam Chambers, *Analecta Hibernica*, xli (2009), 115.

[17] *Dublin Intelligence*: 1 July 1710; *Dublin Gazette*: 1–4 July 1710. The provincial towns were Belfast, Cavan, Clonmel, Coleraine, Cork, Derry, Drogheda, Dungannon, Enniskillen, Galway, Kilkenny, Limerick, Longford, Newry, Sligo and Waterford.

It is the contention of this article that we may detect this unspoken sympathy – perhaps even symptoms of the same kind of fever that gripped the English during and after 1710 – through the adulation paid by Irish tories to two individuals closely connected with Sacheverell, who made a direct impact on the Irish political scene: the first, Francis Higgins, an Irish cleric of a similar stripe, who had become acquainted with Sacheverell on sojourns in England, and who, like Sacheverell, sought and suffered a succession of minor martyrdoms; the second, Sir Constantine Phipps, an English lawyer who had served as one of Sacheverell's counsel at his impeachment before being appointed to high office in the Dublin administration, and who brought with him to Ireland not only a reputation as the defender of the high church hero but also something of his client's political glamour.

2

In 1710, Francis Higgins could fairly claim to be the best known Church of Ireland clergyman outside Ireland.[18] His fiery personality and high church opinions were sufficiently close to the Sacheverellite model for historians, following Sir Walter Scott, have distinguished him as 'the Irish Sacheverell'. Although this phrase does not seem to have been used by contemporaries, the association was clear enough. The anti-Sacheverell pamphlet *A Character of Don Sacheverellio, Knight of the Firebrand . . .*, published in London in 1710, included on the title page a spurious reference to the publisher as 'Francis Higgins, bookmaker' of Dublin, and recommended to the Doctor that if he intended 'to make a second sally' in the lists, he should choose as his 'attender' the Irishman 'Don Higginisco'.[19] Higgins was a regular visitor to England – which may account for the rather odd description of him by Geoffrey Holmes as 'a wild itinerant Irishman'[20] – and was the preacher invited in January 1710 by the imprisoned Sacheverell to substitute for him in the pulpit in St Saviour's, Southwark. The opportunity was lost when the bishop of Winchester prevailed on the other chaplain at St Saviour's to dissuade Sacheverell from what would clearly have been a provocative gesture,[21] but the episode says much for the reputation which Higgins had established among both high and low churchmen in England, despite being no more than a cathedral prebendary in Dublin.

Higgins's origins were relatively humble, as the son of Robert Higgins, a protestant apothecary in the city of Limerick.[22] He later asserted that such 'little fortune' as his

---

[18] For Higgins see the biographical entries in J.B. Leslie, *Ossory Clergy and Parishes . . .* (Enniskillen, 1937), 268–70; *ODNB*; *Dictionary of Irish Biography*, ed. McGuire and Quinn, iv, 681–2.

[19] 'John Distaff', *A Character of Don Sacheverellio, Knight of the Firebrand; in a Letter to Isaac Bickerstaff, Esq.; Censor of Great Britain* (1710), title page and 16. Falconer Madan evidently misread the title page in stating that this work was actually published in Dublin [Madan 59]. See also *Instructions from Rome in Favour of the Pretender Inscribed to the Most Elevated Don Sacheverellio, and his Brother Don Higginisco . . .* (1710) [Madan 411]; Daniel Defoe, *The Review*, ed. John McVeagh (7 vols so far, 2003–), vii, 46.

[20] Geoffrey Holmes, *The Trial of Doctor Sacheverell* (1973), 45.

[21] Holmes, *Trial of Doctor Sacheverell*, 96–7.

[22] Currently this forms the limit of our knowledge of Higgins's ancestry, which renders the allusion to his 'Celtic charm and oratory', in Holmes, *Trial of Doctor Sacheverell*, 45, a trifle overblown. Details of his career can be found in Bodl., MS North, a.3, ff. 237–8: memorial to Queen Anne seeking preferment, [c.1712]. His

father possessed had been 'ruined' during the Williamite wars, but his brother John was able to continue the apothecary's business and eventually climbed the social ladder to become an alderman and mayor of the corporation.[23] Whatever the truth of his own pleas of youthful poverty, there had been enough money to send the 16-year-old Francis to Trinity College, Dublin in 1686, where he was admitted as a sizar. That he was ordained in 1689 while still an undergraduate may be a sign of intellectual precocity, though with the college under jacobite military occupation, this was an exceptional time. Higgins himself wrote that he had been imprisoned by the jacobite regime but, in fact, he seems to have prospered, in so far as he was appointed in February 1690, five months before the Battle of the Boyne, as a reader at Christ Church cathedral – the 'state' church of the Dublin government. After the reassertion of protestant control over Ireland, his career advanced more slowly: he was suspended from his readership in 1691 for neglect of duty, but installed to several livings in the dioceses of Dublin and Ossory, including, in 1694, the rectory of Gowran in County Kilkenny, which was in the gift of the jacobite peer, Lord Rosse (Lady Tyrconnel's son-in-law). In 1695 (according to his own account) he successfully petitioned on behalf of the lower clergy against an obnoxious bill in the Irish house of commons[24] – possibly the bill for building and repairing churches – but it was not until Queen Anne's reign that he came to prominence. When the Irish Convocation was recalled in 1704 he was one of a small group of high-flying clergy who, in the disapproving words of a leading 'low churchman', 'got the management of the clergy . . . into their hands'.[25] In July 1705, he was elected by the tory-dominated chapter of Christ Church into the prebend of St Michael's, and a month later was appointed to preach a sermon before the lords justices in the cathedral at a public thanksgiving for Marlborough's victories.[26] In the world of Irish ecclesiastical politics, he had arrived.

What we know of Higgins's physical appearance and character comes from hostile sources. His enemies ridiculed him as a fat, red-faced, roaring preacher, loud and loquacious but intellectually limited. In the verse satire *The Swan Tripe-Club*, published in Dublin in 1706, he appeared at the head of the table of high-flying tories who met regularly for dinner at the Swan Tavern in Dublin:[27]

[22] *(continued)* sister, at her marriage in 1712 to a Dr Robinson, was described as having been a housekeeper to General Richard Ingoldsby and to lack any fortune (NLI, MS 41589/3: William Burne to William Smyth, 26 Feb. 1711/12; Toby Barnard, *The Abduction of a Limerick Heiress* (Dublin, 1998), 18).

[23] Alderman John Higgins was one of the tories serenaded by the drunken whig officers in 1710 (Lenihan, *Limerick*, 312, 317–20, 704). His house was attacked again by whig soldiers from the garrison in 1718 (Bodl., MS Ballard 36, f. 107: William Perceval to Arthur Charlett, 20 Nov. 1718).

[24] Bodl., MS North, a.3, ff. 237–8: memorial, [c.1712].

[25] Christ Church, Oxford, Arch. W. Epist. xii: Archbishop King to Archbishop Wake, 12 Sept. 1717; see also TCD, MS 2536, p. 165: King to Bishop Crowe of Cloyne, 8 Jan. 1714[/15].

[26] Henry Cotton, *Fasti Ecclesiae Hibernicae . . .* (5 vols, Dublin, 1845–60), ii, 66–8; Francis Higgins, *A Sermon Preach'd before Their Excellencies the Lords Justices at Christ-Church, Dublin; on Tuesday, the 28th of August . . .* (Dublin, 1705).

[27] *The Swan Tripe-Club in Dublin; a Satyr; Dedicated to All Those who are True Friends to Her Present Majesty and Her Government . . .* (Dublin, [1706]), 6–7. See also SHC, 1248/2, ff. 225–6, 234–5: Alan Brodrick to St John Brodrick, 31 Oct., 1 Dec. 1705; J.T. Gilbert, *A History of the City of Dublin* (3 vols, Dublin, 1854–9), i, 42; *The Poems of Jonathan Swift*, ed. Harold Williams (3 vols, Oxford, 1937), iii, 1077–8. Borachio was, of course, the drunken associate of Don John in Shakespeare's *Much Ado about Nothing*. The repetition of 'moderate' in the later lines harks back to Higgins's *Sermon Preach'd . . . on Tuesday, the 28th of August*, where the word was repeatedly used in a pejorative fashion.

Of these the famed Borachio is the chief,
a son of pudding, and eternal beef;
the jovial god, with all-inspiring grace,
sits on the scarlet honours of his face;
his happy face, from rigid wisdom free,
securely smiles in thoughtless majesty,
his own tithe geese not half so plump as he.
Wild notions flow from his immoderate head,
and statutes quoted, – moderately read;
whole floods of words his moderate wit reveal,
yet the good man's immoderate in zeal.
How can his fluent tongue and thought keep touch,
who thinks too little, but who talks too much?

The same physical characteristics were lampooned in the *Character of Don Sacheverellio:*[28]

Does the knight [Sacheverell] want a battering ram? Let him push Higginisco against a town, and it shall immediately drop as flat as the walls of Jericho. Would he challenge a miscreant at ever so great a distance? Higginisco shall reach him with his voice from the Thames to the Nile. Does he want a wallet for provisions? Right before Higginisco there struts a large, capacious conveniency, where there is room for provender for the nags and their masters to the fifth generation.

The satirists' view of Higgins as a blunt instrument is not contradicted by the evidence of his own words and actions. The occasional letter survives, and a few printed sermons. They show that he harboured uncomplicated ideas; and expressed them straightforwardly. Nor, it must be said, was there much, if anything, about his views that we might define as distinctively Irish. In pressing the constitutional rights of the Irish convocation, for example, he imitated the campaign of English high churchmen like Francis Atterbury to advance the rights of convocation in England (although some of his wilder statements in defending the corporate privileges of the Church and the clerical estate might have been too extravagant even for Atterbury[29]). The party-political issues he raised in debates in convocation were also drawn from the controversies agitating English politics, as in the session of 1705, when the lower House – with Higgins to the fore – prepared a loyal address that would have equated Marlborough's triumph at Blenheim with the less glorious naval exploits of the tory admiral, Sir George Rooke.[30]

In the pulpit Higgins pursued three main political themes: hatred of schism and schismatics, that is to say protestant dissenters of whatever stamp; revulsion from free-thinking, which he linked with a general collapse of public morals; and a phobia of the whigs, whom he depicted as republicans and regicides. But this standard tory discourse

---

[28] 'Distaff', *Character of Don Sacheverellio*, 16. See also *The High-Church Bully; or, The Praises of Mr Higgins* [1707?] [Madan 146-7]; *The Curtain-Lecture: or, A Dialogue between Mr H–gg–ns and his L–dy, the Night of his Landing . . .* (Dublin, 1707); *A Letter to Mr H–gg–ns, from a Scholar in the University, on Occasion of his Sermon Preach'd at Christ-Church in the Afternoon, Sunday November 16th, 1718* (Dublin, 1718), 8–10, 13–14.

[29] See, e.g., SHC, 1248/2, ff. 178–9: Laurence Clayton to Thomas Brodrick, 12 Mar. 1704/5.

[30] Hayton, *Ruling Ireland*, 136–7; *Records of Convocation*, ed. Gerald Bray (20 vols, Woodbridge, 2006), xvii, pt 1, pp. 116, 129; *Swan Tripe-Club*, 6.

was not adapted in any significant way to an Irish context. Unlike his friend, William Tisdall, who engaged in close polemical combat with Ulster presbyterians, he had nothing particular to say about dissenters in Ireland. In one denunciation of the heretical writers of the age he picked out three who had been hounded from Ireland – John Toland, John Asgill and Thomas Emlyn – but in any case all had achieved equal notoriety in England, and would have been among the more obvious objects of loathing to English high churchmen.[31] Anyone determined to find a local influence in his words might perhaps seize on the way in which he clarified his idealisation of monarchical government, and demonisation of its historical opponents, by deploring 'the despotic power' of French catholic absolutism; perhaps a reflection of the peculiar circumstances of Irish protestants and the greater risks they would run under jacobite, catholic rule.[32] But the dangers of popery, as such, did not figure in his writings, and, in any case, no self-respecting English high-flyer would have neglected to denounce Louis XIV's regime during the War of the Spanish Succession for fear of sounding unpatriotic.

Higgins's horizons were always broader than Ireland. The cause for which he strove was not that of the Church of Ireland specifically, but of 'the Church interest' more generally across the three kingdoms; centred, in fact, on the Church of England. And the context was the long struggle of the loyal and obedient against the malign forces of anti-monarchical faction. 'We must acknowledge it a very valuable happiness', he preached in 1705, 'to live as we do under a monarchy, hereditary and not elective; and so free from those dismal interregnums, popular tumults, and the avarice of heads of parties, which miserably rend and often sell such elective kingdoms, and make them always subject to fatal revolts, and intestine rebellions.' The danger came from:

the dividing and sharing designs of aristocratical statesmen, or the more fatal attempts of the bell-wethers of the populace, men of democratical principles and profession, avow'd and declar'd lovers of liberty, but underhand laying schemes for anarchy and confusion; and consequently for the most severe and cruel tyranny a deluded people ever groan'd under.[33]

The 'Old Cause' and its consequences – tumult and disorder, civil war, regicide, republicanism and 'levelling' – were always to the forefront of his mind. This obsession prompted the belief that the whigs and their allies, 'the schismatics', were constantly 'at their old game', and encouraged a resort to the language of conflict, and even (in the person of King Charles I) martyrdom.

Like Sacheverell, Higgins was a stormy petrel. He thrived on controversy and seems deliberately to have courted persecution for his beliefs. It is not too far-fetched, given what we know of his character, to suggest that he fancied a kinship, however remote, with the royal martyr, and other victims of faction, such as Archbishop Laud. Admittedly his own torments were minor in comparison with theirs, but were heavily written up,

---

[31] Francis Higgins, *A Sermon Preach'd at the Royal Chapel at Whitehall on Ash-Wednesday, Febr. 26, 1706/7* (1708), 9–10.

[32] See, e.g., Higgins, *Sermon Preach'd . . . on Tuesday, the 28th of August*, 6–7.

[33] Higgins, *Sermon Preach'd . . . on Tuesday, the 28th of August*, 6–7.

presumably with a view to personal advancement. In this respect his experiences resembled Sacheverell's, even to the ordeal of incarceration, in which Higgins's suffering actually preceded the Doctor's.

Higgins's first collision with authority was at a diocesan level, when he was asked to represent the chapter of Christ Church in a dispute with Archbishop King over the status of the cathedral as a royal peculiar. King had been translated to Dublin in 1703 and had immediately attempted to exert authority over the dean and chapter.[34] Political differences between the whiggish archbishop and the high-flying canons added spice to the quarrel. In January 1706 Higgins was sent over to London, where King was staying, to offer a possible resolution of the dispute but, unsurprisingly, the archbishop would not sign the paper presented to him.[35] More useful, as far as Higgins was concerned, was the opportunity the visit afforded him to become acquainted with leading high churchmen in England, where the Christ Church case had 'made a great noise'.[36]

A year later Higgins was in England again, and this time he created an even louder splash. In February, together with William Perceval, archdeacon of Cashel, he appeared before the lower house of the convocation of Canterbury to testify to the powers of the convocation in Ireland. The invitation came from unnamed acquaintances among the high church party in England, among them almost certainly Atterbury, to whom Perceval, himself a product of Oxford University, was well known.[37] Certainly, Atterbury made much of their evidence in a later pamphlet, in order to justify his own assertions about the rights of convocation.[38] The celebrity Higgins had acquired in clerical circles resulted in requests to preach in London churches, including St Bride's, Fleet Street, where Atterbury held a lectureship.[39] Then on Ash Wednesday, 26 February, he delivered a sermon in the Chapel Royal at St James's Palace – at whose suggestion is unknown – which landed him in the trouble he may well have been seeking. The content was predictable, at least if his subsequently printed version is accurate: lamentations for the 'crying sins of the nation', especially the words and actions of those denying true religion and promoting 'faction, schism and rebellion', and a reiteration of the high church cry that the Church was in danger, despite parliamentary votes to the contrary.[40]

All this would have been offensive enough to those in power in Church and state, but it was alleged that he went even further. In April the Middlesex grand jury took evidence from an elderly female member of the congregation that she had heard Higgins say: 'those that brought the royal martyr to the scaffold and the block, such as are now preferred to places of the greatest trust in the kingdom'. As a result, the grand jury found a bill against him for sedition. He was arrested and committed for trial at the Old

[34] Kenneth Milne, 'Restoration and Reorganisation, 1660–1830', in *Christ Church Cathedral, Dublin: A History*, ed. Kenneth Milne (Dublin, 2000), 282–3.

[35] TCD, MS 1995–2008/1193: Archbishop King to Robert King, 29 Jan. 1705[/6]. King had been forewarned by a friend, quite unnecessarily, that Higgins was 'a man of no principle', 'a false insinuating fellow', and 'a great party man' (TCD, MS 1995–2008/1188: Lady Dun to King, 10 Jan. 1705/6).

[36] Bodl., MS Eng. Misc. c.23, ff. 54–5: Thomas Smith to Archbishop Marsh, 23 Jan. 1705/6.

[37] Ralph Lambert, *Partiality Detected: or, A Reply to a Late Pamphlet, Entituled, Some Proceedings in the Convocation, A.D. 1705, Faithfully Represented* . . . (1708), 69, 107.

[38] Francis Atterbury, *Some Proceedings in the Convocation* (1708), 26–9.

[39] [Charles Leslie], *A Postscript to Mr. Higgins's Sermon, Very Necessary for the Better Understanding It* . . . ([Dublin, 1707]), 1 (the British Library catalogue attributes this to Charles Leslie).

[40] Higgins, *Sermon Preach'd at the Royal Chapel* . . . *Febr. 26, 1706/7*.

Bailey.[41] However, either because of the unreliability of the witness, or for fear of a backlash that might upset the forthcoming session of the Irish parliament, the attorney-general issued a *nolle prosequi* and he was released.[42] Higgins was quick to print a text of his sermon, adding a defence in which he denied using the words attributed to him, arguing that what his accuser had misheard had been a denunciation of John Toland, who, he had declared:

> revives and publishes the most republican antimonarchical antichristian treatises he can rummage up out of those magazines of sedition and rebellion, fanaticism, and hypocrisy, which brought the purest church in the Christian world to desolation, overturn'd the happiest constitution of government, and brought our Queen's most pious and most glorious grandfather, our never to be forgotten martyr's monarch, to the scaffold and block in forty-eight.[43]

As a further provocation to his enemies, a brief *Postcript* to the sermon was published, consisting of what purported to be a verbatim transcript of an interview with Tenison of Canterbury before the offending sermon, in which Higgins had insolently rejected the archbishop's feeble injunctions to moderate the tone of his preaching.[44]

Although tories could see little wrong in what Higgins had done,[45] the episode infuriated the episcopal hierarchy in Ireland, in particular Primate Marsh,[46] who ensured that the Irish house of lords ordered the *Postcript* to be burned by the hangman.[47] The English whig, Richard Freeman, who held the Irish lord chancellorship, then turned him out of the County Dublin commission of the peace 'at the request of the justices'.[48] But Higgins had achieved his intention in securing maximum personal publicity. He was in England again in the spring of 1709, at the behest of the Christ Church chapter, to take further their suit against Archbishop King.[49] At the same time, the testimony he and William Perceval had given to the convocation in England in 1707 provoked a pamphlet controversy in Ireland,[50] spilling over into the debates of the Irish convocation in 1709, where the two men were the subject of a complaint of breach of privilege that triggered a major confrontation between the whig viceroy, Wharton, and the high church party.[51]

---

[41] Bodl., MS Ballard 7, f. 7: George Smalridge to Arthur Charlett, 1 Mar. 1706/7; *The Prayer of the Reverend Mr Higgins, before His Text, and His Case* (1707), 7–8.

[42] Narcissus Luttrell, *A Brief Historical Relation of State Affairs* . . . (6 vols, 1857), vi, 143, 177; London Metropolitan Archives, MJ/SP/1707: warrant for *cessat processus* against Higgins, [1707].

[43] *The Prayer of the Reverend Mr Higgins*, 7–8.

[44] [Leslie], *A Postscript to Mr. Higgins's Sermon*; see also *Remarks and Collections of Thomas Hearne*, ed. C.W. Doble *et al.* (11 vols, Oxford, 1885–1921), i, 337.

[45] TCD, MS 1995–2008/1249: [Francis Annesley] to Archbishop King, [1707].

[46] Bodl., MS Ballard 36, f. 43: Perceval to Arthur Charlett, 18 Dec. 1707.

[47] *LJ Ireland*, ii, 172–3.

[48] TCD, MS 2531, p. 70: Archbishop King to Mr Peirson, 20 Mar. 1708[/9].

[49] TCD, MS 2531, p. 70: Archbishop King to Mr Peirson, 20 Mar. 1708[/9].

[50] Lambert, *Partiality Detected*; William Perceval, *Remarks upon a Letter Printed in a Pamphlet Intituled, Partiality Detected* . . . (Dublin, 1709); *A Reply to a Vindication of the Letter Published in a Pamphlet called Partiality Detected* . . . (Dublin, 1710).

[51] BL, Add. MS 61634, ff. 106–13: 'A narrative of some late proceedings in the lower house of convocation in Dublin', [1709]; Lambert, *Partiality Detected*, 80–[1].

When the political revolution of 1710 swept the tories into power, Higgins thrust himself back into the public eye. He was already being identified with Sacheverell, not so much because of his personal connection with the Doctor but because of the notoriety of his own 1707 sermon: a mezzotint published in 1710, for example, grouped medallion portraits of Sacheverell, Higgins and another well-known 'tantivy' preacher, Philip Stubbs (rector of St Alphage and St James Garlickhythe, London), under the heading *The 3 Pillars of ye Church*.[52] Then in the winter of 1710–11 Higgins gave strong support to a converted catholic priest and tory agent provocateur, Dominic Langton (whom he may even have employed as a curate in his Dublin parish[53]), when Langton made wild claims about an alleged republican plot among the whig gentry of County Westmeath, based on loose talk overheard from men who had probably had too much to drink.[54] The anti-monarchical emphasis of the accusation reeked of Higgins's personal obsessions with whig 'sedition', and, indeed, Archbishop King thought that Higgins had himself 'drawn up the narrative',[55] which was presented to the Westmeath grand jury in the hope of a presentment, but was rejected.[56] Whigs did not forgive the insult, and in the autumn tried to take their revenge when Higgins, restored to the commission of the peace for County Dublin, appeared at the assize dinner at Kilmainham, and, presumably somewhat intoxicated himself, insulted various whig justices, drank 'confusion to all Dissenters' and, according to one report, insisted that the assembled company join him in a toast to the principle of passive obedience. This was too much for the whigs present, who persuaded the grand jury to bring in a presentment against him as 'a common disturber of her majesty's peace'.[57]

Whig malice had given Higgins just what he wanted: the privilege of victimhood that his friend Sacheverell had enjoyed. The presentment was printed, as was his answer, which he subsequently elaborated in a published *Case*.[58] This purported to give a verbatim transcript of his exchanges with various whig justices – following the precedent of the published conversation with Archbishop Tenison – and included a reference to his earlier period of imprisonment in England, which he 'gloried in'. The whig peer, Lord Barry of Santry, then raised the matter at the Irish privy council, with the intention of having Higgins removed from the bench once more.[59] Barry of Santry and his party colleagues expected that the Castle administration would simply take executive action,

[52] By John Faber, 1710 (British Museum, Satires 1535); see figure 1. Higgins also features in the satirical print 'Needs Must When the Devil Drives: or, An Emblem of What We Must Expect if High-Church Gets Uppermost', [1710] (British Museum, Satires 1496), which shows a horse-drawn carriage bearing 'Perkin' (the pretender) trampling over liberty, property, toleration and moderation. Sacheverell is the postillion and one of the six horses drawing the carriage is named 'Higginisco'.

[53] TCD, MS 1995–2008/1397: Edward Nicholson to Archbishop King, 19 Jan. 1710/11.

[54] Abel Boyer, *The Political State of Great Britain* (60 vols, 1711–40), ii, 346–66; TNA, SP 63/367, ff. 155–6: to [the earl of Dartmouth], 8 Aug. 1711.

[55] *A Great Archbishop of Dublin William King D.D. . . . .*, ed. Sir Charles Simeon King (1906), 125–6.

[56] TCD, MS 2531, p. 307: King to [Edward] Nicholson, 23 Jan. 1710[/11].

[57] TNA, SP 63/367, f. 214: printed grand jury presentment, 5 Oct. 1711; *Post Boy*: 11 Oct. 1711; *Dublin Intelligence*, 13, 23 Oct. 1711.

[58] TNA, SP 63/367, f. 214: printed grand jury presentment, 5 Oct. 1711; *To His Grace James, Duke of Ormonde . . . the Answer of Francis Higgins, Clerk; to a Presentment Made by the Grand Jury of the County of Dublin . . .* (Dublin, 1711); *Mr Higgin's Case* ([Dublin, 1711]). See also *The New Kilmainham Ballad . . .* ([Dublin, 1711]); *The Song. Dr Higgins's deliverance; or, The Rose T—n Cabal Defeated . . .* [Dublin, 1712].

[59] *Daily Courant*: 1 Nov. 1711.

Figure 1: *The 3 Pillars of y^e Church*, by John Faber, 1710; British Museum, Satires 1535. Published by permission of the Trustees of the British Museum.

but instead, in the words of one whig, the tory government 'in the most extraordinary manner made a formal hearing of the thing'.[60] Each side was summoned to the council board, on successive evenings, accompanied by counsel, after which Barry of Santry's petition was dismissed.[61] Predictably, tories had rallied to Higgins's cause. William Perceval declared himself to be amazed that the whigs had embarked upon 'so violent a prosecution' and the lower house of convocation, of which Perceval was prolocutor, passed a resolution vindicating Higgins's conduct.[62] It was said that in Ireland 'every clergyman makes it [Higgins's case] his own'.[63]

This was the high point of Higgins's career. Anxious to make the most of his Sacheverell-like status as a clerical victim of whig vindictiveness, he appeared in London

[60] SHC, 1248/3, ff. 338–40: [Alan Brodrick] to [Thomas Brodrick], 26 Mar. 1715.

[61] SHC, 1248/3, ff. 338–40: [Alan Brodrick] to [Thomas Brodrick], 26 Mar. 1715. See also Christ Church, Arch. W. Epist. xii: Josiah Hort to Bishop Wake, 7 Nov. 1711.

[62] Bodl., MS Ballard 36, f. 70: Perceval to Arthur Charlett, 1 Nov. 1711; TNA, SP 63/367, f. 21: copy of resolution of the lower house of convocation vindicating Higgins, 9 Oct. 1711.

[63] Bodl., MS Ballard 36, f. 70: Perceval to Arthur Charlett, 1 Nov. 1711.

early in the following year, where a publisher produced a detailed account of his tribulations, and he was observed by Swift, 'roaring that all is wrong in Ireland' and seeking the reward he regarded as his due for defending the church.[64] 'I met your Higgins here yesterday', Swift wrote to 'Stella'. 'He roars at the insolence of the Whigs in Ireland, talks much of his own sufferings and expenses in asserting the cause of the church; and I find he would fain plead merit enough to desire that his fortune should be mended. I believe he designs to make as much noise as he can in order to preferment.'[65] But despite the favourable publicity his case attracted among tories in England, and the personal connections he forged with leading figures like Lord Chancellor Harcourt, his persistent solicitations came to nothing.[66] Nor could he engineer another confrontation with his whig enemies, despite offering provocation. In 1713, he and Dean Clayton of Kildare refused to submit to Archbishop King's visitation.[67] Threatened with punitive action for absenting himself from his cure for over two years without licence, Higgins then disputed the archbishop's authority and declared him to be 'a suspected judge from whom he can't expect justice'.[68] But King was wise enough not to take the bait.

The Hanoverian succession, and the collapse of the tory interest in Ireland, left Higgins and his ilk railing impotently against whiggism and declining into obscurity; in Higgins's case the obscurity, as he put it, of a 'little vicarage' in the country.[69] In 1725, as part of the brief tory revival that followed Lord Carteret's appointment as viceroy, he acquired the archdeaconry of Cashel when his old comrade-in-arms, William Perceval, was raised to a deanery. By this time, Higgins's great days were so far behind him that the promotion excited no comment in the press, and he lived quietly as archdeacon until his death three years later.

3

Before the trial of Dr Sacheverell, Constantine Phipps had achieved a degree of professional recognition as a barrister, and, through appearing in several high-profile cases, notably in defence of Sir John Fenwick in 1696, had become a favourite of the jacobite wing of the English tory party. But it was his performance in Sacheverell's trial that made his reputation, and secured for him the office of lord chancellor of Ireland.[70] Like Higgins, his ancestry was relatively ordinary. His father owned the Bear Inn at Reading, a source of amusement to his enemies in Ireland, who drank 'confusion and

---

[64] *A Full and Impartial Account of the Trial of the Reverend Mr F— H— . . . before . . . the Lord Lieutenant and Council of Ireland . . .* (1712); Jonathan Swift, *Journal to Stella*, ed. Harold Williams (2 vols, Oxford, 1948), ii, 540.

[65] Swift, *Journal to Stella*, ed. Williams, ii, 536.

[66] HMC, *Portland MSS*, v, 113: William Perceval to Francis Gastrell, 17 Nov. 1711; HMC, *Portland MSS*, v, 12: Harcourt to [Oxford], 17 June 1711; Christ Church, Arch. W. Epist. xii: Bishop Kennett to Wake, 17 Nov. 1713; G.P. Mayhew, 'Jonathan Swift's "Preferments of Ireland", 1713–14', *Huntington Library Quarterly*, xxx (1966–7), 298.

[67] *An Answer to D[ean] Clayton's Letter* (Dublin, 1713).

[68] TCD, MS 2536, p. 20: Archbishop King to Bishop Crowe, 14 Aug. 1714.

[69] Worcestershire RO, 705:349/4657/v/6: Higgins to Sir John Pakington, 29 Sept. 1717.

[70] For Phipps's background and career, see the biographical entries in ODNB; *Dictionary of Irish Biography*, ed. McGuire and Quinn, viii, 112–14.

Tyburn to the fat bear of Reading'.[71] There was enough money to send his elder brother to Eton, and eventually into the Church, but not enough for Phipps himself, who although he won a scholarship to Oxford, had not the means to take it up. However, he did manage to secure admission to Gray's Inn, after his father's death, and, following his call to the bar, married in 1684 the orphaned niece of the tory attorney-general, Sir Robert Sawyer, whose patronage transformed his prospects.

Having shown himself to be among the more skilful and self-assured of Sacheverell's counsel, Phipps had every right to expect advancement from the incoming tory ministry in 1710. Probably his previous political associations were too extreme for the new chief minister, Robert Harley, to consider giving him a prominent position in England, so instead, in December 1710, he was appointed lord chancellor of Ireland. Along with the office went a knighthood. Phipps quickly gathered an entourage and set off for Dublin, arriving to a chorus of praise from Irish high-flyers on account of the part he had played in Sacheverell's defence.[72] Others, however, moderate tories as well as whigs, were alarmed that someone should be sent over 'who had exerted all his abilities in defence of that unworthy man Dr Sacheverell, and was well known to be violent in his nature and principles and hate a Whig worse than a papist'.[73] His first steps confirmed both sets of contrasting expectations. He had brought with him as a chaplain Sacheverell's friend, Joseph Trapp, a fellow of Wadham College, Oxford, who had already published several pamphlets vindicating Sacheverell from the aspersions of the whigs. Trapp went on the offensive again in Dublin, preaching a sermon before the chief governors at Christ Church on Restoration Day, 1711, which outdid even Higgins in its intemperate denunciations of faction and rebellion.[74] And once in Dublin, Phipps appointed as his other chaplain, John Clayton, the high church dean who had seconded Higgins in his struggles with Archbishop King, and for good measure restored Higgins to the commission of the peace.

Over the next three-and-a-half years, Phipps amply fulfilled tory hopes and whig fears.[75] First, he deployed in a partisan manner both his judicial authority and the opportunities for patronage that the lord chancellorship afforded. The two most serious allegations made against him, of abuse of power, related to a *nolle prosequi* ordered in 1712 in favour of the openly jacobite publisher, Edward Lloyd,[76] and the contrasting vigour with which a young whig, Dudley Moore, was prosecuted for his part in a political disturbance at the Dublin playhouse. Phipps was also accused of remodelling local government – through appoint-

---

[71] 'An Irish Parliamentary Diary from the Reign of Queen Anne', ed. D.W. Hayton, *Analecta Hibernica*, xxx (1982), 40.

[72] Bodl., MS Ballard 8, f. 82: Bishop Lindsay to Arthur Charlett, 11 Jan. 1710/11; *The Church and Monarchy Secur'd, by the Return of His Grace the Duke of Ormonde, and the Change of the Late Ministry* (Dublin, [1711]).

[73] BL, Add. MS 47087, f. 2: Sir John Perceval's journal, Aug. 1711. See also *The Resolutions of the House of Commons in Ireland, Relating to the Lord Chancellor Phipps, Examined . . .* (1714), p. ii.

[74] Joseph Trapp, *A Sermon Preach'd at Christ-Church in Dublin, before Their Excellencies the Lords Justices: on Tuesday, the 29th of May 1711 . . .* (1711), esp. 18–24. He continued in the same vein in 1712, with a pamphlet expounding the importance of maintaining the royal prerogative (S.J. Connolly, 'The Glorious Revolution in Irish Protestant Political Thinking', in *Political Ideas in Eighteenth-Century Ireland*, ed. S.J. Connolly (Dublin, 2000), 54–5). For Trapp, see *ODNB*.

[75] For what follows see Hayton, *Ruling Ireland*, 163–5.

[76] It is interesting to note that, among his many previous offences against political decorum, Lloyd had printed the Irish edition of the *Postcript* to Higgins's sermon of 1707, and been taken into custody by the house of lords on that account (*LJ Ireland*, ii, 173).

ments to county governorships (the equivalent of the English county lord lieutenancy) and the commission of the peace – in the interests of the tory party. But his most controversial actions were those carried out as a member of the Irish privy council and of the commission of lords justices entrusted with the executive power at Dublin castle in the absence of the viceroy. Whether or not he was really able to exercise the kind of dominance over his colleagues in government that his enemies alleged, he certainly gave that impression. Whigs attributed to him (not always justifiably) personal responsibility for a range of policies designed, as they thought, to weaken the protestant interest, from the deliberate running down of the militia to the systematic exploitation of the privy council's supervisory power over the election of chief magistrates in borough corporations.

By the late autumn of 1711, after the first Irish parliamentary session held under the new tory viceroy, the duke of Ormond, Phipps had established himself as the champion of the tory cause in Ireland. He owed this public reputation principally to his aggressive pursuit of party objectives in government, but also, in part, to the continued afterglow of the Sacheverell affair. For example, he was given the thanks of the lower house of convocation in an address which stated that: 'It was your glory to be instrumental in supporting the distressed when it was not only fashionable but meritorious to depress them. Your undaunted courage, your well-tempered zeal, and your moving eloquence, were then most remarkable when they were most necessary.'[77] That Phipps was aware of the value of the prestige attaching to him as Sacheverell's defender is clear from his selection of Trapp as one of his chaplains. He had also observed, and appreciated, the way in which Sacheverell's 'progress' in the summer of 1710 had fostered popularity, and in turn he made a point of showing himself in a similar way to the Irish political nation, assisted by invitations from local tory interests in the Church and borough corporations. In April 1711, having received the freedom of Dublin in a gold box,[78] he travelled – in what was called by Dyer's newsletter a 'progress' – across to the west of Ireland, having 'great honours paid him in all places where he came'. Accompanied by his chaplains, he stayed with his friend, Bishop Thomas Lindsay, at the episcopal palace at Killaloe in County Clare, and was honoured by the mayor and corporation of Limerick – another gold box – and 'entertained . . . after an extraordinary manner'. A dinner with Bishop Smyth of Limerick followed, and the whole event was topped off with a sermon from none other than Francis Higgins, coming home in triumph to his native city.[79] Phipps returned to Dublin via Cashel, where the dean, clergy and gentlemen waited on him, and the corporation entertained him, and then Kilkenny, the seat of the lord lieutenant, Ormond, at which 'he was met by the sheriff and gentlemen of the county, by the dean and clergy and by the mayor and aldermen, in their formalities, and attended both at his coming and going by the duke of Ormond's regiment of horse'.[80] During the parliamentary recess he travelled again with Ormond to Kilkenny, and both were dined by the Kilkenny corporation.[81] In the

---

[77] *Daily Courant*: 16 Nov. 1711; BL, Add. MS 34777, f. 95.

[78] *Calendar of the Ancient Records of Dublin* . . . , ed. J.T. Gilbert (18 vols, Dublin, 1899–1922), vi, 427; *Post Boy*: 10–13 Mar. 1711.

[79] Bodl., MS Ballard 8, f. 90: Bishop Lindsay to Arthur Charlett, 13 Apr. 1711; Worcestershire RO, 705:349/4739/1/i: Dyer's newsletters, 24 Apr., 1 May 1711.

[80] *Post Boy*: 28 Apr. 1711.

[81] Kilkenny corporation archives (NLI, microfilm P.5136): Kilkenny corporation minute book 1690–1717; TNA, SP 63/367, f. 192: Ormond to earl of Dartmouth, 18 Sept. 1711. In Aug. 1711 the corporation of Cork

years following he was welcomed to other towns and admitted as an honorary freeman: the corporations of Naas in 1712 and Drogheda in 1713 both provided a gold box for the occasion, and Drogheda paid for a grand dinner at the corporation's expense.[82]

By the time the Irish parliament met again, in November 1713, party violence in Ireland had risen to unprecedented levels. Ormond's successor as viceroy, the duke of Shrewsbury, a moderate whig, had been sent to Ireland by Lord Treasurer Oxford in a vain hope of achieving consensus, but neither whigs nor tories were willing to compromise, and the whigs interpreted Shrewsbury's proposed concessions as a symptom of weakness. Moreover, the general election called by Shrewsbury produced a house of commons without a clear majority for either party, with moderate tories holding the balance. The whig strategy was to train criticism on Phipps, in order to expose the tories' Achilles heel, the greater impact of the succession issue on opinion in Ireland. Committees were established to inquire into the judicial leniency shown to the jacobite Lloyd and the supposedly unwonted vigour of the prosecution against Moore, and also to report on the repeated failure of the Irish privy council to approve the election of a whig lord mayor of Dublin, a controversy that had polarised opinion, and in which Phipps had, once again, been to the fore. This campaign culminated in a Commons' address to the queen to remove the chancellor, which, in turn, led Shrewsbury to make a sudden adjournment of the session.[83]

The events of the 1713 parliament turned Phipps into a martyr, of a sort. The whig journalist, Abel Boyer, wrote that in England Phipps had 'vast numbers of champions . . . every Tory thinking himself obliged to vindicate him upon account of his zealous adhering to the church's cause, in Dr Sacheverell's trial' and pamphlets were published praising or denouncing him.[84] Tories in Ireland regarded attacks against him as 'malicious' and 'barbarous', and feared that it was the whigs' intention to mount an impeachment.[85] The Commons' demand for his removal was countered by votes in the Lords and in convocation calling for his retention in office, and a string of county addresses, again reminiscent of the events following the trial of Sacheverell, which (to quote the signatories from County Cork) requested the queen to:

Continue your royal countenance and favour to that great minister, whose impartial justice, consummate abilities, and unbyassed affection to the constitution in church and state, are equal to those great trusts, in which Your Majesty's unerring wisdom, for the safety and honour of Your Majesty's interest, and the common good of your people, has placed him.[86]

---

[81] (*continued*) had voted to give him his freedom (in a silver box) if, as expected, he were to visit the city that summer (*The Council Book of the Corporation of the City of Cork: from 1609 to 1643, and from 1690 to 1800*, ed. Richard Caulfield (Guildford, 1876), 348).

[82] TCD, MS 2252: Naas corporation minute book, 3 Oct. 1712; *Post Boy:* 21 Apr. 1713; *Council Book of the Corporation of Drogheda: Vol. 1: From the Year 1649 to 1734*, ed. Thomas Gogarty (Drogheda, 1915), 316.

[83] Hayton, *Ruling Ireland*, 170–6.

[84] Boyer, *Political State*, vi, 364.

[85] Staffordshire RO, D (W)1778/I.ii/449: Francis North to Dartmouth, 19 Dec. 1713; *How Stands Your Succession Now? You Have Made a Fine Kettle of Fish on't* (Dublin, 1714).

[86] *Post Boy:* 28 Jan., 20 May 1714; Boyer, *Political State*, vii, 90; D.W. Hayton, 'Tories and Whigs in County Cork, 1714', *Journal of the Cork Historical and Archaeological Society*, lxxx (1975), 84–8.

The final link in the chain of association that bound Phipps and Sacheverell in the Irish public mind occurred outside Ireland, and after the death of Queen Anne, when Phipps had been removed from office and had returned to England. In October 1714, Oxford University was prevailed on to confer on him a doctorate in civil laws, *honoris causa*. It was rumoured in Ireland that Sacheverell's influence lay behind this decision.[87] The event itself, which by a deliberate irony took place on the day of the coronation of George I, was a mini-festival of Sacheverelliana, the oration being given by none other than Joseph Trapp, who in his speech harked back to Phipps's defence of Sacheverell in 1710.[88] When the news was reported in Ireland, the obvious connections were made, showing that Irishmen were well aware that in lionising Phipps they had been echoing English tory hero-worship of Sacheverell. Archbishop King wrote from Dublin that 'there's a great glorying here among Sir Constantine Phipps's friends of his reception in England, and he is to be the Sacheverell of the law and to pass a circuit in triumph as the doctor did'.[89]

4

We know from the vigorous Dublin reprint trade that the trial of Sacheverell attracted the attention of the reading public in Ireland. It would, indeed, have been surprising if it had not, given the extent to which Irish protestants in the 'first age of party' were fixated upon events in England, and, indeed, viewed their own party struggles as an extension of the English original. Of course, the Doctor never visited Ireland. Had he done so, it is reasonable to suppose that the floodgates of tory emotionalism would have been opened just as they had been in London and the south and midlands of England during Sacheverell's triumphal 'progress' in 1710. This function, however, could be, and indeed was, performed by others: Higgins, Sacheverell's friend, an indigenous high church champion; and Phipps, whose performance at the trial provided a direct line to Sacheverell himself. Although we have no direct evidence of the expression of the protestant *vox populi*, Archbishop King asserted with some confidence in 1714, that the tory mob in Dublin was devoted to 'the doctor and the lawyer', that is to say Sacheverell and Phipps, which suggests that enthusiasm for the lord chancellor was inextricably bound up in the public mind with the figure of the man he had distinguished himself in seeking to protect.[90] Higgins and Phipps each resembled and recalled Sacheverell in their resolve to take a public stand for their beliefs, and to suffer the consequences: to their enemies they were 'roaring' incendiaries, irresponsible and dangerous; but to fellow

[87] TCD, MS 1995–2008/1535, 1544: Lord Mountjoy to [Archbishop King], 16 Oct., 13 Nov. 1714.

[88] Bodl., Add. MS a.269, p. 36: Edmund Gibson to Bishop Nicolson, 30 Oct. 1714.

[89] TCD, MS 2536, p. 105: King to Mountjoy, 2 Nov. 1714.

[90] TCD, MS 2536, p. 122: King to Mountjoy, 24 Nov. 1714. In 1713 a presentment was brought in by the Dublin grand jury against a whig attorney, Richard Nuttall, for words spoken to one Joseph Cooper and his young son, to the effect that Phipps was 'a canary bird and villain and had set the kingdom together by the ears and ought to be hanged' (an incident that was also taken notice of in the Irish house of lords). Allegedly Nuttall went on to inquire of Cooper *fils* whether he was a whig or a tory. When the boy prevaricated Nuttall asked 'if he loved Dr Sacheverell and the lord chancellor', the affirmative answer to which brought forth another volley of abuse. See *LJ Ireland*, ii, 437–8; Sir Richard G.A. Levinge, *Jottings of the Levinge Family* (Dublin, 1877), 55: Sir Richard Levinge to Edward Southwell, 13 Feb. 1713/14; Public Record Office of Northern Ireland, DIO/4/5/3/55.

tories they set an inspiring example of political and personal courage. Moreover, each had learned lessons from the Sacheverell impeachment and its aftermath, in terms of the way that a political issue could be presented to the public for maximum impact. Higgins courted controversy and exploited victimhood just as Sacheverell had done, without quite achieving the notoriety of his exemplar, while Phipps, who perhaps had victimhood thrust upon him rather than actively seeking it, understood the effect of the Doctor's 'progress' sufficiently to imitate it. The notion that tories in Ireland were wary of aligning themselves with one who had supposedly preached against the revolution does not really seem credible given their support for others with equally extreme views. But even if they had been cautious of doing so, there was, in truth, little need for them to make much of Sacheverell, when the same function – the identification of a political cause with a particular individual, and the manipulation of emotions in support of a political martyr – could be carried out so effectively by others.

APPENDIX: *'Sacheverelliana' Published in Dublin, 1709–15*

The place of publication is Dublin only, unless otherwise stated.

1709
——, *A Letter to Mr Bisset, Eldest Brother of the Collegiate Church of St Catherine's: in Answer to His Remarks on Dr Sacheverell's Sermon* (London; repr. Dublin) [Madan 102].

1710
——, *Aminidab; or The Quaker's Vision, Explain'd and Answer'd Paragraph by Paragraph* . . . (London; repr. Dublin) [Madan 422].
——, *Further Arguments and Debates in the House of Lords, against Dr. Henry Sacheverel, for High Crimes and Misdemeanors* . . . (London; repr. Dublin) [Madan 122].
——, *Dr. Sacheverell Turn'd Oculist, or, Sir William Read's Lamentation for the Loss of his Business* . . . (London; repr. Dublin) [Madan 480, London edn, no Dublin repr. listed].
——, *An Impartial Account of What Pass'd Most Remarkable in the Last Session of Parliament; Relating to the Case of Dr. Henry Sacheverell* (London; repr. Dublin) [Madan 459, London edn, no Dublin repr. listed].
——, *A Letter from an Honest Whigg in North Britain, to His Friend in Dublin; Concerning Doctor Sacheverell, and the Pretender's Landing in Scotland* [Madan 634].
——, *A Letter to Dr. Sacheverell, Suppos'd to be Written by St. James, the First Bishop of Jerusalem* (London; repr. Dublin) [Madan 306].
——, *A Speech without Doors* (London; repr. Dublin) [Madan 376].
——, *The Speeches of Four Managers upon the First Article of Dr. Sacheverell's Impeachment* (London; repr. Dublin) [Madan 415, London edn, no Dublin repr. listed].
——, *A Supplement to The Faults on Both Sides, Containing the Compleat History of the Proceedings of a Party* . . . *And to Shew How Far the Late Parliament were Right in Proceeding against Dr. Sacheverell, by Way of Impeachment* (London and Dublin) [Madan, not listed].
——, *The Trial and Condemnation of Daniel Damaree, one of the Queens Watermen, for High Treason* . . . [Madan, not listed].
——, *A True Answer; or, Remarks upon Dr. Sacheverell's Sermon, March 7th, 1710* . . . (London; repr. Dublin) [Madan 269].

——, *A True List of the Names of the Peers who gave Judgment in Dr. Sacheverel's Tryal, March the 20th, 1709/10* (London; repr. Dublin) [Madan 774, London edn, no Dublin repr. listed].

——, *The Tryal of Doctor Henry Sacheverell, before the House of Peers, for High Crimes and Misdemeanours . . .* (London; repr. Dublin) [Madan 468].

Burnet, Gilbert, *The Bishop of Salisbury His Speech in the House of Lords, on the First Article of the Impeachment of Dr. Henry Sacheverell* (London; repr. Dublin) [Madan 322].

Sacheverell, Henry, *The Speech of Henry Sacheverell, D.D., Made in Westminster Hall on Tuesday, March 7, 1709/10* (London; repr. Dublin) [Madan 265].

Thompson, John, Lord Haversham, *The Lord H[aversham]'s Speech in the House of Lords, on the First Article of the Impeachment of Dr. Henry Sacheverell* (London; repr. Dublin) [Madan 576].

Tilly, William, *A Return to Our Former Good Old Principles and Practice, the Only Way to Restore and Preserve Our Peace. A Sermon Preached before the University of Oxford . . . on . . . May the 14th 1710 . . . With a Letter to Dr. Sacheverell* (Oxford; repr. Dublin) [Madan 458].

1711

——, *The Memorial of the Church of England; with an Impartial Account of What Pass'd Most Remarkable at the Tryal of Dr. Sacheverell* [Madan 463].

King, William, *A Vindication of the Reverend Dr. Henry Sacheverell, from the False, Scandalous and Malicious Aspersions Cast upon Him in a Late Infamous Pamphlet, Entitled The Modern Fanatick . . .* (London; repr. Dublin) [Madan 995].

1713

Sacheverell, Henry, *A Sermon Preach'd before the Honourable House of Commons, at St. Margaret's Westminster, on Friday, May 29 1713* (London; repr. Dublin) [Madan, not listed].

Sacheverell, Henry, *The Christian Triumph: or, The Duty of Praying for Our Enemies . . . in a Sermon Preach'd at S. Saviour's in Southwark, on Palm-Sunday, 1713* (London; repr. Dublin) [Madan 1068].

1715

——, *Sharp Rebuke from One of the People called Quakers to Henry Sacheverell, the High-Priest of St. Andrew's Holborn . . .* (London; repr. Dublin) [Madan 1119-21; no Dublin repr. listed].

Addison's Empire: Whig Conceptions of Empire in the Early 18th Century

STEVE PINCUS

Why did whigs consider the Treaty of Utrecht to be an imperial disaster? Contemporary scholarship makes this a difficult question to answer. Imperial historians insist that it was an imperial triumph. While political historians point to rough-and-tumble party politics that was not about empire. This article aims to recover the rich intellectual history of party political debate about empire in the age of Anne. I suggest that there was bitter conflict between tories who sought territorial empire based on South American mines, and whigs who sought a manufacturing empire based on penetrating South American markets with British manufactures. The Sacheverell trial and its aftermath marked a turning point in British imperial policy. As a result the whigs felt betrayed, venting their anger in the immediate aftermath of the Hanoverian succession.

Keywords: empire; South Sea Company; earl of Oxford; Viscount Bolingbroke; Charles Davenant; Henry Martin; Buenos Aires; Treaty of Utrecht; whig; tory; Sacheverell; Spain; France; New England; Arthur Maynwaring; Jonathan Swift

1

This article examines the corpus of ideas about empire upon which the new tory government drew once it took office in the wake of the Sacheverell affair in 1710 and the rival set of ideas offered by the whigs. It thus explores the ways in which domestic and foreign policy debates intertwined, but also how the rage of party was not simply about religious and constitutional issues. The article seeks to show how the partisanship that had come to a head in 1710 also permeated and shaped conceptions of empire and political economy, and that 1710 had marked a dramatic temporary turning point in imperial visions.

From the whig perspective 1710 witnessed an imperial, as well as a domestic, disaster, leading to the tory-negotiated peace of 1713 which threw away Marlborough's battle-field gains. 'We engaged in the late war with a design to reduce an exorbitant growth of power in the most dangerous enemy to Great-Britain', wrote Joseph Addison in his widely-distributed and eagerly-read periodical, *The Free-Holder*. 'We gained a long and wonderful series of victories, and had scarce anything left to do, but to reap the fruits of them: When on a sudden our patience failed us; we grew tired of our undertaking; and received terms from those who were upon the point of giving us whatever we could have demanded of them.'[1] Why did the whigs believe that the treaties putting an end to the War of the Spanish Succession was an imperial betrayal? Why did they believe that a peace 'granting us', in the words of one fictional tory freeholder, 'Gibraltar, the island of Minorca, St. Christopher's, Hudson's Bay and Straits, Newfoundland, and Nova Scotia' was an imperial disaster?[2] What exactly was the whig imperial project that was abandoned by the earl of Oxford's tory ministry?

Unfortunately the existing scholarship makes it very difficult to answer these questions. Scholars have either insisted that there was a single coherent British imperial policy over which there was little party conflict, or there was party conflict that had little to do with imperial policy.

By and large, scholars who have not focused on high politics have highlighted the coherence of British imperial strategy.[3] Britons across the political spectrum, asserts Linda Colley, remembered the War of the Spanish Succession as a great imperial triumph. 'In return for its participation in the War of Spanish Succession', Colley observes, echoing the views of early-18th-century tories, 'Britain won Gibraltar, Minorca, Nova Scotia, Newfoundland, Hudson's Bay, and trading concessions in Spanish America.' It was this imperial triumph 'that led merchants throughout Britain to push for another war against Spain in the late 1730s'. Britons shared a sense of imperial accomplishment after 1713, in Colley's view, because they shared an understanding of the nature of political economy. 'Most' British patricians, she explains, 'took it for granted that the world's supply of raw materials and markets was strictly finite, that competition to win access to them was bound to be intense, and that if British traders were to succeed in the struggle, they must be vigorously supported abroad and protected at home.'[4]

Political historians argue that the Treaty of Utrecht was a tory, but not an imperial, peace. 'It is doubtful whether any other matter so continuously aggravated relations between Whig and Tory from 1708 to 1712 as the making of peace', insists Geoffrey Holmes. But the issues that divided the two parties were whether there should be a Bourbon on the Spanish throne and whether the peace ending the war should be negotiated jointly with all the members of the Grand Alliance.[5]

In contrast to these views, I suggest that there was a vital and intellectually-sophisticated party political debate over political economy and empire in the late 17th and early 18th centuries.[6] While almost all of the participants in the party political

---

[1] Joseph Addison, *The Free-Holder*, xix, no. 25, p. 178: 16 Mar. 1716 (from repr. 1758 edn). *The British Merchant*, ed. Charles King (3 vols, 1721), iii, 268. The journal was produced by a syndicate of merchants, but King later wrote that Henry Martin 'had the greatest hand in them'. Charles Montagu, earl of Halifax, and junto whig, 'was the support and very spirit of the paper', was central to its intellectual missions, and bankrolled the journal: King, *The British Merchant*, i, pp. xiv, xvi; Perry Gauci, *The Politics of Trade* (Oxford, 2001), 256.

[2] *A Letter from a Tory Freeholder* (1712), 16.

[3] I have not included the careful work of B.W. Hill in this discussion because his argument focuses more on emphasizing the earl of Oxford's central role in a peace process which he describes as fundamentally 'pragmatic': B.W. Hill, 'Oxford, Bolingbroke and the Peace of Utrecht', *Historical Journal*, xvi (1973), 263; Brian W. Hill, *Robert Harley: Speaker, Secretary of State and Prime Minister* (New Haven, CT, 1988), 159–92.

[4] Linda Colley, *Britons* (New Haven, CT, 1992), 62–4, 70–1.

[5] Geoffrey Holmes, *British Politics in the Age of Anne* (1967), 75–81.

[6] It should be clear from what follows that I have learned a great deal from the work of Istvan Hont and Brendan Simms. While I have subtle differences with both of them – I emphasize party and economic principles more than Hont does and unlike Simms I believe political economic and imperial concerns were as important as

wrangling over the War of the Spanish Succession agreed that Britain was a trading nation, they disagreed, and disagreed vociferously, about the proper nature of that trade. As a consequence, whigs and tories developed competing ideals of empire. There was no shared vocabulary with which early-18th-century Britons discussed empire and political economy. And, I suggest, the only way to make sense of that conflict is to accept that party ideology in the early 18th century was constituted as much by economic as by moral philosophical argument. Economic ideas mattered. The signing of the tory Treaty of Utrecht instantiated a party political debate about empire that was to reverberate throughout the 18th century.

2

Party politics permeated everyday life in the early 18th century. While there were certainly some values that most Britons shared, this was not an age of ideological consensus. Party divisions were manifest in parliamentary debates, local elections, company committee meetings, dramatic productions, and coffee-house discussions.

Despite a variety of complex high political manœuvres, party political tensions remained high throughout the War of the Spanish Succession. 'Whig and Tory are as of old implacable', commented Matthew Prior just before the war broke out.[7] The British were 'a nation so divided into parties', wrote the politically-enigmatic former paymaster of the queen's forces, James Brydges, in 1714, 'that no one is allowed any good quality by the opposite side'.[8]

Party divisions cut deeply into British society. Party politics was not a game played only by a rarified metropolitan elite. 'The general division of the British nation is into Whigs and Tories', concluded Joseph Addison, 'there being very few, if any, who stand neuters in the dispute, without ranging themselves under one of these denominations.'[9]

Party political dispute in the late 17th and early 18th centuries was as much about political economy as it was about religion and the constitution. Thousands of Britons now had access to political economic information. Daniel Defoe's *Review* and Charles Povey's *General Remark on Trade* reached thousands of readers each, multiple times per week, in the first decade of the 18th century. Their circulation numbers were almost certainly dwarfed by the wildly-popular competitors, the *Mercator* – a joint Davenant and Defoe production – and Henry Martin's *British Merchant*.[10]

Given the intensity of party conflict, it was hardly surprising that debates over political economy and empire were quickly politicised. Fierce debates in quick succession in the later 1690s over the creation of the board of trade, the Scottish scheme to establish a

[6] *(continued)* were European ones – I am much closer to their perspectives than to most of those who have dealt with the subject.

[7] Yale University, Beinecke Library, OSB MSS fc 37/2/67: Matthew Prior (London) to earl of Manchester, 13 Nov. 1699.

[8] Huntington Library, San Marino, CA, HEH, ST 57/11, p. 10: James Brydges to Nicholas Philpott, 29 Sept. 1714.

[9] *The Free-Holder*, no. 19, p. 107: 24 Feb. 1716; no. 54, p. 379: 25 June 1716.

[10] Gauci, *Politics of Trade*, 165.

colony at Darien in the West Indies, the renewal of the East India Company charter, and ultimately over whether to go to war to prevent the Bourbons from taking over the wealth of Spanish America, helped to map imperial issues onto party politics. 'As of late many controversies have arisen in the English nation', observed a Virginian in 1701, 'so 'tis observable that the two great topics of trade and plantations have had their parts in the dispute.'[11] Addison was convinced that the dispute over whether Britain could make peace without the Spanish West Indies 'has fixed all men in their proper parties'.[12]

Party political dispute in the early 18th century was in large part about political economy and trade. 'Party configurations after 1688' cannot be reduced, as Linda Colley and Mark Goldie have done, to 'attitudes to the Anglican church and the tradition of [the] "mixed constitution" '.[13] 'I divide the care and concern of the nation among these generals, religion, constitution and commerce', explained Daniel Defoe a decade later. 'Trade', he said, 'I rank hand in hand with religion and constitution.'[14] The nature of 18th-century British political thought in general, the contours of the British empire, and the dispute over the peace of Utrecht can only be fully understood if we accord political economy its proper role.

3

What then was the tory theory of empire?

Charles Davenant was the chief tory economic spokesman of the early 18th century. By the early 18th century Davenant had emerged, according to his modern biographer, as 'the leading Tory pamphleteer'. His economic ideas, his close connections with tory City merchants, and his pointed attacks on whig politicians and whig policies all endeared him to leading tory politicians. Unsurprisingly, Robert Harley, who had long been one of Davenant's patrons, helped secure for him the post of inspector-general of imports and exports in June 1703.[15]

Charles Davenant was deeply committed to the notion that national wealth was finite. He agreed, along with Josiah Child and the previous generation of tory economic thinkers, that England needed to engage in overseas commerce. Like them he did not believe in the possibility of infinite economic growth. 'The wealth of a country is finite,

---

[11] *An Essay upon the Government of the English Plantations on the Continent* (1701), 1–2.

[12] Beinecke Lib., Osborn fc 37/13/33: Joseph Addison (Cock-Pit) to Manchester, 27 Feb. 1708.

[13] Linda Colley and Mark Goldie, 'The Principles and Practice of Eighteenth-Century Party', *Historical Journal*, xxii (1979), 243–4.

[14] Daniel Defoe, *Review*, iv, no. 147, p. 588: 20 Jan. 1708.

[15] This paragraph is based on: David Waddell, 'Charles Davenant (1656–1714) – A Biographical Sketch', *Economic History Review*, new ser., xi (1958), 279–88; David Waddell, 'Charles Davenant and the East India Company', *Economica*, new ser., xxiii (1956), 261–4; Istvan Hont, *Jealousy of Trade* (Cambridge, MA, 2005), 201; Beinecke Lib., Osborn fc 37/2/67: Matthew Prior (London) to Manchester, 13 Nov. 1699; Beinecke Lib., OSB MSS 2/Box 2/Folder32: William Blathwayt (Whitehall) to George Stepney, 20 Mar. 1701; Huntington Lib., HEH, ST 58/6, p. 49: Charles Davenant (London) to James Brydges, 12 June 1710; HEH, ST 58/6, p. 65: William Aubrey (London) to James Brydges, 21 June 1710; HEH, ST 58/12, p. 50: Reinier Leers (Rotterdam) to James Brydges, 3 June 1712 ns.

as well as the substance of any private man', he explained.[16] 'There is a limited stock of our own product to carry out, beyond which there is no passing', Davenant elaborated.[17]

Given Davenant's economic premises, shared by Child and other tory writers, the key to England's economic prosperity was to buy cheap and sell dear. This meant, above all, importing overseas products – whether from the East or West Indies, and selling them for a profit on European markets. 'There can be no greater profit to this kingdom than what arises from the vent abroad of what our industry brings to us from other countries', he explained to the tory government in 1711.[18] The 'West and East-India trades', and *not* our 'home product', in Davenant's view, 'have so enlarged our stock, as to get the general balance for many years on our side, notwithstanding all our luxuries'.[19]

Since Davenant believed trade to the Indies was vital to England's, and later Britain's, economic survival, he argued repeatedly that the government should do everything it could to consolidate its imperial holdings. Since slave labour was 'the principal foundation of our riches' in the tobacco and sugar colonies, Davenant argued that 'all probable measures' should be taken to import them on 'easy terms'.[20] Instead of allowing the West Indies to become trading centres, Davenant advocated building 'forts and citadels for security'.[21] Just as Davenant had insisted on the necessity of the East India Company to fortify itself in India in the face of European competition, so he advocated militarising the empire in the Caribbean.

Davenant was just as contemptuous of the northern American colonies as he was enthusiastic about the tobacco and sugar colonies. Should the New Englanders 'pretend to set up manufactures', it would surely prove 'of pernicious consequence'. In particular, Davenant worried that 'by supine negligence, or mistaken measures' New Englanders would begin their own shipping industry. 'Such courses', he opined, would 'drive 'em, or put it into their heads, to erect themselves into independent commonwealths.'[22] Davenant very much hoped that the North American colonies could be drawn into 'a narrower compass' producing only 'commodities not to be had in Europe'.[23]

Davenant's, and by extension the tory, vision of empire was one of hierarchical dependence. He insisted on the radical distinction between the English metropole and the colonial periphery. Were the empire properly organised, he suggested, the colonies 'will be a lasting revenue to the King, an inexhaustible mine of treasure to England in general, and a great means to multiply seamen, and increase our navigation'. But this could only be achieved by keeping the colonies 'dependent upon their Mother country' and not allowing 'those laws upon any account, to be loosened, whereby they are tied to it'.[24]

[16] Charles Davenant, *An Essay upon the Probable Methods of Making a People Gainers in the Ballance of Trade* (1699), 136.

[17] Charles Davenant, *Discourses on the Public Revenues and Trade of England* (2 vols, 1698), ii, 211, 316.

[18] BL, Add. MS 17767, f. 8: Charles Davenant, 'Report of Charles Davenant on the Trade between England and Holland', 1711. I am grateful to Chris Dudley for this reference.

[19] Davenant, *Discourses*, ii, 212.

[20] Davenant, *Discourses*, ii, 255–6.

[21] Davenant, *Discourses*, ii, 254–5.

[22] Davenant, *Discourses*, ii, 105–6, 207, 226–7.

[23] Davenant, *Discourses*, ii, 233.

[24] Davenant, *Discourses*, ii, 207, 231.

Because Davenant believed that national wealth was primarily generated by carrying cheap goods over long distances to places where they could be sold for large profits, he necessarily believed that Britain's chief economic rival was the United Provinces.[25]

Davenant and the tories did not believe that the French were as great a threat. This was in part, as Doowan Ahn has suggested, because the 'French form of government – French absolutism – precluded them from transforming their country into a lasting trading empire.'[26] But Davenant's principle argument was an economic one: nations turned to foreign trade when they had exhausted their native resources.[27] 'The Low Countries were the first straightened in territory', Davenant calculated, so they were 'the first compelled to seek for the reliefs that are to be had from an extended commerce.'[28] Increases in English population forced them to turn to overseas commerce at the end of Elizabeth's reign. But in the French case, the extent of their territory and the decline of population subsequent to the revocation of the Edict of Nantes, meant that 'there will lie no necessity upon 'em to enlarge their foreign commerce'.[29] Because the English and the Dutch were under severe land limitations at home they were natural trading rivals. The logic of Davenant's, and the tories', land-based political economy implied that the French were not England's primary economic competitors. If the English/British economy was well managed, Davenant concluded, the French 'nation will never be able to overtake us in trade'.[30]

Davenant's economic principles led him to outline his vision for a tory territorial empire that would transcend the Spanish empire. The Spanish were right, in Davenant's view, to have sought and seized the American silver mines. Their mistake was 'the strict prohibition' on exporting 'the species' which proved 'an early bar to industry and rendered their treasure useless to the body of the people'. Had they understood that gold and silver were merely 'a commodity' it 'must have put 'em upon methods of turning it to more advantage'. Had the Spanish made proper use of their American mines, Davenant concluded, 'by the help of that vast treasure they were masters of, they might have carried the whole commercial world before 'em'.[31]

The tories believed that at long last they had a chance to reverse centuries of imperial neglect. The early Tudors, tories argued, following Davenant's logic, had abdicated to the Spanish the opportunity to seize the fabulously rich gold and silver mines of South America. 'It was the great oversight and neglect of Henry the 7th that rejected the offers of Christopher Columbus', opined one tory pamphleteer; had the first Tudor monarch not neglected this opportunity, 'what wealth and riches [would] the mines of gold and silver [have] brought into our country'.[32] When Jonathan Swift complained that the

[25] John Shute Barrington, *A Dissuasive from Jacobitism* (1713), 31.

[26] Doohwan Ahn, 'The Anglo-French Treaty of Commerce of 1713', *History of European Ideas*, xxxvi (2010), 180.

[27] Davenant, *Discourses*, ii, 365.

[28] Davenant, *Discourses*, ii, 368.

[29] Davenant, *Discourses*, ii, 370.

[30] Davenant, *Discourses*, i, 203.

[31] Davenant, *Discourses*, ii, 362–3.

[32] *The Considerable Advantages of a South-Sea Trade* ([1711]), 3. One South Sea Company advocate blamed the neglect on earlier English monarchs who had failed to capitalise on a prince of Wales's discovery of America 'long before the days of Christopher Columbus', perhaps around 1190: BL, Add. MS 70163, f. 249r: An Essay

whigs 'have not enlarged our dominions by one foot of land' in 1712, he had his eyes firmly fixed on the vast riches of the South American mines.[33]

By the end of the 1690s, then, the tories behind the intellectual leadership of Charles Davenant were developing a coherent and sophisticated imperial ideology. Since Davenant and the tories believed that the world's resources were limited, it was essential that England could dominate markets by importing valuable commodities and re-exporting them to Europe for vast profits. The only way to guarantee such a possibility was to garrison the valuable tobacco and sugar colonies, and to seize South American mines. England should model its imperial governance on the Spanish council of the Indies, in Davenant's view, because 'whoever considers the laws and politic institutions of Spain, will find them as well formed, and contrived with as much skill and wisdom, as in any country perhaps in the world'.[34] England would defeat its Dutch competitors by mimicking the Spanish empire in every way but one. The English should allow bullion to be exported.

4

Not everyone accepted the tory vision of empire in the early 18th century. Not everyone accepted that the key to prosperity lay in seizing South American gold and silver and exporting it to India and Indonesia. Not everyone agreed that Spanish political and economic institutions should be admired and imitated. In fact, in the first two decades of the 18th century, the whigs outlined a radically-different vision of empire, a vision that drew its ideological energy from a radically-different set of economic principles.

The whigs advocated an integrated commercial empire in which the key to prosperity and power was human labour. Unlike most tories, the whigs did not believe that the world's economic resources were finite, delimited by the amount of land in the world. Britain's economic future depended on the value that labour could add to raw materials, not in monopolising the raw materials themselves. 'The enjoyment of all societies will ever depend upon the fruits of the earth and the labour of the people', argued the whig political economist, Bernard Mandeville. Raw materials mixed with labour, insisted Mandeville in a telling comparison in the context of the War of the Spanish Succession, 'are a more certain, a more inexhaustible and a more real treasure than the gold of Brazil, or the silver of Potosi'.[35]

During the War of the Spanish Succession the whigs gave their labour-based political economy an imperial twist. Since at least the 1680s, whig polemicists had been arguing that labour, rather than land, was the basis of property, that property was, therefore,

---

[32] (*continued*) on the Nature and Methods of Carrying on a Trade to the South Sea, 1711. The tories understood the Tudor failure not as having set the British on an imperial course that would always differ substantively from the Spanish, but as a choice that could be reversed. Cf. J.H. Elliott, *Empires of the Atlantic World* (New Haven, CT, 2006), 411.

[33] Jonathan Swift, *Some Remarks on the Barrier Treaty* (2nd edn, 1712), 21. Thus if Ian Higgins is right to highlight Swift's 'denunciation of colonialism' in the 1720s, it was a newfound anti-imperialism: Ian Higgins, 'Jonathan Swift's Political Confession', in *Politics and Literature in the Age of Swift*, ed. Claude Rawson (Cambridge, 2010), 15.

[34] Davenant, *Discourses*, ii, 240.

[35] Bernard Mandeville, *The Fable of the Bees* (1714), 178–9.

infinite, and that territorial empire therefore made little sense. John Locke, for example, had maintained that 'ninety-nine hundredths' of the valuable goods in the world were owing to human 'labour'. Still, he did not think that labour in the Americas was worth nearly that much. In the 'waste of America', he reckoned, 'a thousand acres yield the needy and wretched inhabitants as many conveniencies of life, as ten acres of equally fertile land in Devonshire'.[36] In 1708, in *The British Empire in America*, the tract that more than any other detailed the whig imperial ideology, the whig polemicist, John Oldmixon, revised Locke's assessment. While Oldmixon, like Locke, believed that labour, not land, was the basis of property, he was far more optimistic about the political economic significance of the Americas. Two decades of development had radically improved the value of Britain's colonies in America. 'A labourer in our American colonies', Oldmixon argued, is 'of more advantage to England though out of it, than any 130 of the like kind can be in it.' Oldmixon's statistical analysis revealed 'that one hand in the plantations is as good as twenty employed at home'.[37] In the American plantations, argued a Virginian in a tract published anonymously by the whig printer and imperial specialist, Richard Parker, 'every man' was 'of great value to England and most of those that come are not able to do much good at home'.[38]

The radical whig political economist, Henry Martin, emphasized that it was precisely by taking advantage of the greater value of labour overseas that the English could guarantee infinite economic growth. Since labour was less expensive in the American plantations or the East Indies, since the value produced by labourers was higher, it made sense to rely on overseas products rather than on more expensive 'manufactures made in England'. Because England's high wages were relatively inelastic, because highly-paid English labourers would be unwilling to accept pay cuts, consumption of goods produced overseas 'may be the cause of doing things with less labour'. Martin was not merely speaking of an industrious revolution, a division of labour that would produce things more inexpensively, he was envisioning a technological revolution. Importation of goods produced with 'less and cheaper labour than would be necessary to make the like in England', Martin suggested, would 'likely be the cause of the *invention* of arts and mills, and engines to save the labour of hands in other manufactures'. Martin's logic was clear. If the colonies could produce goods using less expensive labour, they would encourage Britons to innovate in other areas so that 'the labour will be less, the price of it will be less, though the wages of men should be as high as ever'.[39]

Mandeville, Oldmixon and Martin argued, along with most economic whigs, that economic growth depended on a complex interplay between production and consumption. It was not enough merely to produce goods. The British economy depended on consumers with increasingly high wages and increasingly sophisticated tastes to generate demand for its manufactures. British colonists in America had a voracious demand for British manufactures. Of course, the rapidly growing populations of the northern colonies as they

[36] *John Locke: Second Treatise of Government*, ed. C.B. Macpherson (Indianapolis, 1980), ch. 5, paras 37, 40, pp. 24–5.

[37] John Oldmixon, *The British Empire in America* (2 vols, 1708), i, pp. xxii, xxvi, xxx.

[38] 'An American', *An Essay upon the Government of the English Plantations on the Continent* (1701), 10.

[39] Henry Martin, *Considerations upon the East-India Trade* (1701), 56, 65–7, 72–3. Martin's arguments here are applied to the East India trade, later in the pamphlet he makes it clear that the same logic applies to New England.

developed their own industries and agriculture, had even greater reason than had their southern neighbours to import British goods. Oldmixon, therefore, exclaimed that "tis certain our American plantations take off more of the manufactures of England than any other foreign trade whatsoever'.[40] Daniel Defoe argued for 'improving and extending our colonies and trade in America, Africa, and Muscovy, in order to increase the consumption of our manufactures, and secure an employ to our people, let the accidents of war be what they will'.[41]

Since labour was the basis of wealth, since colonial consumption was central to driving innovation in English/British manufactures, early-18th-century whigs came to very different conclusions about the value of Britain's American possessions than did their tory opponents. Where Davenant had praised the tobacco and sugar colonies and lusted after South American mines, while demeaning the value of New England, whigs argued for the great economic potential of the northern colonies.[42] 'Ships are built in the plantations of cheaper materials, and might also [be] by cheaper labour', agreed Henry Martin, 'materials there for building are cheaper'. 'If ships of materials a great deal cheaper might be built in our plantations by labour of half the price that must be given in Holland', reasoned Martin, 'they must needs be cheaper, and possibly by 20 or 30 per cent.' The benefits to England would be tremendous. Soon the English would 'become the carriers of the world'.[43] Why had the New England shipping industry not yet allowed the British to become independent of Baltic naval stores? The answer, according to Daniel Defoe, could be found in the imperial analysis of tories like Charles Davenant. 'This court whimsy' of keeping colonies dependent on the metropole 'has for 20 years before the Revolution been the bane of our colonies' prosperity. New England had by this time been our storehouse for naval provisions, and a nursery of seamen, and perhaps been twice the magnitude it is now of, but for this fatal and most preposterous jealousy.'[44]

Whereas Davenant and the tories advocated a hierarchically-organised empire in which the colonies provided raw materials and only raw materials that could not be found in Britain, the whigs hoped for an economically and politically integrated empire. Because they believed that the British economy would best be served by taking advantage of higher labour values in the New World, they saw no reason to subordinate the interests of the plantations to those of the metropole. Indeed they rejected any such distinction. John Oldmixon shared with Edward Littleton, whom he quoted liberally and approvingly, the belief that the colonies must be treated as they had been before the restoration of the monarchy in 1660 as 'a part of England' rather than as 'foreigners and aliens'.[45] 'To make our colonies [in America] rich, great, populous and strong', wrote Defoe, 'is the only way to secure them to you forever, and effectually to prevent the Independency' the tories so feared.[46] Whigs argued that the colonies in the New World should have political as well as

[40] Oldmixon, *British Empire*, i, pp. xxv, xxxii; ii, 345. For Smith, see Adam Smith, *The Wealth of Nations*, ed. Edward Canaan (New York, 2000), 671–5 (book iv, chapter vii, part iii).
[41] *Review*, iv, no. 149, p. 595: 24 Jan. 1708. Addison made the point more generally about the importance of consumption in the *Guardian*, no. 9, p. 56: 21 Mar. 1713.
[42] *Review*, iv, no. 135, pp. 539–40: 23 Dec. 1707; vi, no. 46, p. 182: 19 July 1709.
[43] Martin, *Considerations*, 115, 117–18, 121–2.
[44] *Review*, iv, no. 126, p. 504: 2 Dec. 1707.
[45] Edward Littleton, *The Groans of the Plantations* (1689), 1.
[46] *Review*, iv, no. 141, pp. 563–4: 6 Jan. 1708.

economic rights. The Americans, argued one whig, should have 'a true representation in England' so that 'the true state of affairs in America' could be understood.[47]

Whig political economy led to macro-political conclusions radically different from those advanced by Davenant and the tories. Whereas, Davenant, Swift, Robert Harley, Henry St John and other tories were convinced that the Dutch republic represented the greatest economic threat to Britain, the whigs perceived no such threat.[48] The Dutch and British economies simply produced different things.

Early-18th-century whigs, unlike their tory counterparts, believed passionately that the French posed the single greatest threat to British economic vitality and political survival. 'The French, who sixty years ago had never made any tolerable figure in traffic, seem now, especially since their nearer intimacy with Spain, to be next to us, the greatest trading nation in Europe', wrote the whig merchant, Charles King. Because the French 'know the best of any people how to improve their advantages', King warned, "tis to be feared they will outdo even us, if we are not very cautious'.[49] 'The French alone are our rivals in trade', agreed the whig, Viscount Barrington.[50]

In recent years, whigs pointed out, the French had begun to dominate the Spanish American market with their linen and cheap woollen exports. When the Frenchman, Jean du Casse, was granted the *assiento* to supply Spanish America with African slaves, whig observers feared that this would make France 'mistress of the commerce of the Indies'.[51] By the end of the decade, whig fears had become a reality.[52] Whigs were certain that it was the wealth from the Spanish Indies that was financing the French war effort. Without the wealth from the Spanish Indies, one whig merchant told the earl of Sunderland, 'the King of France had been undone before now'.[53]

Should France be able to retain its dominance of the Spanish American trade, whigs insisted in tract after tract, all would be lost. Before the war began, the whig, George Stepney, warned, should Louis XIV gain access to the Spanish Indies 'which furnish all this part of the world with gold and silver' it will 'make it very easy' to realize his dream of 'Universal Monarchy'.[54] Should the house of Bourbon gain 'Spain and the Indies', warned the whig poet and member of the Kit-Kat club, Arthur Maynwaring, 'our own dominions and commerce' will be exposed 'to certain destruction'. Should France retain

---

[47] 'An American', *Essay upon Government*, preface, 47, 76.

[48] Joseph Addison, *The Present State of the War* (1708), 37; John Withers, *The Dutch Better Friends than the French* (1713), 34.

[49] *The British Merchant*, i, p. xxviii.

[50] Barrington, *A Dissuasive*, 31.

[51] Beinecke Lib., Osborn fc 37/6/48: M. de Schonenberg (Madrid) to Manchester, 29 Aug./8 Sept. 1701; *The Duke of Anjou's Succession Further Consider'd* Part 2 (1701), 7.

[52] Addison, *Present State of the War*, 5; TNA, CO 391/21, p. 26: Board of Trade, Journal, 22 Feb. 1709; BL, Add. MS 71143, f. 48r: Marlborough to Heinsius, 16 Oct. 1710; BL, Add. MS 70185 (unfoliated): Reinier Leers (Rotterdam) to Robert Harley, 18 Nov. 1710; BL, Add. MS. 70163, f. 206r: [William Ashurst ?], About the South Sea Trade, 14 Nov. 1711; BL, Add. MS 70164 (unfoliated): Mitford Crowe to Oxford, 11 June 1711; *British Merchant*, iii, 321.

[53] BL, Add. MS 61644A, f. 42v: Thomas Ekines to Sunderland, 17 June 1708; *Observator*, vii, no. 8, p. [1]; 13 Mar. 1708; *A Letter to a Member of the October-Club* (1711), 13.

[54] [George Stepney], *An Essay upon the Government of the English Plantations* (1701), 1–2.

its influence in Spanish America, Maynwaring concluded, 'they will certainly be able . . . to ruin all our plantations'.[55]

Given the gravity of the situation, the whigs wanted to drive 'the French power out of New Spain' and turn the 'channel of that trade to England'.[56] In 1708, whigs at the highest levels of government contemplated a South Sea expedition, along the lines first proposed by the whig poet, John Dennis, in 1703, to drive the French out of the Spanish Indies. Addison, Sunderland and Halifax all discussed a variety of options. Defoe urged them on in print.[57]

The whigs, it should be emphasized, were not advocating a blue water policy. They did not want to seize possessions in Spanish America. And, above all, they did not want a sea war to the exclusion of a land war.[58]

The whigs never unleashed their South Sea expedition because they believed in 1709 that the French had agreed to a peace that would open up the trade of the Spanish Indies to the British and the Dutch. They thought that they had negotiated a treaty that would permanently exclude the French from the Spanish American trade. 'The expedition designed for the West Indies is stopped', Henry Boyle explained to his fellow whigs, the duke of Marlborough and Charles, Viscount Townshend, because they believed that the foundations 'for a general and lasting peace' had been laid at Geertruidenberg.[59] Central to the whig peace demands, demands which they believed the French had conceded, was 'that France should never become possessed of the Spanish Indies, nor send ships thither to exercise commerce under any pretext whatsoever'.[60]

The whig peace treaty was never signed – the whig government fell in 1710 in the wake of the Sacheverell affair before it could conclude the peace – but the whig demands make clear the whig vision of empire. Early-18th-century whigs wanted an empire of commerce and labour, not an empire that sought to monopolise raw materials. In the second number of his wildly popular *Spectator* Addison had his fictional Sir Andrew Freeport – almost certainly a thinly-disguised reference to the radical political economist, Henry Martin – exclaim 'that it is a stupid and barbarous way to extend dominion by arms, for true power is to be got by arts and industry'.[61]

Whigs insisted again and again that they saw no point in seeking territorial concessions in the War of the Spanish Succession. Unlike the tories, the whigs had no desire to

---

[55] Arthur Maynwaring, *Remarks upon the Present Negotiations of Peace* (1711), 9, 15.

[56] *Review*, iv, no. 146, p. 584: 17 Jan. 1708.

[57] John Dennis, *A Proposal for Putting a Speedy End to the War* (1703), 13–14; Beinecke Lib., Osborn fc 37/13/27: Addison to Manchester, 20 Feb. 1708; BL, Add. MS 61644A, f. 42v: Thomas Ekines to Sunderland, 17 June 1708; BL, Add. MS 61644A, f. 59r: Proposals for Carrying on the War with More Vigour in America, 1708; BL, Add. MS 61500, f. 68r: Sunderland's minutes of the cabinet council, 13 Nov. 1709; *Review*, iv, no. 142, p. 567: 8 Jan. 1708.

[58] Dennis, *A Proposal*, p. v.

[59] Bodl., MS Eng. Hist. d. 147, f. 13r: Henry Boyle (Whitehall) to Marlborough and Townshend, 24 May 1709; Bodl., MS Eng. Hist. d. 147, f. 17r: Boyle to Marlborough and Townshend, 24 May 1709.

[60] William Cowper, *Private Diary of William Cowper, First Earl Cowper*, ed. E.C. Hawtrey (Eton, 1833), 39: 23 Jan. 1709; Narcissus Luttrell, *A Brief Historical Relation of State Affairs* (6 vols, Oxford, 1857), vi, 412; Bodl., MS Eng. Hist. d. 147, f. 79v: Boyle (Whitehall) to Townshend, 2 Sept. 1709; Bodl., MS Eng. Hist. d. 147, f. 132r: Boyle (Whitehall) to Townshend, 30 May 1710; Maynwaring, *Remarks*, 5; Arthur Maynwaring, *Vindication of the Present M___y* (1711), 22; *Letter from a Tory Freeholder*, 16–17; *Report from the Committee of Secrecy* [Chaired by Robert Walpole] (1715), 16.

[61] *Spectator*, no. 2, p. [3]: 2 Mar. 1711.

seize the South American mines. William Blathwayt, whose early-18th-century commitment to the whig cause was so well known that he lost his parliamentary seat at Bath to a tory in the post-Sacheverell election of 1710, told the duke of Marlborough that he 'would rather see the Spanish West Indies under the House of Austria with a freedom of trade than in our hands'. 'Nor would I take one foot of ground from' the Habsburgs 'neither on island nor continent', Blathwayt told his good friend, George Stepney.[62] 'It is my humble opinion', wrote the not-so-modest Arthur Maynwaring, 'that if we would obtain either by treaty or by conquest those golden mines we dream of, they would not be half so advantageous to us, as the bare of liberty of trading there, and of exchanging our goods for bullion.' Commerce, not conquest 'is the proper business of our country', Maynwaring insisted, 'thus our people are employed, our manufactures are improved, and our constitution is preserved'. 'The gold and silver mines if we could have them', Maynwaring believed, 'would only destroy our industry, and make us such a lazy generation as the Spaniards.' An empire based on treasure 'may be proper to over-turn a free government, or to support a tyranny'.[63]

Early-18th-century whigs wanted an empire that promoted manufactures, not an empire that sought to parlay territorial possession into trading monopolies. The whigs believed economic prosperity, and hence political power, was generated by maximising the efficiency and productivity of human labour. The best way to achieve this end was to create an integrated commercial empire. Over and over again whigs condemned the Spanish imperial model. Spain had once been 'a fertile country, where trade and manufactures flourished', recalled Bernard Mandeville, but as soon as they had gained 'that mighty treasure, that was obtained with more hazard and cruelty than the world till then had known', 'it took away their senses, and their industry forsook them'. The Spanish, as a direct consequence of gaining mineral riches, had become 'a slow, idle, proud, and beggarly people' for whom 'nothing but the conquest of the world would serve'.[64] The British government, the whigs believed, should develop industry rather than seek mineral wealth.[65] The 'government's first care', insisted Mandeville, should be 'to promote as great a variety of manufactures, arts, and handicrafts as human wit can invent'.[66]

5

When the tories came to power in the summer of 1710 they brought with them the political economic ideas of Charles Davenant rather than those of Addison, Maynwaring and Mandeville. They lamented that the whigs were seeking a peace that granted Britain no territorial gains. They feared that the barrier granted to the Dutch in Flanders would

[62] Beinecke Lib., OSB MSS 2/Box 2/Folder 33: William Blathwayt (Loo) to George Stepney, 8/19 Aug. 1701; Beinecke Lib., OSB MSS 2/Box 2/Folder 33: Blathwayt (Dieren) to Stepney, 26 Aug. 1701; Beinecke Lib., OSB MSS 2/Box 2/Folder 33: Blathwayt (Loo) to Stepney, 9 Sept. 1701; Beinecke Lib. OSB MSS 2/Box 2/Folder 35: Blathwayt (London) to Stepney, 27 Mar. 1702. On Blathwayt's whiggery: Beinecke Lib., OSB MSS 2/Box 2/Folder 32: Blathwayt (Whitehall) to Stepney, 6 June 1701; Huntington Lib., HEH, ST 58/7, p. 4: Henry Brydges to James Brydges, 14 Oct. 1710.

[63] Maynwaring, *Remarks*, 26.

[64] Mandeville, *Fable of the Bees*, 176–8; see also William Wood, *Survey of Trade* (1718), 134–5.

[65] *Review*, iv, no. 149, pp. 595–6: 24 Jan. 1708.

[66] Mandeville, *Fable of the Bees*, 178.

render Britain's chief economic rival invulnerable. Unsurprisingly, the tories sought a very different kind of peace.

The experience of the long and bloody War of the Spanish Succession had taught the tories two things. First, they, too, were convinced that France had been able to sustain its war effort through the wealth of the Indies. Second, they believed, that whig deficit-spending was part of an elaborate ploy to promote social revolution in England. Robert Harley and his allies sought to end both these unpleasant developments.

The new tory ministers had long been obsessed with the South Sea trade.[67] Robert Harley, earl of Oxford from May 1711, had gathered information from a variety of sources to prove the 'great support the French and Spaniards have had to carry on this war by the gold and silver they brought from the Spanish West Indies'.[68] Henry St John, too, had been collecting manuscripts about Spanish America. He, too, concluded that it was 'the immense treasures' that France brought in from 'the Spanish West Indies' that allowed Louis XIV to continue his war effort.[69]

The tories were also convinced that the whig financial mechanisms for fighting that war were effecting a pernicious social transformation in Britain. The tory financier, John Drummond, who very much had the ear of Robert Harley and Henry St John, complained that the Bank of England – at the behest of 'the party' – was promoting 'barbarous republican Revolutions'.[70] At the time of the revolution, St John recalled, 'the moneyed interest was not yet a rival able to cope with the landed interest, either in the nation or in Parliament'. All that had now changed, St John informed Orrery in 1709, because 'we have now been twenty years engaged in the most expensive wars that Europe ever saw'. 'The whole burden of this charge', St John was sure, was paid by 'the landed interest during the whole time.' The result was that 'a new interest has been created out of their fortunes and a sort of property which was not known twenty years ago, is now increased to be almost equal to the *Terra Firma* of our island'.[71] Swift had

<hr/>

[67] The claim that Harley had hoped for a mixed ministry seems invalidated by the plans circulating in 1708. Addison heard that 'Harley and his friends' hoped 'to plant their own party', meaning the tories, into the great offices of state. Given that the rumours Addison heard were almost exactly what occurred two years later, it is hard to imagine that this was a coincidence: Beinecke Lib., Osborn fc 37/13/22: Addison to Manchester, 13 Feb. 1708; Beinecke Lib., Osborn fc 37/13/33: Addison to Manchester, 27 Feb. 1708.

[68] BL, Add. MS 70163, ff. 263–4: DP to Oxford, 8 May 1711; BL, Add. MS 70027, f. 206r: John Drummond (Amsterdam) to Oxford, 12 June 1711; BL, Add. MS 70163, f. 175: C. Dummer to Oxford, 29 June 1711; BL, Add. MS 70163, f. 179r: Thomas Pindar to Oxford, 13 July 1711; BL, Add. MS 70164 (unfoliated): Captain Martin Laycock's proposals, 10 Nov. 1704; BL, Add. MS 70163, ff. 255–8: 'An Essay on the Nature and Methods of Carrying on a Trade to the South Sea', c. 1711; BL, Add. MS 70163, ff. 240–6: 'Explanatory Observations on the South Sea Trade and Company', 1711.

[69] *Letters and Correspondence, Public and Private, of the Right Honourable Henry St. John, Lord Visc. Bolingbroke*, ed. Gilbert Parke (4 vols,1798), i, 40; *Letters and Correspondence*, ed. Parke, i, 10: St John (Whitehall) to John Drummond, 27 Oct. 1710; Henry St John, Viscount Bolingbroke, *Letters on the Study and Use of History* (1752), 301–2, 318–19.

[70] Huntington Lib., HEH, ST 58/7, p. 47: John Drummond (Amsterdam) to James Brydges, 24 Oct. 1710 ns.

[71] Bolingbroke, *Letters on the Study and Use of History*, Letter 8, pp. 267–8, 382–3; Bodl., Eng. Misc. e. 180, ff. 4–5: Henry St John (Bucklebury) to Orrery, 9 July 1709. While I agree on many issues with Isaac Kramnick, I dissent from his view that Bolingbroke's thought was shaped by the credit crisis of 1710 and the later South Sea Bubble. Bolingbroke's social critique was already manifest: Isaac Kramnick, *Bolingbroke and His Circle* (Cambridge, MA, 1968), 63–4. Dickinson is surely right to read this letter as expressing 'the views of the Tory squires': H.T. Dickinson, *Bolingbroke* (1970), 69.

been advancing exactly this case repeatedly in the pages of the tory *Examiner* and in his oft-reprinted *Conduct of the Allies*.

The tories, and one suspects that Robert Harley deserves much of the credit for this, realized that they could solve both problems – French superior financial resources and the social revolutionary effects of whig war finance – in a single blow. They sought to create a new British empire in South America. Harley's South Sea Company was to be the commercial arm of a new imperial project. So, while the whigs hoped to break into Spanish American markets without seizing a single foot of territory, the tories wanted to create a vast new territorial empire that would generate unsurpassed mineral wealth.

Within months of taking office the tories began planning for a new South Sea expedition. It was, the 18th-century editor of St John's papers noted, 'a favourite project of Lord Bolingbroke'.[72] In January 1711, Harley and St John dispatched Sir James Wishart with secret instructions 'for the disturbing and ruining the enemy's trade in the South Sea'.[73] It was surely no coincidence that Swift, who was kept abreast of the tory ministry's plans, suggested later in 1711 that Britain as 'a maritime power' should despatch 'fleets and naval forces' to the 'North and South Seas of America' so as 'to prevent any returns of money from thence, except in our own bottoms'.[74]

The new tory South Sea Company, formed in 1711, depended on a territorial base for its success. The new company intended 'to build forts and castles in the South Sea', Henry Martin later recalled. These settlements – the tories had Buenos Aires on the Rio de la Plata, Valdivia in Chile, and the Tierra del Fuego in mind – would, John Drummond thought, make it so that 'England will not need to envy the mines of Mexico nor Peru'.[75] The South Sea Company, Davenant expected, would soon discover new 'gold and silver' mines.[76] By seizing control of the South Sea trade, by opening up vast new mines (or taking control of those already established), the tories believed that they could cut off the vital French supply lines and also repay the whig debt. France would be kept within bounds and the whig moneyed interest would be brought to its knees.

Treaty negotiations with France put a halt to the tory South Sea expedition, just as earlier negotiations had scuttled plans for the very different whig expedition in 1709. But the tories did not abandon dreams of a South American empire. The tories hoped to secure their vision of empire through the peace they were negotiating with the French. Whereas the whig peace had sought to establish free trade in Spanish America for both the British and the United Provinces to the exclusion of the French, the new treaty – much to the fury of the Dutch – granted the British exclusively some key towns and settlements in the southern cone of South America.[77] "Tis to be hoped',

[72] *Letters and Correspondence*, ed. Parke, i, 40.

[73] *Letters and Correspondence*, ed. Parke, i, 36–7: 'Secret Instructions to Sir James Wishart', 14 Jan. 1711.

[74] Jonathan Swift, *Conduct of the Allies* (1711), 30.

[75] Huntington Lib., HEH, ST 58/9, p. 2: Matthew Decker (London) to James Brydges, 4 July 1711; HEH, ST 58/8, p. 270: John Drummond (Amsterdam) to James Brydges, 21 July 1711 ns; BL, Add. MS 70185 (unfoliated): L. Renaud (Amsterdam) to Oxford, 25 Sept. 1711 ns; BL, Add. MS 70163, f. 241r: Explanatory Observations on the South Sea Trade and Company, 1711; *British Merchant*, iii, 256.

[76] Charles Davenant, *A Report to the Honourable Commissioners* (1712), Part 1, p. 74.

[77] BL, Add. MS 70185 (unfoliated): L. Renaud (Amsterdam) to Oxford, 18 Sept. 1711 ns.

Davenant reported to parliament, referring to the peace negotiations then underway, 'we have an opportunity of procuring to our selves a new branch of trade that will make us amends for what we have suffered by our steady affection to the common cause.'[78] Henry Martin later claimed 'the rewards which were promised to the nation, if we would but make our peace with France and Spain, were mountains of gold in the Spanish Indies'.[79]

Tories and whigs in the early 18th century had radically different visions of empire. Tories hoped for a territorial empire that would give Britain the mines of gold and silver that their Tudor forbears had failed to seize. Whigs, by contrast, wanted no new territory but an integrated commercial empire. These contrasting aspirations were based on competing economic ideologies. There was no mercantilist consensus. There were no common theoretical assumptions or historical lessons learned. Instead, there was deep and partisan ideological conflict about political economy. The tories believed that there was a finite amount of wealth in the world. A nation could become wealthy only by buying cheap and selling dear. The easiest way to do this was to secure valuable raw materials, especially precious metals, through territorial empire.

6

By now it should be clear why it was that whigs were so infuriated by the tory strategy after 1710 and by the peace of 1713. Tories had exchanged, in the whig view, the possibility of penetrating Spanish American markets for the chimera of territorial possession. Indeed, whigs never tired of pointing out, the tories had been so outfoxed by the French and the Spanish that they never received their vaunted foothold in the southern cone of South America.

In pamphlet after pamphlet, the whigs pointed out that whereas the 1709 treaty and the Grand Alliance itself had stipulated that the French were to be excluded from the Spanish American trade, the tories had done nothing to secure Spanish American markets for British merchants. 'France is permitted by the treaty', fumed the whig, Charles Povey, 'to trade to the West Indies, which she never was allowed before.'[80]

The consequences of the tory omission, the consequences of a treaty negotiated on the basis of tory political economy, were of the highest order.[81] Viscount Barrington lamented the 'million' woollen workers who would lose their jobs because the tories had neglected 'the West-India trade'.[82] Henry Martin reported that by 'the universal consent of all our merchants abroad' the 'effect of the late treaty' was 'a universal stop of all our trade to Spain'. 'This', he remarked incredulously, 'that was formerly esteemed as the best flower in our garden, that took off more of our woollen manufactures than any other trade; that enabled greater numbers of our people to live without help from the parish, and paid greater sums for the product of our lands than any foreign trade whatsoever,

[78] Davenant, *A Report*, Part 1, p. 73.
[79] *British Merchant*, iii, 234.
[80] Charles Povey, *An Enquiry* (1714), 20.
[81] *The Balance of Power* (1711), 11: [10 Nov. 1711].
[82] Barrington, *A Dissuasive*, 32.

quite stopped!' Where had all these flowers gone? 'The whole riches of the Spanish nation are thus given up to France.' 'France has engrossed the whole commerce in America', Martin felt obliged to report.[83]

Early-18th-century whigs, in pamphlets, journals and memoranda developed a coherent and radical project for an integrated British empire. The whig project enunciated by Addison, Defoe, Maynwaring, Mandeville, Oldmixon and Martin, among others, envisioned the possibility of remarkable economic prosperity. The whigs did not insist, however, that prosperity should be measured only in the British Isles. Instead, they imagined a global economy in which wealth was generated as much by the New England shipping industry and Jamaican traders with Spanish America as by English merchants and landed gentleman. Indeed, the whig commitment to taking advantage of labour in the locales where it was most valuable, allowed for the possibility that the steepest rate of demographic growth and manufacturing productivity may be in the New World. This was why some whigs were already insisting that inhabitants of the New World needed some kind of representation in Westminster.

This radical whig imperial vision did not die out with the Hanoverian succession or the South Sea Bubble. The Pennsylvania whig, Benjamin Franklin, famously quipped in the 1750s that 'I look on the colonies as so many counties gained to Great Britain.' 'What imports it to the general state, whether a merchant, a smith, or a hatter, grow rich in Old or New England.'[84] Two decades later, Adam Smith would wax eloquent on the same theme. Reasoning that British and colonial wealth were not conceptually distinct, Smith saw no reason why the colonies should be subordinated to the metropole. 'There is not the least probability that the British constitution would be hurt by the union of Great Britain and her colonies', Smith insisted. 'The assembly which deliberates and decides concerning the affairs of every part of the empire, in order to be properly informed', Smith concluded in radical whiggish fashion, 'ought certainly to have representatives from every part of it.'[85] Whigs who believed that wealth was potentially infinitely expandable, and that labour may well be worth more in the New World than the old, were equally happy to argue for colonial integration rather than colonial dependence.

Of course, not all whigs accepted Martin's arguments about the differential value of labour markets. Not all of them accepted that labour may be worth more in the New World. The Walpolean, William Wood, was one such whig. He enthusiastically endorsed John Locke's theory of property enunciated in the *Second Treatise*.[86] But, unlike Oldmixon and Martin, he did not wax enthusiastic about global labour values. As a result he developed a very different vision of empire. He thought that manufacturing in the colonies might be of 'pernicious consequence'.[87] He insisted that 'our Northern colonies can be of no real advantage to us'.[88] Jamaica, Wood reasoned, was 'the most valuable plantation belonging to the crown'. But this was not because it might serve as a staging point to send British manufactures into Spanish America, but because 'the labour of

---

[83] *British Merchant*, iii, 232, 264–5.

[84] Quoted in Alan Houston, *Benjamin Franklin and the Politics of Improvement* (New Haven, CT, 2008), 173.

[85] Adam Smith, *An Inquiry into the Nature and Causes of the Wealth of Nations*, ed. R.H. Campbell and A.S. Skinner (Indianapolis, 1981), 624 (book iv, vii, chapter 2).

[86] Wood, *Survey of Trade*, 161–2.

[87] Wood, *Survey of Trade*, 147.

[88] Wood, *Survey of Trade*, 149.

negroes is the principal foundation of riches from the plantations'.[89] Wood outlined a theory of empire that was embraced by Walpolean establishment whigs. The hierarchical relationship that he posited between Britain and the colonial periphery had many similarities with the tory vision outlined by Josiah Child, Charles Davenant, Bolingbroke, Oxford and Swift. This was why William Wood's *Survey of Trade* was grouped by Sir Charles Whitworth, a pro-government apologist, with Charles Davenant's *Discourse on the Plantation Trade*, and Josiah Child's *The Nature of Plantations* in the 'critical conjuncture' of 1775.[90] Whitworth's point was not to demonstrate an ideological consensus on the political economy of empire – Smith's publication the following year should have put paid to that notion – but to warn the American colonists 'the stake they risk' by their riotous behaviour.[91]

What, then, are the broader implications for this story? What have we gained by recovering the story of the failed tory project for establishing a British empire in the southern cone and the whig alternative of an integrated empire? It seems to me that this story has broad implications for the ways in which we should think and write about the history of the British empire.

First, there was no single moment in which the British became authoritarian imperialists. Historians have long sought the moment in which the British turned away from liberty-loving proponents of a soft commercial empire, into the authoritarians who ruled with such a brutal hand in India and sub-Saharan Africa. Indeed, historians have been so eager to uncover the moment of this remarkable epistemic shift, that they have found *several* of them. In a recent and important work that theorises in innovative ways the nature of the early empire, Alison Games has discovered that a 'cosmopolitan' impulse lay behind English expansion in the 16th and 17th centuries. That initial cosmopolitanism derived from English 'weakness in the sixteenth century', Games assures us, was 'highly decentralized'. By the 1650s, however, there was 'a pronounced shift' in the nature of the empire. This shift that 'challenged the relevance and necessity of an accommodating demeanor', involved a twofold turn toward 'centralization' and 'the use of coercion and force'.[92] The empire, in Games's view, had taken a decisive authoritarian turn by the 1650s.

Historians more focused on the tumultuous events of the 1760s and 1770s have detected an authoritarian turn in their period. This, now familiar, story focuses on the passage of the Sugar Act of 1764, the 1765 Stamp Act, the Townshend duties of 1767, the Tea Act of 1773 and the Intolerable Acts of 1774. The British government turned away from a permissive commercialist attitude towards empire in the earlier period, towards more coercive and authoritarian policies in the wake of the Seven Years War (1756–63).[93]

For others, the period from 1780 to 1830 was the crucial moment in which the British empire began to 'establish overseas despotisms which mirrored in many ways the

[89] Wood, *Survey of Trade*, 173–4, 179.

[90] Sir Charles Whitworth, *Select Dissertations on Colonies and Plantations* (1775), p. iii.

[91] Whitworth, *Select Dissertations*, p. v. Whitworth was a supporter of Lord North. He had published a new edition of Davenant's works in 1771, praising them for laying 'the foundation of our political establishment': Charles Whitworth, *The Political and Commercial Works of that Celebrated Writer Charles D'Avenant* (5 vols, 1771), i, sig. A3r. Compare the rather different spin in David Armitage, *The Ideological Origins of the British Empire* (Cambridge, 2000), 167.

[92] Alison Games, *The Web of Empire* (Oxford, 2008), 289–90.

[93] For other accounts of such a shift, see Edmund and Helen Morgan, *The Stamp Act Crisis* (Chapel Hill, NC, 1953), 21–7, 54; Elliott, *Empires of the Atlantic World*, 298, 301–3, 305.

politics of neo-absolutism and the Holy Alliance of contemporary Europe'. The new British empire that emerged after 1780, according to Sir Christopher Bayly was characterised 'by a form of aristocratic military government supporting a viceregal autocracy, by a well-developed imperial style which emphasized hierarchy and racial subordination, and by the patronage of indigenous landed elites'. 'Constructive authoritarian and ideological British imperialism', in Bayly's view, 'came of age in the years between 1783 and 1820.'[94]

One could go on, citing those who see an authoritarian turn in the 1680s, and others who point to the 1880s. My story of the competing whig and tory imperial projects of the early 18th century, however, suggests that the problem of a British authoritarian empire has been badly conceptualised. In a sense, all of these scholars are right to see an authoritarian turn in their periods. They are wrong, however, to insist on sea changes, epistemic shifts, and pivotal moments of vindictive legislation. Instead, I am suggesting, the contours of the British empire were always shaped by social and political contestation. Some Britons always had an authoritarian impulse. Others, who were no less imperialists, wanted a more integrative and less coercive empire. There were always some Britons who wanted an empire that was commercial, maritime and free. Others wanted a coercive, centralised, blue water empire.

Second, political economic conflict, rather than mercantilist consensus, shaped the British empire. Mercantilism was, from the publication of the influential *The Cambridge History of the British Empire*, thought to be the organising principle of the so-called first British empire. What, then, were the organising principles of mercantilism? What were the concepts about which everyone agreed in the early modern period? The overwhelming majority of scholars agree about the fundamental underlying concept of mercantilism. Mercantilists all believed in the limits to growth. Mercantilists believed that they lived in a world of scarcity – because property and value was defined exclusively with reference to land – in which economic life was necessarily one of vicious competition. They believed, most scholars assert confidently, that trade was a zero-sum game.

These scholars, I have suggested, are not wrong to believe that many subscribed to the zero-sum views which they have called mercantilism. There was, however, no mercantilist consensus. Scholars, by assuming a mercantilist consensus, have obscured the degree to which the shaping of empire was a conscious political choice. In their view, because all governments shared the same goals, the only plausible explanation for empires taking on different shapes were the constraints of environment and opportunity. I show, however, that different parties with different political economic outlooks sought to create different kinds of empires. The tory imperialists wanted an extractive empire in South America because they were committed to the notion that there was a finite amount of wealth in the world, and that it was far better that that wealth be in British, rather than Dutch or Spanish, hands. The tories did not achieve ideological hegemony. The whigs – radical whigs after 1715 – wanted an integrative manufacturing empire devoid of more territorial possessions, because they believed that labour, rather than land, created value. Since

---

[94] C.A. Bayly, *Imperial Meridian* (1989), 8–9, 76–7, 250. With a slightly different chronology, and a different set of emphases, Jennifer Pitts, has also charted 'a turn to empire' in the period 1780–1830, that is 'a sea change in opinions on empire' among liberal thinkers in favour 'of the conquest of non-European peoples and territories'. This was accompanied by 'an increasingly exclusive conception . . . of national community and political capacity': Jennifer Pitts, *A Turn to Empire* (Princeton, NJ, 2005), 2.

they believed that property was potentially infinite, and that manufacturing was the best way to generate national wealth, the whigs thought that the tory imperial scheme was fundamentally misguided. If I am right, then, the best way to understand the ways in which Britons shaped their empire is to pay greater attention to these fundamental political economic conflicts. Britons were divided more by differing political economic conceptions than they were by whether they lived in the metropole or in the periphery.

Finally, this contest over empire in the early 18th century may point to some limits of the so-called new imperial history. The achievements of the new imperial history have, of course, been many and varied. We now understand a great deal more than we did before about 'issues of identity and belonging' in the British empire.[95] The 'new imperial history that is grounded on difference' has alerted us to strategies of domination not accounted for in the older histories. Nevertheless, the focus on 'the ideologies and representations of difference', 'the social, cultural and epistemological networks', and the insistence on the engagement only with softer disciplines of 'literature, anthropology and history, the history of medicine and psychiatry, geography, art history and cultural studies' risks occluding the central sites of political contestation in the 18th century.[96] Contests over institutions were fundamental to the shaping of the 18th-century empire. This was true for three reasons. First, a focus on the ideologies of difference risks making illegible the whig strategy on integrative empire, since that strategy depended so heavily on informal economic links. The new imperial history has invariably focused on areas where the British had territorial sovereignty, not on areas of informal empire.[97] Second, by insisting on the weakness of British imperial institutions, a narrowly-cultural approach to empire risks making incomprehensible the choices made to evade institutional regulation. Piracy only existed because trade regulations were frequently enforced. Third, institutions like the board of trade helped to structure colonial societies. It was the possibility of securing interests through institutions, as Heather Welland has recently shown, that helped to form lobbies that were so central to the 18th-century British imperial polity.[98]

Imperial politics in the 18th century were defined by partisan politics. There was no single imperial project. There was no mercantilist consensus. Party political identities from at least the outbreak of the War of the Spanish Succession were defined, in part, by their imperial visions. Those imperial visions, in turn, were developed through competing political economic understandings, and competing institutions. These positions were not the preserve of a small elite. Instead, party political arguments about political economy and empire were debated in the most popular pamphlets and the most widely-distributed journals of the age. To ignore these arguments, to insist that political argument was restricted to discussion of the Church and the ancient constitution, is to miss the most significant and consequential political theorising of the Augustan age.

---

[95] Catherine Hall, 'Thinking the Postcolonial, Thinking the Empire', in *Cultures of Empire*, ed. Catherine Hall (New York, 2000), 2; Kathleen Wilson, 'Histories, Empires, Modernities', in *A New Imperial History*, ed. Kathleen Wilson (Cambridge, 2004), 5.

[96] Wilson, 'Histories, Empires, Modernities', 5, 10, 13, 19; Hall, 'Thinking the Postcolonial', 24.

[97] The term 'informal empire' occurs twice in Catherine Hall's introductory essay, but nowhere else in her reader. Those two mentions are about what is not discussed in her collection.

[98] It should be noted that in Wilson's view at least the 'new imperial history' is supposed to supplement rather than supplant other imperial histories: Wilson, 'Histories, Empires, Modernities', 3. One worries that all proponents of this cultural approach will follow Wilson's wise strictures.

NOTE AND DOCUMENTS

A Non-Resisting, Passively Obedient Revolution: Lord North and Grey and the Tory Response to the Sacheverell Impeachment*

DANIEL SZECHI

This article is a notes and comments-style edition of two documents written by William North, Baron North and Grey, during the Sacheverell impeachment. The first of these was a response to arguments made by the Commons' managers before the Lords, the second was North and Grey's notes for his own speech in defence of Sacheverell. It is argued that together these encapsulate a strong tory's view of the impeachment and the revolution of 1688. Given the subsequently jacobite trajectory of North and Grey's career, it is suggested that these documents also offer an insight into the tory *mentalité* at the point when the first tory party was on the eve of its greatest political and electoral triumphs and before it turned against the Hanoverian dynasty.

Keywords: North and Grey; tory party; toryism; jacobitism; whig party; Sacheverell impeachment; revolution of 1688; Hanoverian succession; Queen Anne; Harley ministry; William III

Like many other tory peers, William North, 6th Baron North and 2nd Baron Grey of Rolleston (1678–1734), was passionately engaged by the Sacheverell impeachment. Despite the fact that he could only intermittently attend debates in the Lords, North and Grey had by then already developed something of a reputation as an 'important figure' on the tory side. Described by his most recent biographer, Lawrence Smith, as 'extremely active', he first made an impact in the debates in the English parliament on the Union with Scotland in 1706 and 1707, and by 1710 was well on his way to becoming a good, solid subaltern as far as the tories' leaders were concerned.[1] Under the Harley/Oxford

* I would like to express my thanks to Brian Cowan, who generously waived publication of his own edition of the documents below in his forthcoming edition *The State Trial of Doctor Henry Sacheverell* (Parliamentary History Texts & Studies), thus making way for me to publish them here, and provided me with a copy of an early draft of his text. I very much look forward to the publication of Dr Cowan's book, which will revise our understanding of the entire Sacheverell phenomenon with respect to the public sphere in the British Isles in the early 18th century and greatly expand our knowledge of the numerous works which the trial generated.

[1] All the biographic details that follow depend on Lawrence B. Smith's fine, short account in the *ODNB*, online edn [http://www.oxforddnb.com/view/article/20317, accessed 16 May 2010].

administration that supplanted the duumvir-junto government of 1708–10 in the aftermath of the impeachment he was duly appointed a privy councillor and lord lieutenant of Cambridge in 1711, and in 1712 installed as governor of Portsmouth. Despite some unhappiness with aspects of the ministry's conduct he was, like a good many supporters of the queen's (and the century's) last properly tory government, looking forward to a promising future.[2]

For all its frustrations, the period 1710–14 turned out, however, to be the high-water mark of North and Grey's career, and his personal story well illustrates the tories' trajectory between the 1690s and the 1720s. From the age of 24 years, when he was first commissioned as a captain in the foot guards, he was a professional soldier and a loyal officer in the army of Queen Anne, and he proudly claimed in a letter written in about 1712 that since 1702 he had served in a major battle and a major siege at every rank from lieutenant-colonel to lieutenant-general. He was, indeed, especially proud of the fact that, 'In ye most famous action of this war I had ye hottest & most honourable post, closeing ye left in ye attack on Blenheim in ye battle of Hocstadt, where I began ye day wth ye loss of 16 officers and my self wounded.'[3] Such sterling, courageous service, moreover, underlay his rapid promotion to lieutenant-general before 1710. But like so many of his tory fellow officers, North and Grey's professional military career in the British army came to an abrupt end with the Hanoverian succession. Despite his *bona fides* he was suspected of involvement in the jacobite conspiracy that preceded the rebellion of 1715 and was arrested and detained in Brussels.

There is no evidence that he was a jacobite at that time. By 1720, however, North and Grey was deeply involved in the complex of jacobite conspiracies known as the Atterbury plot (so called after the leading light of the English jacobites, Francis Atterbury, bishop of Rochester), was secretly appointed jacobite lord regent and raised to Earl North in the jacobite peerage, the better to exercise his commission as commander when the rising came. The whig government, however, penetrated and then exposed the plot and this led directly to North and Grey's rearrest in 1722 while trying to escape to the continent.[4] Released in 1724, he immediately went into exile. He was very well thought of in jacobite circles by this stage and was, consequently, briefly considered as a potential premier minister to the jacobite King James III in 1727. Instead, he converted to catholicism and entered Spanish service in 1728. In Spain, North and Grey uneventfully commanded Bourbon forces in Catalonia, and finally died in Madrid in 1734. By the end of his life he had made an epic, bitter transition from loyal supporter of the revolution settlement to faithful servant of the Stuarts and the Spanish Bourbons. How the devoutly anglican North and Grey of 1710 came to such a pass is part of a larger process that cannot be considered here, but suffice it to say that this process should not be seen as in any sense inevitable.

---

[2] Daniel Szechi, *Jacobitism and Tory Politics 1710–14* (Edinburgh, 1984), 93–6, 120, 122; Bodl., MS North, a.3, f. 251: North and Grey to Robert Harley, earl of Oxford, [1712?].

[3] Bodl., MS North, a.3, f. 136: draft statement of North and Grey's claim to be retained as a lieutenant-general when the army is put on a peacetime footing, [1712?].

[4] Melville de la Caillemotte de Massue de Ruvigny, marquis de Ruvigny and Raineval, *The Jacobite Peerage, Baronetage, Knightage and Grants of Honour Extracted, by Permission, from the Stuart Papers Now in Possession of His Majesty the King at Windsor Castle, and Supplemented by Biographical and Genealogical Notes* (Edinburgh, 1904), 130.

North and Grey's vision of the revolution and the settlement that followed it, as may be seen from the documents below (taken from the North family papers in the Bodleian Library), is utterly conventional in tory terms. It revolved around God's providential intervention in 1688. According to the standard interpretation, the tories did not resist divinely-constituted authority in the course of the revolution. God's inexorable will, as revealed in the unfolding, inevitable events of the winter of 1688–9, shielded the tories from any breach of their core principles: non-resistance and passive obedience.[5] For all that this version of events almost invariably strikes 21st-century historians as an egregious case of cognitive dissonance, in 1710 it was certainly possible for a committed, ideologically-driven tory to believe that there was no resistance offered to James II at the time of the revolution, and, concomitantly, that the dynastic settlement which followed was divinely approved and should command their loyalty and obedience. That it proved impossible for many tories, like North and Grey, to sustain those beliefs beyond the Hanoverian succession is a salutary reminder of how much the advent of George I transformed the dynamics of British politics and alienated many, hitherto committed, supporters of the post-revolutionary political order.

As the impeachment unfolded in 1710, however, North and Grey's future crisis of loyalty was unforeseeable. He was already a high tory, and faced with the Sacheverell process he simply set out to do the best he could for Church and party. In the first instance the mechanics of this involved North and Grey taking notes on the speeches made by the Commons' managers on 27/28 February 1710.[6] These were, apparently, the better to inform his response when he spoke against the impeachment and in favour of Sacheverell, which he ultimately did on 16 March 1710,[7] the separate notes for which are also to be found in the North papers[8] and are included below. In addition, he supplemented his own notes on the managers' speeches, and Sir Simon Harcourt's defence of the Doctor,[9] with copies of others from commercial sources.[10] Though it is possible he jotted down his notes on the managers' speeches in ink in the chamber, his physical difficulties in writing (he had lost his right hand at Blenheim in 1704[11]) make it more likely that there was a precursor document to the one below [hereafter cited as the notes], probably in pencil, and now lost. What follows is, then, probably North and Grey's later, 'fair' ink copy of the notes, with his 'Observations' added at leisure after the day's business was over. This pattern of note-taking, where North and Grey initially jotted down notes on speeches delivered by political opponents and then drew up a parallel set of responses, seems to have either been, or became, his regular practice when he was preparing to make an important speech in the Lords, as may be seen from the fact that there are a number of subsequent examples in the North papers, notably (with respect to the reign of Queen Anne) on the peace preliminaries of 1711, the Hamilton

[5] H.T. Dickinson, *Liberty and Property: Political Ideology in Eighteenth-Century Britain* (1977), 27–51.

[6] Bodl., MS North, a.3, ff. 137–8; Geoffrey Holmes, *The Trial of Doctor Sacheverell* (1973), 135–40.

[7] Clyve Jones, 'Debates in the House of Lords on "The Church in Danger", 1705, and on Dr Sacheverell's Impeachment', *Historical Journal*, xix (1976), 770.

[8] Bodl., MS North, a.3, ff. 139–40.

[9] Bodl., MS North, a.3, f. 141.

[10] Bodl., MS North, a.3, ff. 142–4.

[11] *ODNB*.

peerage dispute of 1711–12 and the battle in the Lords over the imposition of the malt tax on Scotland in 1713.[12]

The notes he took and the surviving part of the speech he prepared in 1710 are, however, of particular interest in that they offer an unusual insight into the heart of one peer's high tory politics. In his notes of 27/28 February, North and Grey used the first, left-hand, column to write down those elements of the managers' arguments which he considered to be particularly important. In the second, right-hand, column he wrote down his 'Observations'.[13] In general, North and Grey kept the two sections distinct, but occasionally this slipped, and in the entry in the notes on Lieutenant-General James Stanhope's speech on 28 February 1710 he was, significantly, moved to insert an explanatory comment: 'he means Conquest', in parentheses by way of explanation of one of Stanhope's points.[14] Naturally enough, given that the managers all emphasized the affront which they claimed the memory of William III and the revolution of 1688 had received from Dr Sacheverell, the substance of the notes pertaining to the managers' speeches returns again and again to the status of the revolution and the centrality of resistance to James II. North and Grey was, however, also particularly interested in what the managers had to say with regard to the related subjects of non-resistance and passive obedience. These were, indeed, to form the main theme of the surviving part of North and Grey's speech opposing the impeachment [hereafter cited as the speech], and they are also the basis for most of his 'Observations'.[15] Given North and Grey's high toryism, his comments here were always likely to be hostile to the whig managers, but his choice of words: 'Treason', 'Managers pretend to dictate laws', 'Nonsense', 'Ill maners before ye Queen',[16] suggests real anger, and this would certainly tie in with other accounts of the emotional reaction of many tories to what they perceived as a vicious sectarian attack on the Church of England.[17] This impression is reinforced by the language which North and Grey uses in the speech, in which he sarcastically comments on the whigs' implication that men of high tory principles like himself are *ipso facto* 'seditious', 'slavish', 'restless & turbulent' and 'friends to ye pretender'.[18]

The essence of the argument with which North and Grey riposted to the managers' charges against Sacheverell in the speech is that righteous resistance is a popish and fanatical doctrine that is always unlawful and contrary to God's express commands. It is, moreover, an act that contravenes the law of nations and promotes anarchy, which, as in the case of the Great Civil War, naturally leads to tyranny.[19] Resistance to the divinely-appointed authorities therefore promotes the tyranny of the people and is correspond-

---

[12] Bodl., MS North, a.3, ff. 192–7, 199, 248.

[13] Bodl., MS North, a.3, ff. 137–8.

[14] Bodl., MS North, a.3, f. 138r.

[15] We know that North and Grey's speech dealt with more than simply resistance because he is recorded as also having: 'insisted on the insolence of some pamphlets and writers on t'other side, and I think it was he that mentioned the boldness of Mr Hoadly who had made the people the sourse of power and Justice' (Jones, 'Debates in the Lords', 770). None of this is present in the part of his speech that survives in the North papers.

[16] Bodl., MS North, a.3, ff. 137–8.

[17] Jones, 'Debates in the Lords', 769.

[18] Bodl., MS North, a.3, f. 140v.

[19] Bodl., MS North, a.3, f. 139r.

ingly condemned in all polities. The revolution, moreover, did not constitute an act of resistance. William of Orange denied he was promoting resistance or conquest and James II abdicated the crown voluntarily.[20] Since non-resistance and passive obedience are central tenets of both good government (notably that of Queen Anne) and the Church of England, the impeachment of Dr Sacheverell must be an attack on both, and the vehemence with which this attack is being carried on is threatening the civility and amity necessary for the proper conduct of business in the Lords.[21] In all this, North and Grey was very much in tune with the tories who spoke against the impeachment in the Lords, in that his defence of Sacheverell, non-resistance and passive obedience was *sui generis*. The tories completely failed to sustain a common case for the Doctor's acquittal beyond the basic argument that resistance was generally bad, but the revolution was generally good, and North and Grey's notes for his speech are very much of a piece with this diversity of tory opinion.[22] Ominously for the tory party, and despite the efforts of Francis Atterbury and others to build up the providentialist interpretation, in 1710 the revolution was still clearly a subject on which the tories found it hard to maintain a united front, and in the aftermath of the Hanoverian succession the whigs would use this to damn them in the eyes of the new dynasty.[23]

In the documents that follow,[24] I have retained the punctuation, spelling and commonplace contractions, but added additional punctuation where this elucidates North and Grey's meaning. I have also uniformly capitalised the beginnings of sentences, inserted full stops in the few places where he appears to have missed doing so, and silently expanded other abbreviations. Both manuscripts have been damaged at some point and words and parts of words have been erased. Where possible I have deduced what the partially missing or damaged word was and inserted my conclusion in square brackets, but on other occasions the damage has defeated me and I have simply noted where the text breaks off. Possibly because of his physical disability, North and Grey's handwriting is, too, sometimes very difficult to read. I have noted in the footnotes those occasions where it has proved impossible for me to do so.

---

[20] Bodl., MS North, a.3, f. 139v.
[21] Bodl., MS North, a.3, f. 140v.
[22] Holmes, *Trial of Doctor Sacheverell*, 218–20; Jones, 'Debates in the Lords', 769–71.
[23] Dickinson, *Liberty and Property*, 36–8.
[24] Published here with the kind permission of Piers Edward Brownlow North, earl of Guilford, and the Bodleian Library.

APPENDIX 1: *Bodl., MS North, a.3, ff. 137–8: North and Grey's Notes and 'Observations' on the Speeches of the Commons' Managers, 27/8 February 1710*

[Notes on Managers' Speeches]	*[North and Grey]* 'Observations'

[f. 137r] *Mountague:*[25]
Sacheverell by his doctrine endeav^d to sett on side ye succession. Commissioners sorry to be oblidgd to prosecute this cause themselves, but only because 'tis in diffence of ye religion establish'd by law. Y^e whole scope of the sermon is to prove ye church in dainger & reflect on ye minestry. Y^e 5th of November was an improper day for such a discourse being ye time of King William's comeing over. King William disclaimed not resistance comeing over wth an armed force. Y^e 1st Parliament of King William allowed ye Tolleration; Dr Sacheverell against it. What occasion of ye Doctrine of passive obedience now? Answer what occasion for ye House of Commons to oppose it.

The succession canot be set on side but by resistance.

Question: whither where itt's principals are attaqued openly it is not in danger?

Lechmere:[26]
Great regard to be had to all accusations of ye Commons cald impeachments. One motive of this impeachment is y^t their opinions of ye revolution may be recorded. Revolution right sustained out of duty to ye Queen, but ye foundation of her right is undermined by Doctor Sacheverell. A limited monarchy wth an originall contract. W^n ye executive power dose not its duty we are free from our alegiance. Magna Charta sustain by ye resistance of ye Barons. Statute of Henry VIII y^t England is subject to noe laws but itts owne, &c. The Homilys mean only a civill obedience. Desires a mark of infamy upon all beleiving ye Doctrine of Passive obedience. [f. 137v] Sachaverell's design to raise Sedition & rebellion, to weaken ye Queen's title. Commissioners are oblidged to persue till they have publick satisfaction & justice. When Sacheverell names hereditary right he means ye pretender. Our successes are witness y^t our proceeding justly [*sic*].

He seems to carry it wth a high hand, as in ye case of Ld Strafford, but L^ds not to be threatned nor to go beyond justice.

Treason.

That is to say as to ye mayor of a town.

} Managers pretend to dictate laws.
That is contrary to his own doctrine of passive obedience. A title by succession ye strongest. Two titles stronger than one. Perhaps changing an impeachment to an attainder.

---

[25] Attorney-General Sir James Montagu, MP for Carlisle.
[26] Nicholas Lechmere, MP for Appleby.

APPENDIX 1: (*continued*)

[*Notes on Managers' Speeches*]	[*North and Grey*] 'Observations'

Sr Joseph Jekell:[27]

We must give up our right to ye law or injoy it precariously. All depend on this article; y^t is on ye justice of ye Revolution. Zeal for ye Queen shewed by ye Whigs, for ye Protestant succession. Y^t doctrine of Passive Obedience of noe use to good princes. Law not to be mixt wth religion. People have a right to ye laws, example: Restoration and Revolution. That they'l support all rights of ye throne. Quoats ye acts of repealing ye old oaths of alleagence & of setteling ye succession to prevent vexatious evils. Resistance if in generall unlawfull, *then y^f Revolution* in particular. An armed force to oblidg King James to call a free Parliament as well as to secure him self against evill ministers.

Those who offend against by rebellion &c doe.
The Prince of Orange disclaiming resistance made the Revolution more just. W^t zeal ye Whigs showd for ye Queen in ye reign of King William is notorious. It counsels dutifull obedience, and curbs ambition . . .[28] & murthering of Charles 1st Or y^t taking away ye cheif y^t ye person of ye King or Queen is sacred.

If it was founded on resistance.

If King William had made use of armed force ye Parliament could not be free.

Mr [Eyre], Solicitor General:[29]

Restless & turbulent spirits enemys to ye revolution. This doctrine preached up chiefly since the designed invasion. Noe acts of parliment can be good, not even ye succession if hereditary right takes place, nor exclusion of papist [min]isters[?][30]

Nonsense.
Therefore y^t invasion being over where is the hopes even [of] traitors?
He can not mean ye Queens right.

[f. 138r] *Sir John Holland:*[31]

Y^t the Revolution ye friends to it traitors, ye Queen an usurper; if Passive Obedience is sustained 'tis a daingerous spiritt to be reformed by his example to terrifie others as ye sabath for man, so government.

Negat[ive].

No danger in obedience.

Walpoole:[32]

Church of England enimys to ye constitution. Sett up an hereditary right y^t can never be soposed to be in behalf of ye Queen. They give ye people an ill impression.

---

[27] Sir Joseph Jekyll, MP for Eye.

[28] Indecipherable text.

[29] Robert Eyre, MP for Salisbury. NB: North and Grey's hand is so hard to read here that my attribution of Eyre is dependent on his being noted as solicitor-general and his position in the sequence of managers between Jekyll and Holland.

[30] MS damaged, text missing.

[31] MP for Norfolk.

[32] Robert Walpole, MP for King's Lynn and future premier minister.

APPENDIX 1: (*continued*)

[*Notes on Managers' Speeches*]	[*North and Grey*] 'Observations'
Major General[33] *Stanhop*:[34] Doctrine of passive obedience undermining her majesty['s] titl[e] . . .[35] behalf of a prince on t'other [side of the] water. All religions are against passive obedience. All government founded either upon an originall contract; or resistance (he means Conquest). The people having ye power of ye legislature, have a right to exercise and defend y^t power. Y^e Queen's part in ye Revollution. Prince of Wales a competitor. Ends of Government are ane peace att home and reputation abroad. Aris[totle?] says y^t we may rebell for Religion. Sermon not only to weak & silly women.	Granted (as Cicero says) except Church of England. 'Tis her disinguishing carecter. Lett him shew ye originall contract, I'le shew ye conquest. He would invade the Queen's right of makeing war. Our reputation abroad very good for every thing but our fidelity & obedience. Ill maners before ye Queen. I ask have noe seperate Hyrarchy.

APPENDIX 2: *Bodl., MS North, a.3, ff. 139–40: Part of North and Grey's Speech Opposing the Impeachment, 16 March 1710*

Resistance

[f. 139r] 2. [*sic.*] Against Nature. Religion.
1st. Self deffence much [*sic.*] (les resistance to supream powers) no law of nature, for then not to doe it in all cases would be a sin. Even ye worst malifactors object ye good of ye society, but upon y^t account we must not act contrary to a law of nature. 2. Resistance is contrary to reveald religion, ye practice of Christ himself & of his church, of Primitive Christianity, of ye begining of ye Reformation & ye principalls y^n established in ye Church of England, daingerous upon account of scripture minaces [*sic.*]. 3. Resistance is a doctrin introduced wth transubstantiation by ye papists (in ye 11th century by Gregory VII), preached by ye Jesuits for religion's sake, practisd by sectarys of all sorts. Anabaptists in Germany, Presbyterians here & in Scotland. Non-resistance is comanded ye slaves [*sic.*] towards their cruell masters, to ye Heathen persecuting conquerors *a majore ad minus*. 4 [*sic.*].[36] Against ye laws of all nations even elective monarchys & Republicks. 1st in Poland it appears King Augustus insists upon his former wright [*sic.*] to ye throne through y^e *pacta conventa* although they had chose another king; & even there ye resistance is not by ye people but Palatins, Castalans, Waiwood, &c petty tyrants. 2^[nd] not in Hungary, it being rebellion against our allie. 3^[rd] Resistance punished in Holland by millitary exicutions therefore not lawfull.

---

[33] *Recte* lieutenant-general; an interesting slip on North and Grey's part.
[34] James Stanhope, MP for Cockermouth.
[35] MS damaged; text destroyed.
[36] '3' erased and '4' inserted.

3 [sic.].[37] Against y^e nature of Goverment. 1st Goverment in y^e people collect[ive]ly is anarchy. 2$^{[nd]}$ y^e people collect[ive]ly have not a greater right to power over each other y^n seperately, nor so great n[ei]ther according to y^e new imaginary scheams of Power & Goverment in y^e people by y^e right of self diffence, &c. 3$^{[rd]}$ y^e power of y^e sword not from y^m because they have it not, neither to kill y^{m}selvs nor neheibours. 4$^{[th]}$ their never was any Comonwealth or Monarchy so constituted.

5. Noe good effect can be of y^t docterin of Resistance. 1st 'tis y^e interest of all Goverments as far as possible to be consientiously obeid, especialy y^e Crown of England y^t has not y^e same hold on their people as formerly by teneors, Wardship, &c. 2$^{[nd]}$ people apt enough to rebell. 3$^{[rd]}$ what tyranny so bad as anarchy? Example: y^e rebellion of '41. 4$^{[th]}$ Anarchy y^e mother of a tyrant as Cromwell.

6. Resistance contrary to y^e law of England. 1st y^e king can doe noe wrong. 2^{ndly} Treason acts. 3^{rdly} y^e very acts ceated in y^e preamblule to impeachment to setle y^e right of y^e subject & prevent vexatious suits shew y^t y^e people claim noe such right of deposeing & y^t absolvetory laws wear necessary for y^m who acted in y^e late revolution. 4$^{[th]}$ y^e law impowers no one more y^n another to resist as in Aragon. Chief Justices y^e *censores merum*, &c. 5$^{[th]}$ on y^e contrary then [the] most impowrd are most oblidgd to obey, acting by vertue of y^t commission . . .[38] [f. 139v] 6$^{[th]}$ Princes might be deposd for y^e faults of their ministers since they act all through them.

7. Resistance not y^e principall of y^e Revolution. 1st disclaimd by y^e king when Prince of Orang in his Declaration. 2^{ndly} by y^e Bishopps y^t invited him over & many other Lords. 3$^{[rd]}$ not y^e ground of y^e throne being vacant but y^e abdication. Therefore they reflect on y^e king & Revolution who make him come over not for our good but his own benifit.

8. This dispute of Passive Obedience & non resistance can have [no] good effect for: 1st it takes away y^e Queen's ancient hereditary right. 2$^{[nd]}$ seems to suppose some right in y^e pretender, wch is high Treason by a late act of Parliament.

9. Passive obedience most usefull to good princes. For: 1st makeing a duty of obedience it curbs ambition & makes it ease boath to y^e Prince & subject y^t y^e ministers should obey too. Example: y^e Earles of Esex & Leicester seem to have wanted this vertue, for though one was a good t'other a great subject & boath oblidged infinitely to ye Queen, y^t upon fancying y^t ye Queen had faild one flew to ye weak armes & lost his life. T'other more cuning closed in wth ye disguisd rebells of those times & so endeavoured to [him]self feared.

[f. 140v] *Ad mutandem de andure regni negonis* [sic.]

Noe excuse for speaking now being accused as being w^t they call [a] High church man.

1st of seditious principall & slavish.

2 of restless & turbulent spiritt.

3 of being friends to ye pretender.

Therefore not to speak would now be criminall, to retort ye falsity as far as ye dignity of Parliament will permitt.

---

[37] '4' erased and '3' inserted.

[38] Incomprehensible.

Their charge is generall, not against a pittyfull tooll of a party, as a manager calls ye prisoner, but ye established church, excepting only of [the] flying squadron y^t call themselves low & pretend to . . .^{39} One would think they were not verie [sure] of their majority. They would now venture to accuse so many of y^r Lordships to themselves. Have we noe affinity, noe relation between Lords of different partis? I'm sure their are severall Lords amongst ye Whigs y^t I should be sorrie to see so awkerdly booked in for treason. I might in justification of my principalls plead my EDUCATION & ye DOCTRINS PREACHD UP in my youth, but I had rather avow y^t upon ye examination of y^m I found y^m true.

The things to be spoak of before I come [to an end?]: the douting of Passive Obedience and Non Resistance; 1st ye manour of this impeachment; ye Heat & threatnings. 2^{ndly} ye time. 3^{rdly} the person against whom 'tis brought, a private man.

All Goverments founded upon *Originall Contract* or on Resistance. Noe Original Contract but ye laws, wch Sir Joseph Jekell grants to be all for passive obedience before Resistance.

2. By Resistance you must mean of some forain power or conquest; els noe goverment founded on such resistance but Oliver Cromwell & . . .^{40}.

Docterin of Passive Obedience or non resistance to be considered as it relates
1. to Goverment in Generall 1.2.3.4. [*sic.*]
2. to England   5.
3. to ye Revolution   7.
4. to ye Queen   8.
Abdication y^e *causa proxima* or *sine qua non* of ye revolution.
. . . ad^{41} & law declared y^e king elective none . . .^{42}

---

^{39} Word partially destroyed: '. . . spiration'.
^{40} Name indecipherable.
^{41} MS damaged; one or more words destroyed.
^{42} MS damaged; one or more words destroyed.

Index

Printed and bound by CPI Group (UK) Ltd, Croydon, CR0 4YY

09/06/2025

14686132-0004